PRAISE FOR *PRESIDENTS AND THE MEDIA*

Communication technologies have fundamentally changed how the president interacts with the public, transforming the nature of representative democracy. This book offers a cutting-edge portrayal of how changes in media affect presidential actions and his ability to influence the public. It is a must-read for anyone interested in representative democracy.

James N. Druckman, *Northwestern University*

Timely and relevant amid cries of fake news, Stephen Frantzich's thorough overview of the connection between the presidency and media shows how their relationship has existed and continues to evolve under the Trump administration. This book is accessible to undergraduate students, and it is also a useful compendium for scholars of the presidency and news media.

Matthew Eshbaugh-Soha, *University of North Texas*

Presidents and the Media: The Communicator in Chief is a thorough and thoughtful treatment of an increasingly important topic. It should be required reading for those who want to understand the twenty-first century version of the public presidency.

Irwin Lester Morris, *University of Maryland*

Stephen Frantzich's compelling new book offers a wealth of important insights on the evolving relationship between modern American presidents and the media. This comprehensive account illuminates this symbiotic, tension-filled relationship from the perspectives of the nation's chief executive, the media, and the public. Frantzich's crisp writing and engaging analysis shed important light on the changing strategies and techniques that presidents and the media use in their efforts to inform and shape the opinions of the American people.

Brendan J. Doherty, *United States Naval Academy*

PRESIDENTS AND THE MEDIA

Is Donald Trump's "War on the Media" new news, fake news, or business as usual? Presidents have always "used" the media and felt abused by it. Tried and true vehicles such as press conferences, routine speeches, and the State of the Union address have served presidents' interests and received significant coverage by the print media. As new technologies have entered the media spectrum, the speed and pervasiveness of these interactions have changed dramatically. President Obama ushered in the social media presidency, while President Trump has become the tweeter in chief. This book shows how each of these developments affects what is communicated and how it is received by the public.

Stephen E. Frantzich is Professor Emeritus of Political Science at the United States Naval Academy, where he was selected as outstanding civilian professor in 1990. He is the author of over two dozen books and has served as a consultant to the US Congress, Dirksen Center, C-SPAN, and a variety of foreign parliaments. He also runs Books for International Goodwill (www.big-books.org), which has distributed over 8 million books to underserved populations around the world.

MEDIA and POWER

Series Editor: David L. Paletz
www.routledge.com/Media-and-Power/book-series/MP

Media and Power is a series that publishes work uniting media studies with studies of power. This innovative and original series features books that challenge, even transcend, conventional disciplinary boundaries, construing both media and power in the broadest possible terms. At the same time, books in the series are designed to fit into several different types of college courses in political science, public policy, communication, journalism, media, history, film, sociology, anthropology, and cultural studies. Intended for the scholarly, text, and trade markets, the series should attract authors and inspire and provoke readers.

Published Books

PRESIDENTS AND THE MEDIA

THE COMMUNICATOR IN CHIEF

STEPHEN E. FRANTZICH
UNITED STATES NAVAL ACADEMY

Routledge
Taylor & Francis Group

NEW YORK AND LONDON

First published 2019
by Routledge
711 Third Avenue, New York, NY 10017

and by Routledge
2 Park Square, Milton Park, Abingdon, Oxon, OX14 4RN

*Routledge is an imprint of the Taylor & Francis Group,
an informa business*

Library of Congress Cataloging in Publication Data
Names: Frantzich, Stephen E., author.
Title: Presidents and the media : the communicator in chief /
Stephen E. Frantzich, United States Naval Academy.
Description: New York, NY : Routledge, 2019. | Series: Media
and power | Includes bibliographical references.
Identifiers: LCCN 2018011591| ISBN 9781138479807 (hbk) |
ISBN 9781138479814 (pbk) | ISBN 9781351064743 (ebk)
Subjects: LCSH: Presidents—Press coverage—United States. |
Mass media—Political aspects—United States. | Press and
politics—United States.
Classification: LCC JK516 .F58 2019 | DDC 070.4/49320973—dc23
LC record available at https://lccn.loc.gov/2018011591

ISBN: 978-1-138-47980-7 (hbk)
ISBN: 978-1-138-47981-4 (pbk)
ISBN: 978-1-351-06474-3 (ebk)

Typeset in Galliard
by Florence Production Ltd, Stoodleigh, Devon, UK

To Tyler, Emalja, and Connor
Whose generation will reap the results of our continuing attempt
to improve the relationship between the president,
the media, and the public

CONTENTS

SPECIAL FEATURES

Boxes

Figures

Photos

Tables

CHAPTER 1

PRESIDENTS AND THE MEDIA IN A
REPRESENTATIVE DEMOCRACY

Representative democracy is a multidirectional conversation between citizens and elected officials. Presidents play a preeminent role in this conversation, suggesting topics, promoting solutions and reacting to events. In order to play a role, the president's message must be received by the target, understood, seen as relevant and credible.[1]

The Public's Need for News

Many of the president's efforts fall into the category of "munication," that is, communication without the "co." If no one is paying attention, or sloughing off the messages as irrelevant or not credible, the president's efforts are wasted. It is the media that help identify issues, frame problems, outline solutions, and crystallize opinions.

Effective conversations are based on the exchange of valid information. A fully informed electorate is a luxury to be sought but seldom reached:

> The founders of our country saw a well-informed citizenry as the bedrock of our system, and assumed that the communication among citizens and between citizens and elected representatives would take place in a way that lifted the best available evidence to the top, where it received more attention than all the noise below.[2]

Unless we share some information it is impossible to carry on a meaningful political conversation. We need to define terms and share some assumptions about how the world works. These shared islands of understanding fill in the gaps between bits of new information we glean in the political conversation. The media play an important role in creating these shared understandings on which useful conversations are based.

Few of us experience American politics directly. "Almost all of what Americans know about national politics, the U.S. Government, their fellow citizens, and the larger world is communicated through the media . . . for practical purposes, media reality *is* political reality."[3] In our vicarious viewing of politics and government we are dependent on media choices and interpretations. As Grossman and Kumar stated in their classic study, presidential "[r]eality as refracted through the lens of the news media is for most people their only glimpse at what is going on at the White House."[4]

It is hard to overestimate the importance of the media in a political system. "Democracies are fragile. . . . They need informed and engaged citizens to survive."[5] Citizens cannot form their views or make an educated choice among candidates without good information. The media are the only feasible way to spread objective information to the public. Relying on political leaders alone to raise issues and promote solutions threatens to provide biased information supporting current policies and regimes.

Political participation has relatively little value in the abstract. Politics is a method by which societal problems are discovered and support for solutions created. From the individual citizen's perspective, participation is important when the issue is relevant to them and they have the tools to affect the outcome. If one cares little about an issue and its possible solution, participation is little more than a hollow ritual. On the other hand, failure to participate in the development and solution of an issue of personal interest creates frustration and dissatisfaction. There is such a thing as "rational apathy" when the individual has no interest in an issue that will not affect him or her and/or lacks the knowledge and tools to participate. Knowing that the issue has already been decided or that the system is completely stacked against your interests is an invitation to concentrate one's efforts elsewhere. It is the media that helps individuals understand the issues under consideration, the potential impact of proffered solutions, and the tools for getting one's voice heard.

Political observers both among the public and the media are tempted to ask, "Why can't the media and the president just work together to provide the information needed to understand what is going on?" Such a position ignores the inherent tension stemming from the different goals of each of the three players. From the public's perspective the goal is to "satisfice" one's information, gathering enough to understand realms in which they are interested. Few news consumers seek to maximize information for fear that it will overwhelm them. For many members of the news audience, the goal lies in reinforcing one's current opinions rather than challenging them. For the president, the goal lies in good media coverage to undergird his leadership capabilities. The media, on the other hand, seeks to make a profit by maximizing both the size and content of its audience.

While this book will focus primarily on presidents in office, numerous commentators have pointed out that modern presidents are involved in a "permanent campaign," with every action taking into account either their reelection and/or the fate of their fellow party members in congressional campaigns.[6] Drawing the line between presidents acting as presidents and them acting as candidates becomes more difficult to draw.

In a representative democracy, the public plays a role in selecting, directing, and evaluating the president. Ideally the media "peels back the curtain," to provide the public the ability to carry out their task. In the words of George W. Bush, "We need an independent media to hold people like me to account."[7]

The President's Need for Media Coverage

Presidents do not crave media attention for the sake of attention. Positive media attention has the potential for increasing the president's power relative to other political players and to eventually lead to the adoption of his preferred policy outcomes. Negative media attention, on the other hand, has the opposite effect, threatening to take resources away from the focus of the president and his staff on the issues in which they are most interested. The ability to use the media to set the agenda has the potential to enhance the president's success in Congress.[8]

Discussions of contemporary presidents' "permanent campaign" activity[9] point out the difficulty of separating campaigning from governing. As Bill Clinton's press secretary put it:

> Campaigns are about framing choices for Americans. ... When you are responsible for governing you have to use the same tools of public persuasion to advance your program, to build public support for the direction you are attempting to lead.[10]

From the earliest days, presidents have used the news media to communicate with the public. At George Washington's request, his farewell address was published in a daily newspaper. Two centuries later, President Ronald Reagan chose the medium of the day—television—to give his farewell address.[11] President Jefferson played a key role in developing a new newspaper for the nation's capitol when he encouraged the creation of the *National Intelligencer* as an outlet to get his message to the people.[12]

Presidents are acutely aware of the importance of positive media coverage and the support it generates among the people. President Clinton pointed out that the key to political success was the president's unparalleled "access to the people through his communications network."[13] Clinton viewed positive coverage as the ability to "create new political capital all the time."[14] His staff sought to "deliberately and relentlessly communicate [the president's] program to the public."[15]

Presidential Approval

A president's popularity, whether measured by specific public opinion polls or in general terms by the media, is more than a vehicle for massaging the president's ego or warning him of shortcomings in his performance. Popularity is "said to be a political resource that can help him achieve his program, keep challengers at bay, and guide his and other political leaders' expectations about the president's party's prospects in presidential and congressional elections."[16] When the president receives positive coverage, his approval remains high, while negative coverage is associated with a decline.[17] Correlation, though, does not necessarily mean causation. A president's news coverage may be negative *because* of declining popularity, rather than vice versa. It is also clear that high presidential popularity is associated with legislative success,[18] but again it is not clear whether popularity leads to success or vice versa.

Two decades ago, researchers concluded that "a president's overall reputation, and to a lesser extent, his apparent competence, both depend upon the presentation of network news programs."[19] Today that is still true with television news being augmented by other news venues such as blogs and news alerts. Presidential approval by the public is an important power resource for a president. As one staff member put it, "When you go up to the Hill and the latest polls show [the president] isn't doing well, then there isn't much reason for a member to go along with him."[20] A member of Congress chimed in his support by saying, "The relationship between the President and Congress is partly the result of how well the President is doing politically. Congress is better behaved when he does well."[21]

There is a temptation to view seeking fame and adulation as a self-serving activity incompatible with the idea of unselfish public service. As far back as the Constitutional Convention, James Wilson argued that:

> the love of honest and well-earned fame is deeply rooted in honest and susceptible minds. Can there be a stronger incentive to the operation of this passion than the hope of becoming the object of well founded and distinguishing applause?[22]

Thus the promise of fame can be seen as a psychological motivator for presidents to do well.

Policy Leadership

Presidents have a choice of how they carry out their task as a national leader. They can deal with other power holders directly through a bargaining approach or they can attempt to use the media to indirectly put pressure on members of Congress and the bureaucracy by harnessing the power of the citizenry through "going public."[23] While few argue that presidents are not going public, there is considerable disagreement as to its effectiveness and consequences. Edwards[24] questions the ability of the president to change public opinion, arguing that the so-called "bully pulpit" is "more baloney than bully."[25] It may well be that presidents are "mainly effective when [they] are pushing Congress to do something the public already favors."[26] Farnsworth worries that the demands of going public encourage presidents to simplify issues, papering over the nuances and making compromise more difficult as the media focuses on who wins and who loses.[27] There is more consensus on the assertion that presidents use the media to set the policy agenda, even if they cannot control public attitudes (see Chapter 9). Agenda setting is crucial to presidents. "If presidents cannot affect news coverage of their top priorities, then they are even less likely to influence the public's priorities."[28] Lacking awareness of an issue means the lack of public opinion and the motivation to act. As Maxwell McCombs put it, "If the media tell us nothing about a topic or event, then in most cases it simply will not exist on our own personal agenda or in our life space."[29] No president uses only one approach, but they differ in the amount of emphasis they give to inside-the-Washington-Beltway bargaining versus broader public appeals through the media.

Bargaining and the Media

Even the bargaining model requires some use of the media. The targets for many presidential media initiatives are members of Congress or bureaucrats. Presidential statements carried by the media send signals as to what the president is willing to bargain over and his starting position. The media also play an important role in setting the national agenda, by pointing out problems in need of presidential attention (see Chapter 9) and by reporting public reaction to suggested solutions.

Harnessing public support is often difficult. Media attention to the president and his preferences means little in the abstract. The goal of positive coverage lies in its potential to effect and activate the public. In his policy battles with Congress, the president attempts to use the media to put pressure on Congress to support the president's policy initiatives. This two-step influence strategy is fraught with many challenges. Negative media stories may well undermine the president's goals. The public may not be paying attention. The routines of everyday life often crowd out concerns for public policy. "For many citizens budgets are boring, lawmaking is tedious and international problems seem distant."[30] Even if citizens are listening they may not be motivated enough to take action. For many, the costs seem too great and the payoff too remote. Lack of attention, or the public's low potential for activation, makes citizens less likely to affect their member of Congress. All that said, presidents work on the assumption that the media provide the best way to gain the attention and support of members of Congress. While public indifference exists, presidents see it as a challenge to overcome rather than an impossible hurdle.

Typically discussion of the media focuses on the impact of news coverage to the broader audience outside the Washington Beltway. In reality, the elites in Washington talk to each other *through* the media. Lawmakers attempting to get through to President Trump point out that "a TV appearance [is] as nearly on par with an Oval Office meeting in terms of showcasing their standing or viewpoints to the president."[31]

Going Public: The Policy Connection

Traditionally, analysis of presidential policy-making focused on a model emphasizing inside-the-Beltway bargaining and deal-making. The power to persuade only slightly involved the media.[32] The public largely played its role at election time, with presidents and members of Congress seeking compromises without much public input. Richard Neustadt saw the media's impact on the Washington community as it made judgments about the president and his public support from the media.[33] A few decades later, President Clinton's press secretary asserted that: "The modern presidency revolves around this question of how you use or how you penetrate the filter of the press to go directly to the American people, which is your ultimate source of political strength."[34] Samuel Kernell argued that, by the 1980s, a strategy of "going public" began to overtake the bargaining model. Increasingly a "president promotes himself and his policies in Washington by appealing to the American public for support. . . . Forcing compliance from fellow Washingtonians by going over their heads to appeal to their constituents."[35] The going public strategy relies much more heavily on the president's ability to use the media to get his preferred issues and policy preferences into the public dialogue. The president seeks to create a coalition of supporters among the public in the hope they will put pressure on other political players.

Bargaining strategies depend on flexibility, and on insulation of the bargaining partners from the short-term swings of public opinion. Numerous aspects of the structure of American government were premised on insulation more than consultation. Staggered elections, the Electoral College, the indirect election of Senators (since abandoned), and a bicameral Congress were all chosen by the Founders to temper public input.[36] Under such a system, politicians saw their jobs much more as trustees looking out for the interests of the public than as delegates responding to the short-term wishes and whims of their constituents. Going to the public through the media made little sense if the president had to deal with members of Congress, for whom the public played a minimally constraining role.

Going public can be done in at least two different ways. Some presidents "go national," relying on nationally televised addresses to sway public opinion. Such national appeals tend to be relatively moderate given the lack of homogeneity of the audience. Other presidents "go local," using addresses to clearly defined groups of the public to push a targeted message thorough. These groups may represent particular interests, or involve traveling to local destinations to give a speech of particular relevance to that area (see Chapter 6). Local appeals tend to result in more extreme rhetoric as the president tries to appeal to more limited interests.[37]

Going public is not an entirely new phenomenon, but it remained relatively rare until recent decades. Franklin Roosevelt used his fireside chats to highlight his legislative agenda, but only once did he ask the American public to put pressure on Congress to pass desired legislation.[38]

The shift to the going public strategy resulted from a number of interrelated factors. (1) The growth of the welfare state with its multitude of government programs gave an increasing percentage of the population a clear and apparent stake in what the president proposed. (2) Emerging communications and travel technologies gave presidents the tools to make their case widely and to travel to locations best suited to promoting a particular policy position. (3) The decline of political party organizations during the last half of the twentieth century made a larger percentage of members of Congress susceptible to presidential influence.[39] While partisanship and party-line voting have increased in recent years, presidents have accommodated themselves to relying less on party and more on public support.

There are so many variables in the presidential–congressional relationship that it is difficult to definitely prove that going public is an effective strategy. Presidents act as if positive media coverage and public support are important—and complain bitterly if they do not get the coverage they desire (see Box 1.1). It makes sense that policy initiatives gaining public support will put pressure on members of Congress with marginal political support. On the other hand, the relatively few members of Congress winning by small margins may well have to show their own independence on some issues favored by the president of their party.

Going public is far from a foolproof strategy. It is simply one of the tools in the presidential arsenal. Used effectively and judiciously, going over the heads of Congress directly to the people can have a positive effect. Going public is more important for setting the agenda of issues that should be of concern to the media and the public, more than directly changing their viewpoints. Presidents tend to be more successful in setting the agenda on issues where there is currently little public concern.[40]

Box 1.1
Presidents Talk about Their Frustration with the Media

Presidents describe the Washington media context in a number of unique but related ways.

President Carter bemoaned the media's lack of focus on the substance of public policy rather than the emphasis on personalities.[41]

President Clinton expressed frustration over his inability to "cut through the fog"[42] and described press conferences as being "peppered" by the media.[43]

President George W. Bush often called the media a "filter" of reality.[44]

President Obama talked about the difficulty of "breaking through the noise" to get his message out through the media.[45]

President Trump's epithets toward the media include calling them liars and "enemies of the people"[46] (see Chapter 5).

Experienced in the "art of the deal," President Trump seems more comfortable with behind-the-scenes negotiating or with building alliances among natural supporters than with broadening his base. In the battle for health care reform, he failed to "make a full-throated case to the country about [the] legislation." Rather, he played "the role of partisan cheerleader or frustrated onlooker."[47] President George W. Bush was much more active in generating public support for tax reform, while President Obama garnered significant media coverage for his health care plan.[48]

The effectiveness of going public to broaden one's policy support has declined somewhat in recent years. With the explosion of media sources, presidents have lost their monopoly of news coverage. News audiences have shrunk and the public displays less trust in the media. Second, interest groups have seen the past effectiveness of presidents and imitated presidential use of the media by adopting their own public relations initiatives. Finally, the growing ideological divisiveness of the electorate produces members of Congress committed to the views of their base supporters, which may or not be those of the president—even if of their own national party.[49]

Going Public: Symbolic Leadership

The president serves as the manifestation of the nation, responding to crises more for symbolic than for policy purposes. Natural threats and disasters force the president onto the public stage to become a symbolic first reactor.

The attacks of 9/11 confronted President George W. Bush with both a strategic and public relations challenge. Lacking knowledge of the extent of the attack, prudence suggested protecting the president at all costs—a task the Secret Service took on by having him fly to undisclosed locations. President Bush recognized that his job at that time was to reduce the public's "angst" by reassuring them "that I was safe . . . not me, George W., but me the president; reassuring them that our government was functioning and that we're going to take care of the American people."[50] With that in mind, the president countermanded the Secret Service and returned to the White House, where he could speak to the American people through the media and present a semblance of order and competency.

Natural disasters provide unique opportunities to show the presidents' power and concern, while delayed or ineffective action loom as potential dangers. Since presidents have become our responders in chief they reap rewards for timely action, with the media creating a timetable for what is acceptable. Presidents who hesitate to get engaged after natural or manmade disasters face criticism from the media for not "minding the ship." President George H.W. Bush's limited response after Hurricane Andrew hit Miami led to considerable criticism.[51] His son, George W. Bush, was quick to go to Florida shortly after Hurricane Frances to hand out bottled water. It was not lost to observers that Florida was a key state in the upcoming presidential election.[52] On the other hand, President George W. Bush's five-day delay in any personal involvement after Hurricane Katrina hit New Orleans led to a barrage of criticism by the media. In their view, his behavior lacked "strength, decisiveness and national unity."[53] The criticism fell on fertile ground. President George W. Bush, who had maintained strong popularity, in part boosted by the events of 9/11, increasingly saw negative media coverage and a decline in popularity. The tragedy in New Orleans had the kind of "human face" the media like to cover. Real people in misery having lost everything made for extensive coverage. For many, federal help was too little too late. Flying back to Washington from a vacation, Bush did not stop in New Orleans to assess the damage. A photograph of the president looking out the window of Air Force One at the damage seemed to send the message of limited concern. President's Bush's delayed visit to New Orleans could have been framed as an attempt not to get in the way of rescue operations, but it was seen more as disinterest. When Bush did travel to New Orleans, one comment became a catchphrase for the president's priorities. Rather than admitting shortcomings or focusing on the flood victims, Bush singled out the Federal Emergency Management Administration director, Michael Brown, saying "Heck of a Job, Brownie." To the media, Bush seemed more interested in complimenting his executive agency staff than showing compassion for those who had lost lives and property.

A president's "I care" message after a disaster may well be affected by a strategic decision of who he wants to be seen as caring for. Since Louisiana is not a swing state in presidential elections, its residents may not be as relevant as those in other states.[54]

Mindful of George W. Bush's slow response to a national emergency, President Obama took quick action to appear sympathetic and appear at memorial services for victims of mass shootings in places like Aurora, Colorado, and Newtown, Connecticut. President Obama also went on the air shortly after the Boston Marathon bombing and traveled to Boston to express his sympathy to the victims and their families. President Trump also was quick to respond to a series of hurricanes in 2017 (see Chapter 5). In the role of responder in chief, the president speaks for the nation expressing grief and motivating action.

Presidents are dependent on the media to transmit their images to the public. As the media environment has changed, the White House is challenged to utilize new opportunities while maintaining tried and true vehicles for public persuasion.

The Contemporary Media Environment

Presidents may make news, but they do not make the media environment in which they must operate. They are dealt a set of technologies and operating procedures and must adapt to their opportunities and potential pitfalls. Early media in America were largely partisan, with presidents relying on the paper of their party to make their points. Presidents rewarded their partisan paper with lucrative government printing contracts—a practice that became obsolete with the creation of the Government Printing Office in 1860. From the 1830s onward, improvements in printing led to the creation of the "penny press," lowering the cost of newspapers and ushering in a revised business model. By expanding the base of its readers in both size and demographics, newspapers were able to rely on advertising more than government contracts.[55] The emergence of wire services such as the Associated Press, serving newspapers with widely divergent political views, found that partisanship was a bad business plan.[56] The ethic of objective reporting spread through most outlets during the first two-thirds of the twentieth century.

Toward the end of the nineteenth century appeals to a wider and better-educated readership required toning down the partisan rhetoric, but added to the temptation to use sensational headlines to grab the attention of potential readers. By the 1890s, breathtaking headlines and stories came into full bloom in what became called "yellow journalism."[57]

The written press, largely in the form of newspapers, dominated American politics for much of the first two centuries of the American Republic. With the emergence of television, news readership began to decline and the number of distinct newspapers fell dramatically. Cities with two or more independent newspapers became a rarity and newspaper syndicates produced papers for a number of cities.

The Era of Mass Media

From World War II until the 1980s, we lived in the era of true *mass* media. Television was the vehicle of choice and the three major government-authorized networks (ABC, CBS, and NBC) dominated as news sources. By the 1960s, "more homes in America had television than indoor plumbing and virtually all viewers (including early cable subscribers) depended on the networks for programming."[58] The three networks news programs consistently garnered the vast majority of the households with their televisions on. Since the networks dominated and covered the president without questions, he "possessed an enviable tool of persuasion." Government regulations such as the "Fairness Doctrine" and the "Equal Time Provision" reinforced objectivity in reporting on broadcast television.

On any particular night there was a great deal of overlap in the stories carried by each network and in the way in which they covered them. The "consonance"[59] created shared islands of understanding and facilitated political conversation. One could begin a "water cooler" discussion at work or school with comments about the previous evening's stories and be relatively assured that everyone was up to speed. In this previous age of homogeneity, a president who could get his story on the evening news had pretty good assurance that he was using the most efficient way to reach the general population on a regular basis.[60]

The New Media Era

Observers have argued that current changes in media delivery technology are as significant as was the shift from handwritten to printed text.[61] Technologies do not impact on political behavior like two ships colliding at night. There are no inevitable laws of physics that determine the nature and extent of the consequences. The impact of technology is more dependent on choices made by human actors in determining when and how the technologies will be used. The pressure to use emerging technologies stems more from "demand-side" than "supply-side" factors. The existence of a technology does not guarantee its use.

Beginning in the 1980s, the news audience became more and more fragmented. Presidents retained "all the accoutrements of high office, but . . . no longer commanded the public stage."[62] Gone are the days when a president could "appear simultaneously on all national radio and television networks at prime, national-audience evening hours, virtually whenever and however the president wishes."[63]

The first wave of change affected television in the form of cable TV which lured away viewers toward specialized channels, often with little or no news content. Within the news realm, twenty-four-hour news channels such as CNN (1980), Fox News (1996), and MSNBC (1996) changed the method and timing of news gathering. For those with the deepest interest in politics, C-SPAN (Cable Satellite Public Affairs Network, 1979) began broadcasting congressional sessions. Later C-SPAN added speeches and press conferences by presidents and other political leaders in their entirety.

The arrival of the VCR (and, later, "on-demand" recording services) in the 1990s allowed viewers the chance to capture presidential statements and review them at their leisure. The Internet spawned a whole new set of applications with the potential for changing both the content and format of presidential communications. YouTube's arrival in the 2000s allowed interested viewers the ability to seek videos of presidential events and commentary on them. YouTube also increased the archive ability of presidential statements for the general public. By "sharing" or "liking" a post, average citizens could attempt to change the political dialogue. The networks had long kept an archive of presidential statements to compare with contemporary comments. Social media added a new twist: individuals could share favorite video segments, news stories, and comments with others in an attempt to inform and influence. Twitter and news feeds to one's smartphone serve as alerts to what is trending in segments of society in which one is interested.

Unlike previous technologies, contemporary vehicles are driven more by demand than by supply. Individuals must opt in to specific apps both for initial utilization and continuing involvement. Applications such as Facebook, Twitter, and Instagram add a potential interactive element to political communication. While the White House website provides a highly controlled broadcast capability, it remains useless unless people go to it for their information.

With readers and viewers more able to opt for varying content, the new technologies have created a "buyer's market" for information as consumers are able to pick and choose their information platforms and content. With the total audience relatively stable, each media venue competes with the other for a market share that will sustain their endeavors. The net result has been the discontinuation of many newspapers built on the objectivity goals of a previous era. Many of the remaining sources followed a strategy of appealing to consumers with a particular partisan or ideological bent, or to merge more entertainment (infotainment) into their hard news reporting.[64] Only slightly before the strong emergence of Fox News and MSNBC, one set of scholars asserted that "partisan news organizations are nearly nonexistent in the United States,"[65] but things have changed.

Many observers bemoan the new technologies and their seemingly negative impact on the legacy media, especially newspapers. Younger members of the public are most likely to eschew the reading of hard-copy newspapers, adding concern as to print media's long-term survivability. As the public shifts toward increased use of the Internet for news there is a presumption of print and television irrelevance. What tends to get forgotten is that much of the raw material on the Web comes from hard-copy sources. Few news aggregation sites such as the *Drudge Report*, *Huffington Post*, *Newsmax*, or *Buzzfeed* create content of their own. Only a few of the legacy print sources such as the *New York Times*, the *Washington Post*, and the *Atlantic* have accomplished significant financial success with their electronic versions.[66]

In the realm of television news, we must also remember that, despite the decline in audience size over time, the national network evening news still garners a significant audience of over 24 million viewers, far more than the 2 million that Fox News or 1 million CNN receives during prime time.[67] It is also important to remember that users of the legacy media are less likely to have their minds made up and more likely to participate in the political process.[68]

Presidential Reaction to the New Media Environment

Presidents are not free agents when it comes to utilizing the media. Situational factors help determine which medium is available and the very nature of the existing media system. Presidents did not drive viewers away from network television news or newspaper utilization, but had to accept the conditions of the new media era. The old media environment of dominant newspapers and three television networks "are no more likely to make a triumphant return than are big bands."[69] Presidents unwilling or unable to take advantage of new media potentially lose out to their opponents who have figured out how to use the new media to their advantage.

Communications technologies have created opportunities for presidents to get their message out, but do not mandate their use or the messages they purvey. Transportation technologies increased the ease of the president to travel around the country to make news. Communications technologies such as satellites allowed the utilization of town hall meetings with broad participation. The Internet gave presidents more control over the timing and content of their messages, but it is important to recognize that the White House use of vehicles such as web pages and Twitter focused more on controlling the message than on utilizing the technology's other potential for increasing interactivity and citizen involvement (see Chapter 7).

Presidents dissatisfied with their ability to get their message out in the form they desire using existing technologies will demand the use of new approaches. The public plays a role in establishing expectations of what it means to be a modern president. Presidents not using widely accepted current technologies will be seen as "out of touch." Most new technologies are add-ons, adopted without fully displacing the existing technologies.

It took a while for presidents to master each new technology. President Herbert Hoover tended to shout his speeches into the microphone as if he really could not believe that his words could be heard everywhere.[70] It took Franklin Roosevelt to recognize the power of radio and its ability to build a personal tie between the president and the public. His famous "fireside chats" showed him more as a beloved uncle explaining the world than as a detached world leader. Dwight Eisenhower came across on television as a "wooden" leader, while it is widely accepted that Richard Nixon's inability to master the new medium cost him the 1960 election. "JFK was to television what FDR was to radio."[71] He came across as confident and courageous. His first use of televised news conferences portrayed him "like a gladiator in the arena; on the other side, a crowd of reporters hurling what appeared to be sharp verbal spears at him, which he fended off with seemingly heroic grace and skill."[72] Barack Obama was literally the first Twitter president, but it took Donald Trump to make it into a governing tool (see Chapter 7). Previous presidents did not have the luxury of technologies not yet available.

The new media environment confronts the president with a number of challenges. In the age of legacy media, deadlines were relatively fixed and predictable. Newspaper reporters focused on the necessary lead times for either morning or evening editions. National television reporters needed to get their stories filed by late afternoon to make it on the evening news. With the arrival of all-news channels on cable television and the Internet blogs, reporters present an almost insatiable demand for new information and fresh perspectives. More and more reporters are multitasking, preparing their primary story for one format such as print and blogging information or appearing on television.[73]

Cable television with its all-news networks created a significant larger news "hole" requiring content. The White House responded by producing "dramatic settings for the president to deliver carefully scripted appearances for delivery throughout the day, not just for the evening news broadcasts."[74] The modern era requires the "White House staff to be ready to dispense information virtually around the clock."[75] Speed of delivery of news comes with its own problems. As President Clinton's press secretary put it, "the faster you report, the less reliable the information will be. Because it hasn't been tested and verified, and determined to be authentic."[76]

The fragmented media market may well have positive results for politicians. The efficiency of dealing with a limited number of television networks and a few major newspapers might look desirable in retrospect, the limited news holes in these outlets limited the voices that could be heard and expanded the power of a relatively few journalists. In the current "factionalized and unstable universe, credible policy makers have even more opportunity to communicate directly with the public and to promote their own visions and answers to the public and to other policy makers."[77]

Presidents must remember that information providers on the Internet are less constrained by economic necessities or professional norms. The low entry cost to create a website, Twitter presence, or blog reduces the barrier to getting one's viewpoints distributed. Stories that the mainstream media might back away from serve as fodder for the new media. The legacy media's fact checkers and legal offices emphasize caution over distribution of questionable stories. While the mainstream media dragged its feet in covering Bill Clinton's inappropriate behavior with a White House intern, the story was broken by *The Drudge Report*, an online blog. With the story out, the mainstream media rushed to catch up.[78]

Presidents are only partially masters of their own media presence. They must take into account the question of "Who is paying attention to what?" and direct their media efforts to those media outlets they believe will communicate to those they perceive as important.

The Potential Impact of the Media

The news media serves as an inter*media*ry (emphasis intended) standing between reality and news consumers. The media have both a "gatekeeping" and "interpretive" function. In choosing which stories to cover and how to cover them, the media construct reality. In the selection and presentation of the news, the media often evaluate and modify politicians' messages. The media serve as "the eyes and ears of the public, determining what the public sees and hears.[79] The news media are "managers of meaning."[80] They place activities and political actors into context and suggest how we as viewers and readers should reasonable react to them. The very fact that a story gets into the news suggests it is important for an intelligent person to know. Common story lines confront us with conflict (who is battling whom?), duplicity (who is being inconsistent?), and accomplishment or failure (who is winning and who is losing?).

While some citizens have well established information and opinions on the president and his performance, others receive important clues from elites especially in the media. "Prominent journalists serve as important opinion leaders in establishing the president's reputation."[81] The public uses two different ways to evaluate presidents. On the one hand, some members of the public line up a president's *policy* positions and compare them with their own. Given the complexity of policy positions and the public's limited knowledge, *character* seems like the most effective yardstick. If an individual approves of the president's character and style, he or she is more likely to show support for him and his policies.[82] The public, and even the media, want to believe the president:

> A president perceived as honest can get away with a multitude of errors, but a president perceived as dishonest will have every mistake magnified. . . . The jury in deciding all this, of course, is the White House press corps, which sets itself up as defender of the truth and prosecutor of all liars.[83]

Shock and Awe

There are at least two ways in which news stories can impact on the public. Some stories are so big they break through indifference and inattention through a process of "shock and awe." Presidential resignation or assassination attempts fall at the far end of the continuum, demanding media coverage and almost forcing public attention. Less significant stories fall on a continuum ending with the irrelevant. Most news stories fall somewhere in between.

Stalagmite

"Our picture of reality does not burst upon us in one splendid revelation. It accumulates day by day and year by year in mostly unspectacular fragments from the world scene, produced mainly by the mass media."[84] Just as stalagmites grow in caves through constant dripping leaving a hard residue, many news stories lack an immediate and dramatic effect. It is only over time that related stories build up a strong presence. "Presidents are best able to sustain public and media attention to their policy priorities by speaking about issues frequently over several months."[85] On the negative side, a series of unflattering stories may well create an impression of a president that exaggerates his weaknesses. Even though he was an accomplished athlete, President Ford's tripping over his own feet became a story line of his tripping over his duties as president. President Bill Clinton's serial womanizing led to an overall judgment of his moral weakness. President George W. Bush's grammatical errors became a question of his overall intelligence. President Donald Trump's first few months as president led him to complain about his communications staff and the "steady drip of damaging headlines."[86] "Bad news travels through the press with a greater velocity and intensity than good news. Bad news stories can stretch for days and weeks. Good news stories are often one-day events."[87] For the White House, there is nothing worse than the drip, drip, drip of an ongoing negative story.

Using an analogy similar to the stalagmite description, BBC commentator Alistair Cook discussed the nature of looking for presidential scandals. He felt that looking for the smoking gun that would prove to everyone the president's misbehavior was misdirection. He asserted, "We've been conducting the wrong kind of search. The object in question is the body of the constitution. When we find it with a hundred stab wounds, there's no point in looking for a smoking gun."[88] With each "stab" wounding the president's legitimacy, the ultimate effect is the same as a political life-ending revelation.

While individual news stories are important, the development of a theme leads to a pattern of conventional wisdom that may have a broader and long-term influence on the president's ability to control the news and lead the nation. During the Vietnam conflict, a series of stories led to a credibility gap in which President Johnson was seen as shading the truth. Each new story was evaluated with that "reality" in mind. Journalists were quick to point out that "Bill and Hillary Clinton had a particular tendency to fudge the facts."[89] The media made a big deal about President's George W. Bush's mangling of the English language and created the image of a person not intellectually capable of being president. This image dogged him through his presidency and affected media and public evaluations of his policy actions. President Trump's intemperate reaction to others led to an image of emotional instability, which was then used to frame other stories and establish a mindset among some of the public.

Selectivity

The president may make legitimate news and the news media report it, yet the impact is minimal. News consumers are fickle, seeking to reinforce currently held views, not to challenge them. Humans are not objective observers of the world or purely open-minded consumers of the media. In many realms, we confront the world with a full complement of biases. As Francis Bacon put it, "The human understanding when it has once adopted an opinion draws all things else to support and agree with it."[90] Public reaction to positive or negative stories about the president is filtered through previous political commitments. The president's supporters tend to either dismiss the negative stories or blame the media for focusing on them. As the title of an article discussing President Trump's son meeting with a Russian lawyer put it, "Smoking gun or distraction? All depends on whose side you're on."[91]

Bias

While it is well beyond the scope of this book to provide a comprehensive discussion of media bias, a few factors closely associated with the presidency and the media deserve mention. Bias refers to a misrepresentation of reality. If a president acts in an unwise manner, it is not bias to report it. But if the media only seeks out missteps and ignores the positive actions of a president, bias is at play. Lack of bias implies fairness: "the best way to be fair is not to be falsely evenhanded, giving equal weight to unequal sides. It is to push for the truth, and tell it both accurately and powerfully."[92] When the president "makes news," he deserves coverage, but little is gained in providing coverage for coverage's sake.

As Box 1.2 points out, even when the same event is described by a journalist, the headlines placed on the article or the lead-in to the story on television create a mindset which affects how the article is interpreted.

Ideological and Partisan Bias

A continuing conundrum in media studies involves the question of ideological and partisan bias. There is little question that in their personal beliefs the majority

---

Box 1.2
Head-Lying

Newspaper headlines and television lead-ins help create a mindset as to how the story is read or viewed. They may be the only things to which many readers attune. In this age of news services, local papers purchase stories from other sources and add their own headlines.

The range of headlines on the same story varies considerably. On the same day, the following headlines about health care appeared over the same basic story:

"Bush Opposes Bill for Patients' Rights" (*U.S.A. Today*, March 22, 2001)[93]

"Bush Seeks Compromise on Patients' Rights" (*Washington Post*, March 22, 2001)[94]

"Bush Backs Patients' Bill of Rights, with Caveat" (*New York Times*, March 22, 1001)[95]

After a series of hurricanes hit the U.S. in 2017, the *exact same story* was published by a number of different newspapers with the following headlines:

"Trump administration earns cautious praise for early response to hurricanes" (The original story in the *Washington Post*)[96]

"Trump gets broad praise in initial storm responses" (The story as it was headlined in the more conservative *Capital*)[97]

While only two key words differed, the meaning of "cautious" and "broad" send two different signals to the reader.

---

of journalists lean toward the left and prefer Democratic candidates.[98] The key question lies in determining whether these personal preferences spill over into their reporting. The majority of studies using content analysis come to the conclusion that factors other than personal bias drive journalistic decisions as to what to cover, and how to cover it.[99]

Not all research explains away partisan and ideological bias. When journalists were asked how they would cover particular events, one study found that there was "substantial evidence that partisan beliefs intrude on news decisions."[100] Patterson and Donsbach do not attribute such bias to a conscious effort to take partisan sides, but rather hidden results boiling up through reporting decisions without the reporters' awareness.[101]

The Negativity Bias

For many members of the media, the key assumption that conflict "sells" leads to White House dissatisfaction with received coverage of mistakes and short-comings. A smooth-running White House with widely accepted policy decisions seldom makes news. Negative stories are used to draw public attention. It makes sense that the audience will remember the headline and closing comments to a story, more than the internal content. Television uses a "tease" to get us to watch and stay tuned after breaks. As an example, the media hope that by saying "stay tuned; the president has shaken up the White House staff" the viewer won't shift to another channel. Headlines in a newspaper or on a website not only attempt to draw in an audience but also to help frame how they will view the rest of the content. Observers in the White House also point out that television reporters "on all the broadcast and cable networks sum up their stories with a gloomy, negative, conflict-driven final sentence."[102]

In their attempt to provide context and explain presidential behavior, journalists often rely on parallels. While no two events are identical, they may share enough characteristics to make the comparison enlightening. Most comparisons have a great deal of negative content. Recent presidents attempting to use U.S. troops and weapons in places like Iraq, Afghanistan, North Korea, and Syria face the potential of having their efforts compared to Vietnam.[103] In dealing with issues of international military involvement, the media force the president to battle against the phantom of previous engagements.

The Conflict Bias

Contemporary media are biased toward conflict and the unique since they are competing for an audience or readership. Journalists seek out stories that will be of interest to their audience. "Because interesting is found on both the left and the right, any journalist who values what all journalists value makes a poor vessel for ideological or partisan bias. . . . To the reporter . . . interesting is the currency of the realm."[104] Covering conflict fits the bill.

The Public Weighs In

While the debate about how liberal the media are rages without a definitive answer, the public does perceive significant bias. Almost two-thirds of the public perceives the media as favoring one party or ideology over the other. Among those holding that belief, 64% see the media as favoring Democrats and 22% Republicans. Republicans are much more likely to see partisan bias, with 77% of them seeing favoritism as opposed to 22% of Democrats. Over time, the Republican perception of bias has increased.[105] In terms of general views of media bias, Republicans perceive it as much more of a problem than do Democrats (see Figure 1.1).

Intentional Bias

The newspapers of the nineteenth century were literally conceived in partisanship. Thomas Jefferson urged the creation of the *National Intelligencer*, which became the "house organ of the Jeffersonian party."[106] Andrew Jackson granted subsidies to *The Globe* and it provided positive coverage to his party, making him "the first [president] to manipulate press coverage on such a grand scale."[107] The shift to more objective reporting began in the middle of the nineteenth century and lasted until the 1970s.

A number of factors came together to challenge the idea of objective journalism. The Vietnam Conflict and Watergate seemed to invite investigative journalism in which reporters "looked at what officials said and did publicly," and shifted more to what they "did behind closed doors."[108] Investigative journalism usually begins with the assumption that something is wrong. Presidential missteps such as the Clinton–Lewinsky scandal and President George W. Bush's abortive search for weapons of mass destruction created the opening for more interpretation rather than pure description.

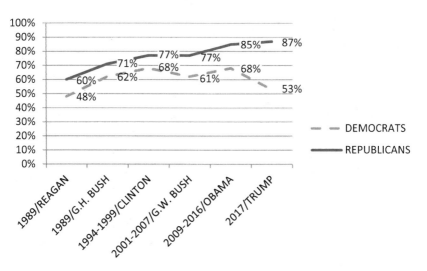

Figure 1.1 Percentage of Partisan Group Saying the Media Is Likely to "Favor One Side"

Source: Data from the Pew Research Center, "Americans' attitudes about the news media deeply divided along partisan lines" (www.journalism.org/2017/05/10/democrats-republicans-now-split-on-support-for-watchdog-role/)

There is more room today for journalists and media outlets with a clear partisan or ideological leaning. In the not-so-distant past journalists were "anxious to preserve their own credibility," and "most cannot make a living if they are not seen by sources, readers, viewers, and bosses as trying to be fair."[109] With publications and television news outlets finding a market for news that leans in one direction, more journalists have taken this approach to job security and enhancement.

It was not until the early 2000s that networks such as Fox News and MSNBC found a viable business model in presenting news with a clearly ideological twist. Later even more ideological news organizations such as Breitbart News (conservative), *The Drudge Report* (conservative), *The Guardian* (liberal), and the *Huffington Post* (liberal) emerged.[110] Even the legacy media look more opinionated. The media have never reported "just the facts," but some key observers like the executive editor of the *New York Times* admits that "what we publish on the front page of the *New York Times* today—a fair amount of it would have been regarded as excessively opinionated twenty years ago."[111] While we have not come full circle to a system of an almost exclusively partisan press, early presidents would have some empathy for the challenges of the contemporary president to get his message through to the bulk of the population.

Conclusion

Presidents and the media exist in a symbiotic relationship. They each need the other. The president needs to get his messages out in order to build popular support for his initiatives and to influence the other branches of government. The media need to cover the president on a daily basis to meet the expectations of their readers and viewers. The role of these two institutions is critical, especially in a representative democracy. "Alone, the president and the media are influential. Together, they are invincible."[112] Roderick Hart goes a step further, arguing that, beyond needing each other, the media and the president are "parasitic," in that neither could exist without the other. The public stands as critical targets for presidential and media efforts.[113]

Presidents and the media compete to control the message to the public. The nature of that competition has changed over time with the arrival of new relationships, technologies, and behavior patterns. In the following chapters, we will look at how the media, the public, and the president have developed strategies for reaching their goals.

Notes

1. Jeffrey E. Cohen, *The Presidency in the Era of 24-Hour News*, Princeton, NJ: Princeton University Press, 2008, p. 181.

2. Juliet Elperin, "Gore's Faith in Reason Endures," *Washington Post*, March 11, 2017, p. C1.

3. Bartholomew H. Sparrow, "Who Speaks for the People? The President, the Press, and Public Opinion in the United States," *Presidential Studies Quarterly*, Vol. 38, No. 4, 2008, pp. 578–579.

4. Michael Baruch Grossman and Martha Joynt Kumar, *Portraying the President: The White House and the News Media*, Baltimore, MD: Johns Hopkins University Press, 1981, p. 299.

5. Margaret Sullivan, "A Chaotic News Cycle Creates Bewilderment," *Washington Post*, May 15, 2017, p. C1.

6. Sidney Blumenthal, *The Permanent Campaign*, New York, NY: Simon and Schuster, 1982; Norman J. Ornstein and Thomas E. Mann, *The Permanent Campaign and Its Future*, Washington, DC: American Enterprise Institute Press, 2000.

7. http://thehill.com/homenews/321295-former-president-george-w-bush-media-essential-to-democracy.

8. Brandice Canes-Wrone, *Who Leads Whom? Presidents, Policy and the Public*, Chicago, IL: University of Chicago Press, 2006.

9. See Brendan Doherty, *The Rise of the President's Permanent Campaign*, Lawrence, KS: University of Kansas Press, 2012.

10. Samuel Kernell, *Going Public: New Strategies of Presidential Leadership*, Washington, DC: Congressional Quarterly Press, 1997, p. 34.

11. Matthew Kerbel, Dom Bonafede, Martha Joynt Kumar, and John L. Moore, "The President and the News Media," in Michael Nelson (ed.), *Guide to the Presidency*, Washington, DC: CQ Press, 2008, p. 940.

12. Ibid., p. 941.

13. Lawrence R. Jacobs, "The Presidency and the Press: The Paradox of the White House Communications War," in Michael Nelson (ed.), *The Presidency and the Political System*, Washington, DC: Congressional Quarterly Press, 2010, p. 237.

14. Ibid.

15. Ibid.

16. Richard Brody, *Assessing the President: the Media, Elite Opinion and Public Support*, Stanford, CA, Stanford University Press, 1991, p. 3.

17. Jeffrey Cohen, "The Presidency and the Mass Media," in George C. Edwards and William G. Howell (eds.), *The Oxford Handbook of the American Presidency*, New York: Oxford University Press, 2009, pp. 254, 271.

18. See Han Soo Lee, "Analyzing the Multidirectional Relationships Between the President, News Media, and the Public: Who Affects Whom?" *Political Communication*, Vol. 31, No. 2, 2014, pp. 261, 266.

19. Kernell, 1997, p. 219

20. Quoted in Kernell, 1997, p. 38.

21. Richard Cheney, quoted in Ibid.

22. David Haven Blake, "Hollywood, Impersonation and Presidential Celebrity in the 1990s," in Peter C. Rollins and John E. O'Connor, *Hollywood's White House*, Lexington, KY: University of Kentucky Press, 2003, p. 324.

23. Kernell, 1997. For the revised edition, see Samuel Kernell, *Going Public*, Washington, DC: CQ Press, 2007.

24. George C. Edwards, *On Deaf Ears: The Limits of the Bully Pulpit*, New Haven, CT: Yale University Press, 2003.

25. George C. Edwards, "More Baloney than Bully," *Public Perspective*, September/October, 2002, p. 7.

26. John Wagner and Ashley Parker, "As going in D.C. gets tough, Trump hits road," *Washington Post*, June 21, 2017, p. A2.

27. Stephen Farnsworth, *Spinner in Chief: How Presidents Sell Their Policies and Themselves*, Boulder, CO: Paradigm, 2009, p. 14.

28. Matthew Eshbaugh-Soha and Jeffrey Peake, *Breaking Through the Noise: Presidential Leadership, Public Opinion and the News Media*, Stanford, CA: Stanford University Press, 2011, p. 19.

29. Maxwell McCombs, "Agenda-Setting Research: A Bibliographic Essay," *Political Communication Review*, Vol. 1, No. 1, 1976, p. 3.

30. Farnsworth, p. 60

31. Philip Rucker, Ashley Parker, and Devlin Barrett, "Trump Lawyers Finding He Prefers His Own Advice," *Washington Post*, July 14, 2017, p. A1.

32. See Richard Neustadt, *Presidential Power*, New York: John Wiley and Sons, 1980.

33. Ibid.

34. Mike McCurry, quoted in Eshbaugh-Soha and Peake, p. 8.

35. Kernell, 1997, p. 3.

36. Kernell, 1997, p. 13.

37. Jeffrey E. Cohen, *The Presidency in the Era of 24-Hour News*, Princeton, NJ: Princeton University Press, 2008, p. 189.

38. Kernell, 1997, p. 23.

39. See Kernell, 1997, p. 28.

40. See Chapter 8 and Eshbaugh-Soha and Jeffrey Peake, 2011.

41. Quoted Martha Joynt Kumar, *Managing the President's Message: The White House Communication Operation*, Baltimore, MD: Johns Hopkins University Press, 2007, p. 182.

42. Ibid. p. 36.

43. Ibid. p. 269.

44. https://books.google.com/books?id=sqU1TKKblrcC&pg=PA164&lpg=PA164&dq=george+w.+bush+media+filter&source=bl&ots=vWEiEgATUS&sig=-3pw8cfZouISDXOinFs87QxNtM&hl=en&sa=X&ved=0ahUKEwiE0MT0muPTAhVIeSYKHU-eABMQ6AEIVTAL#v=onepage&q=george%20w.%20bush%20media%20filter&f=false.

45. Matthew Eshbaugh-Soha and Jeffrey S. Peake, *Breaking Through the Noise: Presidential Leadership. Public Opinion and the News Media*, Stanford, CA: Stanford University Press, 2011.

46. www.politico.com/magazine/story/2017/04/28/poll-trump-white-house-press-corps-journalists-215051.

47. Abby Phillip and Robert Costa, "Republicans Waiting for Trump to Use That Bully Pulpit," *Washington Post*, July 15, 2017, A4.

48. Ibid.

49. Kernell, 2007, pp. 215 and 234.

50. Quoted in Jeff Smith, *The Presidents We Imagine: Two Centuries of White House Fictions on the Page, the Stage, Onscreen and Online*, Madison, WI: University of Wisconsin Press, 2009, p. 266.

51. Farnsworth, 2009, p. 67.

52. www.cbsnews.com/news/florida-cleans-up-frances-mess.

53. Joseph R. Haden, *A Dubya in the Headlights*, Lanham, MD: Lexington, 2009, p. 177.

54. Farnsworth, 2009, p. 68.

55. Nancy Beck Young, "The Presidency and the Press," in Nancy Beck Young (ed.), *Encyclopedia of the U.S. Presidency*, New York, NY: Facts on File, 2013, p. 151.

56. Kerbel et al., p. 946.

57. Ibid. p. 154.

58. Matthew A. Baum and Samuel Kernell, "Has Cable Ended the Golden Age of Presidential Television?" *American Political Science Review*, Vol. 93 [March], 1999, p. 110.

59. Cohen, *The Presidency in the Era . . .*, pp. 56, 177.

60. James B. Lemert, "Content Duplication by the Networks in Competing Evening Newscasts," *Journalism Quarterly*, Vol. 51 (Summer), 1974.

61. Smith, 2009, p. 269.

62. Tom Rosenstiel, *The Beat Goes On: President Clinton's First Year with the Media*, New York, NY: The Twentieth Century Fund, 1994, p. xxiii.

63. Ibid.

64. Ronald M. Peters, "The Media in Our Partisan Era," *Extensions*, Winter, 2014, p. 3.

65. Thomas Patterson, *Doing Well and Doing Good: How Soft News and Critical Journalism are Shrinking the News Audience and Weakening Democracy—And What News Outlets Can Do About It*, Cambridge, MA: Joan Shorenstein Center for Press, Politics and Public Policy, 2000, p. 435.

66. Terence Smith, "Say This for Trump: He Has Given Us a Journalism Renaissance," *The Capital*, March 12, 2017, p. A12.

67. www.journalism.org/2014/03/26/state-of-the-news-media-2014-key-indicators-in-media-and-news/ and www.adweek.com/tvnewser/evening-news-ratings-week-of-may-22-2/330626.

68. Margaret Sullivan, "Scott Pelly Is Showing His Bias for the Truth," *Washington Post*, March 26, 2017, p. C1.

69. Sidney Blumenthal, "A Letter from Washington," *The New Yorker*, April 5, 1993.

70. Michael Nelson, "Why the Media Love Presidents and Presidents Hate the Media," *Virginia Quarterly Review*, Vol. 76, No. 2, 2000, p. 255. Available online at www.vqronline.org/essay/why-media-love-presidents-and-presidents-hate-media.

71. Ibid.

72. Ibid.

73. Martha Joynt Kumar, *Managing the President's Message: The White House Communication Operation*, Baltimore, MD: Johns Hopkins University Press, 2007, p. 92.

74. Ibid., p. xxxi.

75. Ibid., p. xx.

76. Quoted in Ibid, p. 3.

77. Bartholomew H. Sparrow, "Who Speaks for the People? The President, the Press, and Public Opinion in the United States," *Presidential Studies Quarterly*, Vol. 38, No. 4, 2008, p. 590.

78. Smith, 2009, p. 271.

79. Lee, pp. 261, 266.

80. Smith, 2009, p. 268.

81. Kernell, 1997, p. 67.

82. Farnsworth, 2009, p. 57.

83. Marlin Fitzwater, *Call the Briefing*, New York, NY: Times Books, 1995, p. 198.

84. Ben.H. Bagdikian, *The Media Monopoly*, Boston: Beacon Press, 1983, p. x.

85. Eshbaugh-Soha and Peake, p. 189.

86. Noah Bierman and Brian Bennett, "Spicer Resigns amid Shake-Up," *The Capital*, July 22, 2017, p. A2.

87. Ari Fleischer, *Taking Heat: The President, The Press, and My Years in the White House*, New York, NY: HarperCollins, 2005, p. 99.

88. Quoted in Marc Fisher and David Nakamura, "Smoking Gun or Distraction? All Depends on Whose Side You're On," *Washington Post*, July 13, 2017, p. A8.

89. Howard Kurtz, *Spin Cycle: Inside the Clinton Propaganda Machine*, New York, NY: The Free Press, 1998, p. 17.

90. Quoted in R. Nisbett and L. Ross, *Human Inference: Strategies and Shortcomings of Social Judgment*, Englewood Cliffs, NJ: Prentice Hall, 1980, p. 167.

91. Fisher and Nakamura, p. A8.

92. Margaret Sullivan, "In Journalism, Relaying the Truth Takes Precedence over 'Both Sides'," *Washington Post*, August 17, 2017, p. C8.

93. P. 12A.

94. P. A6.

95. www.nytimes.com/2001/03/22/us/bush-backs-patients-bill-of-rights-with-caveat.html.

96. www.washingtonpost.com/politics/trump-administration-earns-cautious-praise-for-early-response-to-deadly-hurricanes/2017/09/12/57c3376e-97be-11e7–87fc-c3f7ee4 035c9_story.html?utm_term=.51c69bba3f5f.

97. David Nakamura, *The Capital* (Annapolis, MD), September 13, 2017, p. A3.

98. Pew Research Center, 2007 Survey of Journalists.

99. David Niven, "An Interesting Bias: Lessons from an Academic's Year as a Reporter," *PS*, April 2012,p. 33.

100. Thomas Patterson and Wolfgang Donsbach, "News Decisions: Journalists as Partisan Actors," *Political Communication*, Vol. 13, No. 4, 1996, p. 465.

101. Ibid., p. 466.

102. Fleischer, p. 88.

103. Haden, p. 157.

104. Niven, pp. 260, 263.

105. www.gallup.com/poll/207794/six-partisan-bias-news-media.aspx.

106. Nelson.

107. Young, p. 151.

108. Nelson.

109. Richard Reeves, "The Question of Media Bias," in Shanto Iyengar and Richard Reeves (eds.), *Do the Media Govern?* Thousand Oaks, CA: Sage, 1977, pp. 40–41.

110. www.washingtonpost.com/news/the-fix/wp/2014/10/21/lets-rank-the-media-from-liberal-to-conservative-based-on-their-audiences/?utm_term=.a73665c64bad.

111. Quoted in Fleischer, 2005, p. 83.

112. Roderick Hart, *The Sound of Leadership*, Chicago, IL: University of Chicago Press, 1987, p. 111.

113. Ibid.

CHAPTER 2

THE PRESIDENT AS A NEWS HOOK
THE FIRST "W"

One of the first things journalism students learn about writing a story is to include the five "Ws"—Who? What? Where? When? and Why? The American media focuses on personalities. It is important to note that the "who" comes first in the journalistic formula. The president is the most important, authoritative, and familiar figure in the nation. This makes the president and his actions newsworthy and the most readily available personality on which to tie a story. Because of their high level of recognition, presidents serve as a much better "news hook" than members of competing political institutions. Reporters can hang their stories on the president since the public knows a significant amount about the president's background and political preferences. Stories about the president do not have to include a great deal of background information and can dig into contemporary issues and behavior. There are so many members of Congress to watch that most Americans do little more than react to Congress as an institution. "Most American could not pick more than a few members of Congress out of a police lineup."[1] Even when it comes to their own members of the House or Senate, less than half can usually recognize their names and even fewer can remember their names without prompting.[2] When the president acts, the media almost always covers the event, while members of Congress struggle for visibility (see Box 2.1).

Even though the public knows more about the president than other officials, what they purport to know is not always correct. Well into his term, 29% of Americans incorrectly identified Barack Obama as a Muslim and 20% asserted that he was born outside the U.S.[3] During the 2016 campaign, 10% of respondents incorrectly saw Barack Obama as a conservative while 21% incorrectly labeled Donald Trump a liberal.[4]

Box 2.1
Guess Who Is Coming to Dinner?

The primacy of the president as a news hook can be seen by the varied media reaction to visits by key policy-makers to Iraq in 2003. Although Senator Hillary Clinton received relatively little coverage on her four-and-a-half-day fact-finding mission, President George W. Bush's two-and-a-half-hour highly secret trip to serve Thanksgiving dinner to the troops garnered extensive coverage.[5] Much of the coverage focused on how the president snuck away from his ranch with Air Force One taxiing on departure and arrival with its lights off. Most coverage gave Bush credit for the visit and included the results of a photo op with the president carrying in a platter with a turkey. One might even get the impression that the president of the United States had cooked and basted the bird on the way over in Air Force One.

The efforts of presidents to show concern for the troops and secure positive media coverage by entering war zones has happened a number of times. President Lyndon B. Johnson made an unscheduled stop in Vietnam at the height of the war shortly before Christmas in 1967. President Richard M. Nixon went to Vietnam in 1969. On an earlier Thanksgiving, in 1990, President George H.W. Bush visited U.S. troops deployed in Saudi Arabia in the run-up to the 1991 Persian Gulf War. President Bill Clinton visited Bosnia in 1997.[6] Each visit led to extensive positive media coverage. While the military is a good target audience, unlikely to embarrass their commander in chief, not all troop visits result in positive coverage (see Box 5.3 on George W. Bush's visit to the USS *Lincoln*).

It is more than idle curiosity or massaging the president's ego that drive us to look at the president's coverage by the news media. The quality and quantity of presidential news coverage "affect the president's ability to lead the mass public."[7]

The Quantity of Presidential Coverage

The statistic that remains most consistent in the contemporary era is the imbalance of presidential coverage versus that of other institutions of government. The president gets at least twice as much coverage as Congress and nearly five times more coverage than the Supreme Court, no matter which medium one looks at[8] (see Figure 2.1). Awareness of the president and some basic information about him allows the journalist to begin a story without having to cover the personal context. No other political leaders share anything like the widespread public familiarity of the president.

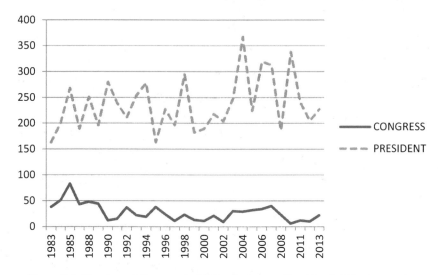

Figure 2.1 Number of Congressional Stories versus Presidential Stories on the Network News

Source: Data from the Vanderbilt Television News Archives (https://tvnews.vanderbilt.edu)

Even stories about Congress tend to mention the president prominently.[9] Other national personalities also suffer inattention. The president receives over ten times more coverage than the vice president or the secretary of state.[10]

When the president's party controls Congress, the attention focuses on the president. Under conditions of divided government, the opposition party emerges as a viable competitor to the president.[11] President Trump can hardly feel ignored by the media. Analyzing major news outlets, the Shorenstein Center found that during his first 100 days in office President Trump received 41% of all national coverage, three times the volume received by previous presidents.[12] Volume of coverage, though, can be a mixed blessing. With the exception of Fox News, a large percentage of the news coverage was negative (see later discussion).

The Shift to a Presidency-Centered Focus

The top-billing modern presidents receive in the news has not always been the case. Early presidents received considerably less coverage than Congress except during periods of crisis such as the Civil War and World War I.[13] It does not matter which form of media one looks at; presidential coverage dominates the modern era. The contemporary Congress, unlike a century ago, plays second fiddle to the president. "Congressional investigations and sharp legislative rhetoric can generate a headline from time to time, but Capitol Hill is too diverse and too disorganized to mount an effective media counterattack to presidential spin over the long haul."[14]

Media attention to the presidency emanates from the waxing and waning of presidential power. Our early presidents were active in shaping public policy and received considerable media attention. With the exception of Abraham Lincoln, presidents serving from the 1830s to the early 1900s played a much less critical role and coverage of Congress relative to the presidency increased. Teddy Roosevelt embodied the activist presidency. He invited members of the press on his travels across the country, giving interviews and allowing himself to be photographed presiding over the most media-friendly administration up until that point in time.[15] Franklin Roosevelt added impetus to the presidency-dominated coverage of the modern era.[16] FDR's "effective use of the mass media led to a new era of presidential marketing."[17]

Expanding expectations about presidential responsibilities such as a centralized budget and foreign policy management made the president the natural news hook. As the most widely recognized political leader, presidential coverage benefited from the nationalization of political news. While news was once largely limited to local concerns, national news services, national television networks, and social media platforms gravitated toward subjects recognized by the widest audience. The increased U.S. role in foreign affairs provided the president with a venue in which he is uniquely capable of performing. Public expectations that presidents will serve as the governmental reactors in chief focus attention on the timing and character of his reactions to natural disasters and human tragedies. The contemporary media almost immediately look to the president for a response. The lack of a timely reaction leads to negative media coverage.[18]

Changes in the media itself also drove them toward more presidential coverage. The expansion of the national network news to 30 minutes in 1963 required more national news and covering the president fit the bill.[19] The growth of newspaper syndicates and the relative size of national network news staffs meant that covering national stories in general and the presidency in particular were efficient ways to fill the news hole.

The Quality of Presidential Coverage

It is one thing to get coverage and another to get "good" coverage. John Kennedy popularized the sentiment that "success has a thousand fathers and failure is an orphan." When it comes to media coverage of the president, that should probably be rewritten to "success has a thousand fathers and failure shows up as the lead on the evening news." Bill Clinton bemoaned the fact that "success and the lack of discord are not as newsworthy as failure."[20]

To a large degree, winning the presidency carries with it the potential for a positive image. From the "ruffles and flourishes" played when the president enters the room to the pack of adoring aides making each event look good, symbolism gives the president an advantage. As others defer to him, there is little question who is in charge. Presidents associate with the "beautiful people" and are given many opportunities to say the right things at crucial times. All that said, the negativity of the media can be at least partially explained by the fact that "[w]arts on an ugly person are of far less interest than the appearance of blemishes on someone who is expected to look beautiful."[21] Since Grossman and Kumar wrote those words almost forty years ago, the media's hunt for imperfections of every type has only increased. When it comes to both their personal and public life, investigative journalists tend to view the president as guilty until proven innocent. The media dredges up decades-old statements and cries "inconsistent," not accounting for changed conditions. Alleged hypocrisy turns into a major news story before its validity or importance are proven. While presidents should not be immune to criticism, both the media and the public need to be judicious about the amount of emphasis they put on each example in evaluating the president.

From the very beginning, the media have criticized presidents. George Washington found himself disparaged for his domestic policies and political principles. Despite chafing at the assessment, Washington took a strong position on freedom of the press, saying "the freedom of Speech may be taken away—and, dumb and silent we may be led, like sheep, to the Slaughter."[22] Despite rude and inaccurate statements about him, Washington simply avoided public response to his detractors' claims.[23] What is new is the increased emphasis on negativity.

The Growth of Negativity

In a previous era, the media and the president were on very good personal terms. "The camaraderie between journalists and the president meant that reporters tended to cut President Kennedy some slack, even protecting him by holding back potentially damaging rumors about his sexual escapades, illnesses, and [legal] drug use."[24] Despite receiving relatively positive media coverage, Kennedy was not beyond frustration with the press. He once cancelled his subscription to the New York *Herald Tribune*, feeling that it provided biased coverage.[25]

The modern escalation of adversarial journalism has a variety of sources. Seeds of distrust have been scattered throughout the modern presidency. When the Soviets shot down an American spy plane in 1960, the Eisenhower administration tried to pass it off to the media as a weather plane. The capture of the pilot and plane belied the White House prevarication and forced the president to explain. President Johnson's handling of the Vietnam conflict led to a "credibility gap" recognized by the public and popularized by the media. He gave overly optimistic estimates of success and misled the public about an attack on a U.S. ship. This led Congress to pass the Gulf of Tonkin Resolution, giving the president a virtual blank check in pursuing the war. It is important to point out that Johnson served at a time period in which the media tended to be relatively supportive of the presidency. The term "credibility gap" is a polite way of saying that the president misled the public and Congress. Later presidents would simply be charged with lying.[26]

The Watergate cover-up during Richard Nixon's administration led to increased conflict between the White House and the media. The very cover-up itself undermined public and media trust in the presidency. Second, much of the media recognized that they had missed the boat in uncovering Watergate. Given the status of White House reporters and their desire not to jeopardize their access, it fell to two junior *Washington Post* reporters to seek out and nail down the story. Other journalists did not miss the fact that the efforts of Carl Bernstein and Bob Woodward led to Pulitzer Prizes. Investigative journalism became the new normal.

Far from simply being recorders of the facts, investigative journalists seek out weaknesses, shortcomings, and/or deceptions. As one journalist put it,

> My job is like that of your dentist. When you open your mouth you don't want him to brush you off with "everything is ok," when it is not. You go to the dentist to discover problems and have them corrected.[27]

In another journalist's words, "[I am at the White House] in part, to compel the government to explain and justify what it's doing . . . we're the permanent in-house critics of government."[28]

President Bill Clinton's misrepresentation of his relationship with White House intern Monica Lewinsky shattered his promise that "he would always be honest with the press and the people."[29] As one reporter put it, "both Clintons believed that Washington should take them as they presented themselves and they felt violated when the press corps would not go along."[30]

George W. Bush and his administration's insistence on the existence of weapons of mass destruction in Iraq became another marker along the road of media distrust. The media's generally positive reaction to Bush's warlike reaction to 9/11 turned to belated self-chastisement over the media's own lack of vigilance in discovering the truth.

Donald Trump waged a virtual war on the media, questioning their motives, patriotism, and capabilities (see Chapter 7). The media on the other hand has returned the criticism of their craft by pointing out the president's tendency to play fast and loose with the facts.

New producer's gravitation toward negative stories could be related to the existence of more questionable behavior on the part of the presidents. Alternatively journalists may hold the perception that audiences find negative stories more appealing and that covering them will promote their careers and help their organization's financial bottom line.

Negativity toward the president is matched by increased negativity toward other institutions in American society. Negative coverage of the president does him little good, but it is tempered by negative views of the media that deliver the story. "The battle between the president and the press [is] viewed as a clash between two morally ambiguous forces, not a shoot-out pitting the sheriff against the bad guys."[31]

For much of presidential history a cozy reciprocal relationship existed between the president and the press. The president largely held the upper hand and the media bolstered the presidential image. In the golden age of presidential television (the 1940s to the 1970s), the media tended to show deference to the president. When negative stories were reported, they tended to be so rare and unexpected that they seemed more credible to the public. In the subsequent era, negative stories became the norm.[32] In the modern era the relationship resembles much more of a competition with the media giving the president little slack and the president attempting to manipulate coverage.[33]

Modern journalists have taken to heart the perspective of turn-of-the twentieth-century humorist Peter Dunne, who argued that the "newspaper's job is to comfort the afflicted and afflict the comfortable."[34] In their evening the playing field, the president often finds himself directly in the media's sights.

Variable Levels of Negativity: The Overall Picture

According to a detailed analysis of the last four presidents, increased media negativity is clearly evident. The tone of news coverage for each president's first 100 days in office was almost twice as negative for Trump (80%) as it was for Obama (41%), and well above those recorded by Presidents G.W. Bush (57%) and Bill Clinton (60%). The negative tone of stories on Trump never fell below 70% and rose as high as 90% during his first 100 days in office (see Figure 2.2 and Box 2.2). Even President Jimmy Carter recognized President Trump's situation, commenting, "I think the media have been harder on Trump than any other president certainly that I've know about. I think they feel free to claim that Trump is mentally deranged and everything else without hesitation."[35] As President Trump's administration has progressed the volume and range of negative coverage has not subsided.

As for the individual U.S. news outlets, CNN and NBC led the pack with 93% negative coverage of President Trump, followed closely by CBS (91%), the *New York Times* (87%), the Washington *Post* (83%), the *Wall Street Journal* (70%), and Fox News (52%)—which should debunk the liberal notion that Fox is in the tank for Trump.[36] The opposite pattern developed for Barack Obama, who garnered positive treatment by the major networks except for Fox News.[37]

Not all criticism of Prescient Trump has come from sources usually considered more liberal. Even the more conservative *Wall Street Journal* harshly commented on Trump's continued and unproven assertion that the Obama administration had him wiretapped by using the metaphor of Trump "clinging to his assertion like a drunk to an empty gin bottle."[38]

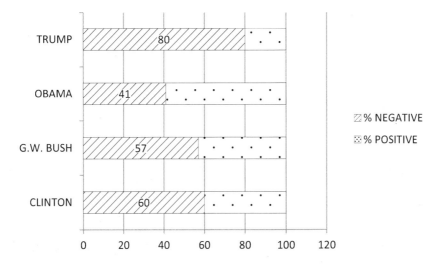

Figure 2.2 The Tone of Presidential Coverage during the First 100 Days

Source: Data from https://shorensteincenter.org/news-coverage-donald-trumps-first-100-days, Figure 4

White House correspondents are relatively upfront about what they see as bias in covering the Trump administration. Forty-five percent saw their colleagues as presenting a negative bias and only 2% a positive bias. The remainder felt that the media has been balanced in its coverage.[39]

If there is a bright spot for President Trump in his relationship with the media, it is the fact that more people (37%) believe that the White House has been more forthright than believe that about the media (29%). Almost half of the respondents believe that reporters have been more negative toward President Trump than was the case for previous administrations. Less than 20% of voters feel the media has let President Trump off easy.[40] In another national poll 51% of Americans believed the media had been too critical of Trump, while 41% thought news coverage had been fair and objective, and 6% said the media hadn't been tough enough. The evaluation of the media split clearly along partisan lines with Republicans much more likely to see the media as too critical.[41] The vast majority (81%) of Americans believe that President Trump's relationship with the media is worse than previous administrations and that it has hurt his ability as president.[42]

Variations in Negativity over Time

The tone of media coverage early in a presidential term is important since a president's ability to set and carry out his agenda declines over time. Most presidents arrive with a reservoir of goodwill, with even many of those who voted against them taking the position that "He is our president now. I will give him a chance."

BOX 2.2
Measuring the Media

It is one thing to present impressionistic evaluations or single examples of media coverage, and another to offer hard empirical data. Content analysis involves a laborious, but precise, empirical measure of the volume and/or tone of media coverage. It may focus either on the quantity or quality of coverage. Researchers read or view each article (headline, photo, paragraph), recording it as positive, neutral, or negative. Coding is often checked by having multiple researchers rate the same story (called "inter-coder reliability"). The degree of positive evaluation is normally related to how the subject of the story might rate it. Articles using terms such as "an ineffective president" or "an angry occupant of the Oval Office" would rate as negative. A pure descriptive statement such as "The president met today with the Canadian prime minister" rates a neutral tone. Calling the president "delighted with the outcome" or "basking in his recent success in Congress" are clearly positive. A positive a story about a president's trip might describe the crowds as large and enthusiastic. On the other hand, rather than simply describing upcoming presidential travel in a neutral way, a story might end with the snarky negative tag line "And tomorrow the president goes to Cleveland and no one knows why."[43]

Recent presidents have received both different levels of coverage and different degrees of positive and negative attention. Using the first fifty days of each administration, a study by the Center for Media and Public Affairs generally found that more coverage was negative than positive on the evening news programs. While President Obama was the exception, they found that even his coverage became more negative over time. After his first 100 days in office, only 43% of the stories about him were positive.[44]

Table 2.1 Quantity and Quality of Recent Presidential Media Coverage on Television

	Amount	% positive
Clinton	15 hours 2 min	44%
Bush	7 hours 42 min	33%
Obama	27 hours 44 min	58%

Source: Data from https://cmpa.gmu.edu/media-boost-obama-bash-his-policies

The presidential "honeymoon" is clearly borne out in terms of presidential support both among the public and other political actors. Bad media coverage tends to chip away at the armor of presidential adulation.

There is a great deal of truth in the assertion that presidents who want to leave office with the greatest media and public support should resign on inauguration day. Barring major events such as assassination attempts and national security challenges, presidential support tends to decline over time. During the first few months of an administration the media and the president are feeling each other out. In the "honeymoon stage," both have a stake in transmitting stories about the president's personality and policy initiatives that have a "gee whiz" character. As the novelty wears off, it becomes clear that the president and the media will be competing with each other to reach their goals. Generally, toward the end of a president's term there is a period of "detachment, or virtual cold war between the president and the media."[45] President Trump seems to have largely missed the first stage, jumping right into confrontation and conflict. All recent presidents have seen their coverage become more negative over time.[46]

Many observers conclude that Donald Trump's honeymoon looked more like it was on the path to a divorce. There was little attempt on either side to hide their mutual disdain. There is plenty of blame to go around. The media was still stinging from Trump's declaring them as the enemy during the 2016 presidential campaign. The fact that most of the media got it wrong when speculating about a potential Trump win undoubtedly stuck in their craws. The ideological disconnect between much of the media's personal views and Trump's brand of conservatism failed to make them natural allies. Trumps calling the media on the carpet for underestimating the inaugural crowd and the media firing back with its own photographic evidence led to a spitting contest over whose facts were real. Kellyanne Conway, one of Trump's key staff members, threw gasoline on the fire by talking about "alternative facts," undermining her credibility and that of her boss among large segments of the media and the public.

What is unique about President Trump's coverage is not only its extremely negative tone, but also the fact that he is given the opportunity to speak for himself. Presidents and other news sources have often complained because the "talking head" journalists and the individual's opponents fill out most of the story, leaving little room to explain themselves directly to the public. During the first 100 days, President Trump was the source of nearly two-thirds of the sound bites in stories about the presidency. The problem has been that much of the time the comments have been defensive, with the president trying to explain himself.[47]

The president's ability to control the news and get good coverage varies with the policy realm. Presidents tend to get more positive coverage on foreign versus domestic policy issues for a number of reasons. Presidents are able to control more of the foreign policy information under the blanket of national security concerns. When it comes to domestic policy, journalists can tap a much wider variety of sources to compete with the information provided by the president.[48] Also, both competing power centers—Congress and the media—are more hesitant to take on the president on foreign policy issues for fear of being seen as unpatriotic. The "rally around the flag" phenomenon tends to temper criticism.[49] The deference to President George W. Bush's claims during a press conference about Iraq's weapons of mass destruction stem partly from pressure on the media. As *New York Times* reporter Elisabeth Bumiller put it:

> [I]t's live, it's very intense, it's frightening to stand up there. Think about it, you're standing up on prime-time live TV asking the President of the United States a question when a country is about to go to war. . . . No one wanted to get into an argument with the President at this very serious time.[50]

Journalists are supposed to play the role of impartial "referees" determining what information the public receives. After 9/11, the media gave George W. Bush the "home team advantage" equating patriotism with letting one's guard down. In retrospect the media and Congress criticized themselves for not showing more skepticism toward the assertions of the George W. Bush administration about weapons of mass destruction in Iraq. Presidents may "enjoy foreign policy rally effects as a result of major military actions, yet even these are hard to sustain."[51]

What Is News to the News Media?

The word "news" is the plural of the word "new," so news involves new revelations about someone or something important. The large news hole reserved for anything presidential leads to a temptation of defining anything as news. The rehashing of old stories without any real update fails on the first test of newsworthiness. In the desire to provide context and establish a pattern, many presidential stories take the form of "in another example of. . ." There was little question that George W. Bush garbled some sentences and created plausible but incorrect words (such as "misunderestimated"),[52] but a good case can be made that there were other more important stories to cover on the days these were highlighted. Despite the danger of trivializing news, it became a cottage industry to find and point out these gaffes in books such as *The Bush Dyslexicon* by Mark Crispin Miller.[53] "In the quest for 24/7 news, what's novel is more important than what matters. Context and nuance are lost."[54]

Just as important as avoiding defining old phenomena as news, is the focus on the wrong things. Do we really need to know that Bill Clinton wore boxers rather than briefs, George H.W. Bush disliked broccoli, that Barack Obama liked to play basketball, and that Donald Trump eats fried chicken with a fork?[55]

"The kinds of stories that news editors assign and news reporters write are fairly predictable. They deal with conflict, disaster, policy setbacks, personal turnarounds, and reversals of political fortune."[56] There may be a silver lining in this assessment.

When such stories don't emerge, things must be going pretty well in the president's running of the country.

News media outlets compete with each other in defining news. There is clearly a hierarchy of news sources in America. One might consider the size of their audience, the composition of their readership or viewership, or their reputation. Despite some chinks in its armor, the *New York Times* plays a crucial role in defining what news is. Like a rock thrown into a pool creating a ripple, coverage by the *New York Times* sends a signal to the White House and more importantly to other media outlets as to what must be covered. Editors around the country scour its pages each day to make sure they are not missing something.[57] When it comes to national politics, the *Washington Post* plays a similar, if slightly less comprehensive, role. Recognizing the mutual benefit, the *New York Times* and the *Washington Post* share front pages of the next day's first edition early enough in the evening to allow compensation for a missed story in later editions. Regular news alerts throughout the day send signals about what is trending on other news venues encouraging their competitors to get on the emerging story.

Although the president is a good news hook, presidential stories must compete with other things going on in the world. Editors make judgment calls as to the importance of presidential stories relative to other stories that might crowd them off the page or keep them from airing. Even presidential scandals and major policy initiatives are less likely to get coverage when other events are seen as more important.[58]

Framing the News

Journalists fall back on established patterns in choosing stories to cover and how to cover them. These "frames" help to predetermine the way in which the president is viewed.

The Conflict Frame

The primary frame is one of conflict and competition. Presidents are represented as clashing with competitors in the other branches of government over public policy in their attempt to override the constitutional separation of powers and prevail with their political reputations and accomplishments in tack. When it comes to conflict, President Trump "is the journalist's dream. Reporters are turned on to what's new and different, better yet if it's laced with controversy." As one network executive put it, Trump "may not be good for America, but [he's] damn good for us."[59]

The conflict frame invites journalists to define the "good" guys and the "bad" guys. It focuses on motives, strategies, and effectiveness. Presidents are judged on their ability to win the conflict.

The Horserace Frame

Much research[60] has validated media focus on the "horserace" aspects of presidential campaigns. Most directly this appears in the form of fascination with the polls telling us who is in front and who is behind and with the internal machinations of the campaign. Reporters carry with them the horserace frame once they begin to cover the president.

Once in office, the competitive advantage of each president is replaced with media emphasis on presidential popularity measures. Presidents are evaluated in the abstract and relative to previous presidents at a particular point in their term. In the broader sense of the horserace, the media ponders whether a particular president will live to rule another day. President Obama stated that among the media there is a tendency to consider that the "job description of elected officials is to get reelected."[61] From the day a first-term president arrives in office, each action is weighed against its potential impact on how it will affect their desire for a second term.

The unprecedented number of cabinet and staff firings and resignations during the first two years of the Trump administration has been the subject of a barrage of media coverage. Each new departure has led much of the media to portray an administration in disarray.

President Trump's former press secretary Sean Spicer outlined his frustration with the media, saying, "No matter what you do, what you wear, it gets amplified to a degree you couldn't imagine." The media has an:

> obsession with who's up and who's down . . . versus the substance. . . . I understand that there's always going to be a little palace intrigue, but I think that the proportion that I've seen of palace intrigue versus policy is a little out of whack.[62]

A second variant of horserace coverage deals with the president's success or failure in dealing with the media itself. Stories in this realm portray the presidential/media competition as a race for access by the media and positive coverage for the president. The media itself becomes part of the story, either reporting on its own coverage biases, or more often on the shortcomings of the president's dealing with the media. This type of coverage most often appears when relations between the media and the president are particularly sour.[63] The contemporary media reveals a fixation with a president's support among the media and the public. For the news media, "every question boils down to one. 'How is the president doing?' That simply was not the case during most of our history."[64]

Third, in the legislative realm presidential success is measured by the portion of the president's legislative program that gets passed into law. Specialized organizations such as Congressional Quarterly even calculate presidential "batting averages," comparing the legislative support from one president to the next. Presidents seek to claim credit for enacting public policies that solve recognized problems, while avoiding blame for governmental inaction. In most cases, presidents receive more media credit for positive outcomes than they deserve and more blame than they are due.

Presidents attempt to take credit for outcomes coming to fruition on their watch even if they could more rightfully be credited to their predecessors. President Trump condemned the Bureau of Labor Statistics unemployment figures during his campaign, and then claimed credit for improved figures once in office, even though the data was based on a time period before any of his policies took effect. He also took credit for reducing the cost of the F-35 jet fighter, even though the agreement was negotiated before his inauguration.[65]

It takes a big ego to run for office. It is like the sandlot baseball player standing up and screaming "pick me, pick me" as teams are being formed. Presidents want their policy proposals to win both because of their commitment to them and to bolster their ego. Presidents unwilling to share some of the credit are tempted to expand their role in a particular compromise, leaving nothing for anyone else to brag about. While President Truman's famous observation that "a lot can be done in Washington if you let someone else take the credit"[66] contains a great deal of truth, presidents often do not want to share the credit. The media add to the problem by focusing on the wins and losses of a particular president, often not acknowledging other key players.

Modern presidents face the challenge of riding an immense roller coaster of media-facilitated high promises and troughs of dashed hopes. During the campaign or after major policy crises, the media want definitive answers to the question "so what are you going to do about it?" The answer becomes a criterion for future success or failure. Few policies fully solve identified problems and, even if some progress is made, some segments of the population remain dissatisfied. Opponents of the policy route taken receive considerable media attention, given the media's penchant for raising the question of who won and who lost. In the process, public support for the president declines. Each group of dissenters withdraws their support challenging the president's overall level of approval.

Journalists love to play the "blame game," attempting to determine whether presidents deserve credit or censure for their actions.[67] In telling the story, it is always easier to clearly point out the effective participants and the dolts. Americans tend not to accept fatalistic explanations of why particular events happened. They want to know who should be held responsible. One explanation emanates from the very nature of the English language, which embodies a cause and effect pattern. Subjects act (verb) on objects. We are less likely to say "the president's bill failed" (a fatalistic description) than to say "the president failed to get his bill passed."

We live in a visual age and have become used to television screens with multiple pictures and "crawls" across the bottom of the screen. Ari Fleisher describes another example of the blame game. Cable news networks used a small up or down arrow in the lower right corner to send a message as to whether the stock market was on the way up or down. When the market began to slide in 2002, coverage of President George W. Bush's speeches on the economy utilized a split screen with a down arrow filling half the screen, giving the clear indication that President Bush should be held responsible for the decline. A year later, when the market began to improve, a similar up arrow failed to appear.[68]

The "blame game" frame turns the president into a target for the media. Finding fault remains news well after the events in question. Eight months after 9/11, CBS ran a story indicating that President George W. Bush knew about the impending attacks before they happened. As it turns out, the CIA's daily briefing of Bush weeks before 9/11 did outline the general concept of terrorists hijacking air planes but did not conceive of using airplanes as missiles to attack buildings. The media and other politicians began to question why Bush had not acted to thwart the attack. The story became a "feeding frenzy" for weeks, leading to question both the president and his spokespersons.[69]

Another aspect of horserace coverage focuses on uncovering the presumed strategies of the president and his staff. Few, if any, policy decisions are evaluated by the media at face value. Decisions are not presented as good or bad in societal terms but relative to the president's political standing. Potential political gains or losses are attributed to each action. The White House staff is not seen as honest brokers of objective information, but rather partisan operatives promoting the president's interests who "launder the news—to scrub it of dark stains . . . and present it to the country crisp and sparkling white."[70] For journalists, focusing on the horserace aspect of presidential politics is less risky than delving into the complex world of policy analysis.[71]

Closely related to the horserace coverage is the "inside the bubble" analysis of who in the campaign and later on who on the White House staff is on the ascent and whose prospects have dimmed. The reassignment, resignation, or firing of a staff member receives considerable media attention. Such events are seen as signals of which policy preferences will succeed and/or signs of disarray in the political organization:

> Journalists' focus on the Washington power game—who's up and who's down, who's getting the better of whom—can be a fascinating story but at the end of the day, it's food for political junkies. It is remote enough from the lives of most Americans to convince them that the political system doesn't speak for them or to them.[72]

Criticism of the media for focusing on the internal politics of the White House more than the content of policy is recognized by the media. As one journalist complained, they want us to cover policy and not the palace intrigue. That challenge is that the White House itself is very, very focused on palace intrigue, and who's up and who's down. It is not just the press that's engaged in this . . . 70% of the content that gets asked about and discussed in these White House briefings is the press corps asking about who's doing what to whom inside the White House.[73]

White House personnel decisions are of special interest to the media. They are always looking for who is on the way up, and whose future is faltering. A leak or rumor that someone is about to resign or be fired often puts their White House career and effectiveness in a tailspin. For the press secretary, there is only one right answer to a question about a staff member's future employment in the White House: "The president has full confidence in everyone in the administration, right up until the day he fires them."[74] Presidents often allow departing staff to save face by resigning "to pursue other opportunities" or "to spend more time with their families," so as not to reflect badly on the president's initial decision to hire them. When key Trump advisor Steve Bannon was forced out, the official line from the White House was that the departure was a "mutual decision" and the president thanked him for his service. Bannon's "sins" included battling with other White House insiders and stealing some of the attention from President Trump.[75]

The combined impact of these horserace frames with their emphasis on strategy and outcome largely stripped of policy content leads the public to conclude that "it's all politics." Such a view is fertile ground for the growth of cynicism.[76]

Bad News and Gaffes

Given the media's negativity toward the president, sometimes the best a president can hope for is avoiding bad news. The American public has competing desires when looking at the president. In one sense, they want someone who stands out above the crowd in terms of intelligence, effectiveness, and morality. On the other hand, they desire a president with a "common touch" with whom they can identify.[77] Wise presidents must remember that every word of their utterances will be parsed and every one of their public actions searched for meaning and importance.

In general, bad news tends to make news more than good news. Research has shown that negative coverage tends to dominate the choice of what to cover. Failures in the legislative arena are more likely to receive coverage than successes. Changes in presidential popularity "are more likely to garner media attention when they are in the negative direction than when they are in the positive direction."[78] The "very real danger for presidents [is] that their good results will garner less attention that their bad results and that the American people will be given a quite misleading picture of their performance."[79]

Two types of negative stories, gaffes and scandals, draw journalists like ants to sugar. Gaffes refer to self-inflicted wounds that question the president's motives, character or intelligence.[80] Potential scandals emerge when a president is charged with illegal or immoral acts.

Individual gaffes such as misstating a fact, making a foolish statement, or stumbling over one's words (see Box 2.3) are simply human shortcomings that are often forgiven—especially by a president's supporters. It is unrealistic to expect that any president will always say what he means to communicate. Humans are not perfect. As one former CIA staff member put it,

> It is not unprecedented to people anywhere in the bureaucracy to have to clean up or to deal with in other ways statements that are short on veracity from the man at the top. What you are talking about with [President Trump] is a substantial difference of degree in which some of these things happen.[81]

When such gaffes represent a pattern, the president's character and intelligence may come under attack. When coupled with the easily refutable assertions about the size of the inaugural crowd, President Trump's insistence on disagreeing with the photographic evidence seemed to feed the media's attempt to paint him as reckless and short on truthfulness.[82]

Other gaffes have the potential to "draw back the curtain" and reveal the character of a sitting president. Getting a clue as to a president's intelligence, empathy, or the way he treats other people helps the public to evaluate the president as a person.

While many of President Trump's gaffes have occurred in his Facebook and Twitter postings (see Chapter 7), others have related to his behavior with foreign leaders. For example, President Trump garnered headlines when he seemingly pushed the Montenegrin prime minister out of the way to reach the front at a NATO summit as the participants gathered for a group photo.[83]

Whether these were simply mistakes or representative of policy or personality factors remains is subject to debate. Whatever the case, media attention to gaffes raises questions about any president and siphons off attention to other presidential actions.

Scandal stories are especially appealing to a negative media and cynical public. They fit the story line of good guys versus bad guys, with the media attempting to serve as referees who will let justice prevail. While no one—except probably those directly involved—support sweeping scandals under the rug, scandal coverage has the potential to overwhelm news about social problems and potential policy solutions.[84] Reporters and editors assume, with a degree of evidence, that the public finds such revelations interesting. Journalists don't believe they have to justify covering a scandal because each one is considered out of the ordinary and deserving some sort of punishment for breaking laws or moral standards.[85] Presidents caught in the crosshairs of media attention must walk a very careful

BOX 2.3
Bush League Grammatical Gaffes

No one questions President George W. Bush's mangling of the English language. Among his verbal gaffes one finds:

1. "Our enemies are innovative and resourceful, and so are we. They never stop thinking about new ways to harm our country and our people, and neither do we."—Washington, DC, August 5, 2004.
2. "Rarely is the question asked: Is our children learning?"—Florence, SC, January 11, 2000.
3. "You teach a child to read, and he or her will be able to pass a literacy test."—Townsend, TN, February 21, 2001.
4. "There's an old saying in Tennessee—I know it's in Texas, probably in Tennessee—that says, fool me once, shame on—shame on you. Fool me—you can't get fooled again."—Nashville, TN, September 17, 2002.
5. "And there is distrust in Washington . . . and I'll work hard to try to elevate it."—speaking on National Public Radio, January 29, 2007.
6. "Families is where our nation finds hope, where wings take dream."—LaCrosse, WI, October 18, 2000.[86]

George W. Bush's verbal gaffes led to two different conclusions. For his supporters they added some charm and a human face to a national leader who could make minor mistakes and laugh at himself for them. His detractors painted a darker picture, questioning his overall intelligence and capability for the highest office in the land.[87]

Presidents attempt to make virtues out of their shortcomings. George W. Bush readily admitted that "Sometimes I mangle the English language. . . . But all the time, whether you agree with me or not, you know where I stand and where I'm going to lead the nation."[88]

line. The media are interested in both the substance of the scandal and how the president reacts to it.

When charged with improper relations with Monica Lewinsky, President Clinton went through three stages of news management. At first he attempted to deny the relationship, but that failed to quell the attention. He then focused on discrediting his accusers by blaming them. The White House sent out Hillary Clinton to NBC's *Today* show to claim "a vast right wing conspiracy that has been conspiring against my husband since the day he announced for president."[89] When denial or redirection did not work, President Clinton admitted the improper relationship, but reframed the issue by distinguishing criteria by which to judge a president versus the private life of a caring, but philandering, husband and father attempting to protect his family from embarrassment.[90]

Most recent presidents have been charged with purportedly scandalous behavior. Some have led to serious attempts to remove the president from office (Nixon and Clinton). Others, such as questions of illegal aid to the Nicaraguan Contras (Reagan), the misrepresentation of facts about weapons of mass destruction in Iraq (George W. Bush), and ties with Russia (Trump), festered for years, drawing attention away from other presidential stories.

Hard News versus Soft News

The definition of legitimate news about the president is difficult. In the human desire to know the president as a person "news" stories emerge about the president's family, pets, book preferences and eating habits. It is not so much that presidents don't receive adequate media coverage, but rather that soft news coverage has increased at the expense of hard news dealing with public policy and presidential performance. Given their commitment of staff to the White House, the mainstream media is forced by their investors to justify such an allotment of resources by posting White House stories every day. It is still true that "No matter how pedestrian his day may have been, no matter what other matters of great moment may have imposed themselves on the nation that day, an American president will be seen, heard and read every twenty-four hours."[91] The result is that more and more soft news and "feel good" stories make it through the production and editing process.[92]

The growing overall emphasis on soft news stories about celebrities and personalities has added a word to our vocabulary, "infotainment." Thus a president trying to push stories about policies finds the media more interested in his personality, meetings with celebrities, and lifestyle.[93] As an example of "soft" news, a number of reporters commented on the first lady Melania Trump's choice of wardrobe when visiting hurricane victims, especially pointing out the incongruous wearing of three-inch heels for the visit rather than focusing on her interaction with the victims.[94]

Fascinated with presidents as persons, journalists often ask them about their favorite historical figure or the most recent book they have read. George W. Bush opted for the Bible, while Barack Obama chose *Self Reliance* by Ralph Waldo Emerson.[95] The fact that Donald Trump is not a great reader has not gone without notice.[96] Presidential heroes most often include one or two of their predecessors. Barack Obama found inspiration in Lincoln, while President Trump is a fan of Andrew Jackson and Ronald Reagan. Pressed for his rationale as he ruminates about his political heroes, President Trump receives criticism from the media as they conclude that he "often gets the facts wrong or comes up with interpretations sharply at odds with the historical consensus."[97]

Public fascination with the "soft news" side of the presidency, and the media's compliance in feeding the public stories about presidential lifestyles and peculiarities, may well shortchange the role of citizens in a representative democracy. Without adequate hard news about presidential policy goals and strategic behavior, the public may lack the necessary tools to hold the president accountable.[98] Part of the president's power lies in his ability to monopolize the public space.[99] Presidents who get shortchanged by the media in the coverage of their policy role suffer the potential of becoming less politically influential and relevant.

The Presidential News Audience

The creation of media stories means little unless there is a readership or viewership to consume it. Potential audiences make choices about what to attune to based on trust and political opinions.

Public Trust in the Media

Trust in the media in general, or in particular media outlets, is important since "individuals trust information coming from well-known or familiar sources and from sources that align with their worldview."[100] In general, the public is far from enamored with the media and its performance. When asked "if the news media helps society to solve its problems, or if the news media gets in the way of society solving its problems," 58% felt they got in the way, compared with 31% who felt they helped solve problems.[101] Trust in the media to report news accurately has eroded over time. Only about one-third of Americans have a "great deal" or "fair amount" of trust in the media. That figure drops to less than 15% among Republicans. The future of trust in the media looks bleak since younger citizens have significantly less trust than older citizens[102] (see Figure 2.3).

When it comes to trust, the public has more confidence in local media than other outlets. National media suffers in comparison, with less than 20% having a "great deal" of trust in its product. Social media has yet to earn the trust of the general public[103] (see Figure 2.4).

Evaluation and use of various media vary with one's partisan and ideological proclivities. Liberals (more likely to be Democrats) have a more positive impression and lean toward CNN and MSNBC for their news. Conservatives (more likely to be Republicans) are over ten times more likely to tune in to the more conservative Fox News[104] (see Figure 2.5).

In more general terms, Democrats (liberals) are more supportive of the media than are Republicans (conservatives). When their party controls the presidency, Democrats are more positive toward the media than when Republicans occupy the White House. The opposite is true of Republicans.[105] During the early months

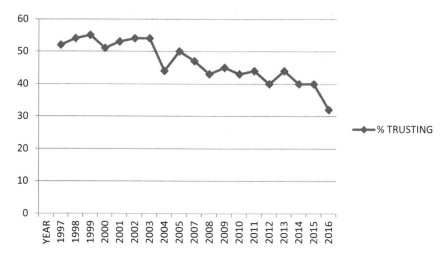

Figure 2.3 Trust in the Media

Note: "Great deal" or "fair" trust in the media to report news accurately.

Source: Data from www.gallup.com/poll/195542/americans-trust-mass-media-sinks-new-low.aspx

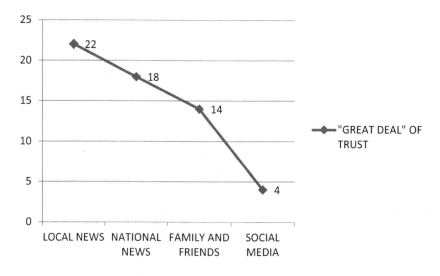

Figure 2.4 Trust in Media Outlets

Source: Data from the Pew Research Center, "The Modern News Consumer," www.journalism.org/2016/07/07/the-modern-news-consumer

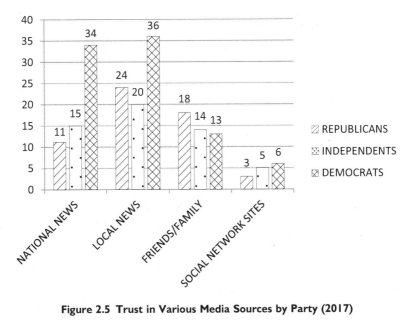

Figure 2.5 Trust in Various Media Sources by Party (2017)

Source: Data from the Pew Research Center, "Americans' Attitudes about the News Media Deeply Divided along Partisan Lines," http://journalism.org/2017/05/10/media-attitudes-appendix-a-detailed-tables

of the Trump administration, Democrats evaluated the media much more positively than did Republicans.[106] Republicans tend to have a basic distrust of freedom of the press, with 49% of strong Republicans believing "we have gone too far in expanding the right of freedom of the press," as compared with 6% of strong Democrats taking the same position.[107] Over 60% of Republicans believe that the media "keeps political leaders from doing their jobs," with independents and Democrats much less likely to take that position.[108]

Public evaluation of the quality of news coverage of the president tends to be relatively low, with the evaluation colored by one's partisan preferences. Overall, about 40% of the public approves of the way the media covers President Trump. That figure drops to 7% among Republicans and rises to 71% for Democrats. Independents fall in between at 36%.[109] It is telling that polling firms did not ask similar questions about previous presidents and their treatment by the media. The public did have a measured opinion on whether President Obama was treated fairly. Forty percent of the public felt he was treated easier than previous presidents, with about the same percentage feeling he received the same treatment.[110]

From the president's perspective, distrust in the media does not necessarily translate into trust in the president. In a head-to-head evaluation a much larger percentage of the American public trusted the news media (52%) than Donald Trump (37%) when it came to the presentation of important issues.[111] In taking out his frustrations on the media, President Trump does not inevitably bolster his own position. To add confusion, another national poll reported Trump viewed as more trustworthy than the media, with both well below 50%.[112] What is clear is that neither President Trump nor the news media ranks high in trust among the American public.

News Gathering Routines

Despite the president's potential to lead the mass media, the possible impact of the president on public opinion must take into account the decline of the traditional mass media. If the public is increasingly attuned to other sources of political news, or show no interest in such information, being able to set the agenda for some segments of the media fails to guarantee a president's ability to affect the national agenda.[113]

Since the 1970s, broadcast television and newspapers have chased a smaller and smaller news audience as individuals used an increasing number of information sources on cable television and the Internet. It is not so much that people today are uninformed, but rather that they are informed about other things—many of which have little to do with politics in general or the presidency in particular.

While television remains the public's primary source of news, online access is growing especially among younger citizens. Radio and television have declined rapidly and appeal most to older members of the public[114] (see Figure 2.6). Although the number of people securing their news from the major networks has declined, they still represent big players in the media game. The arrival of cable

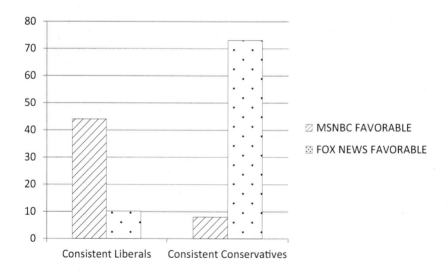

Figure 2.6 Cable News Favorability and Ideology
Source: Data from www.people-press.org/2014/06/12/views-of-msnbcfox-table

television alternatives created a need for a new strategy on the part of the White House. Even though only a few hundred thousand people might be watching a particular cable program at a particular time, those who watch are likely to be some of the most interested and active citizens who "get the buzz going."[115] While the concept of "going viral" became popular after the Internet emerged, the rapid spread of stories to the wider population predates the Internet.

The increased variety of news sources and the reemergence of opinionated outlets across the political spectrum "allows people to gravitate to a news provider that reinforces their preexisting political orientations."[116] Thus Republican consumers can find stories to strengthen their commitment to Republican presidents, while during times of a Democrat in the White House Democratic supporters can acquire stories to reinforce their preferences. It is clear that Republicans find Fox News more pleasing and credible, while Democrats gravitate toward MSNBC.[117] The ability to find and utilize websites with a supportive set of political views is even more convenient. The increasingly fragmented news audience in America feeds conflict and partisanship making evaluations of the president more and more divergent. The availability of slanted news reduces in the number of people receptive to objective presidential news and the increases number of people resistant to change.[118]

Securing an Audience

With the increased competition for "eyeballs," the news media has ushered in an age where a broader range of media attempt to capture the attention of audiences. Print media and Web stories use extreme headlines a graphics to lure users to read particular stories rather than skipping over them as they scan the page. For the Web, the strategy even has a name, "clickbait." Television uses its own set of strategies, particularly relying on anticipation to keep viewers attuned. The beginning of newscasts is filled with "teases" as to what one will see if they "stay tuned." Increasingly, everything becomes "breaking news," even stories that have been around for a number of days. Viewers are threatened that if they don't tune in they will miss something important. For presidents this means that only their most dramatic statements will make the cut.

Conclusion

The quantity and quality of presidential news serves as a surrogate measure of his importance both to the media and the public. By pushing out other political players, an extensively covered president makes it more difficult for competitors in both the public and private sector to make their case.[119] In recent years, the media have become more negative in their coverage, leading to more conflict in what and how they cover the president. The media use a relatively limited number of story lines to portray the president to the American public. Media stories do not necessarily fall on fertile ground. Readers and viewers make choices about which media they wish to attune and how to react to it.

Notes

1. Stephen Farnsworth, *Spinner in Chief: How Presidents Sell Their Policies and Themselves*, Boulder, CO: Paradigm, 2009, p. 3.

2. http://news.gallup.com/poll/162362/americans-down-congress-own-representative. aspx, and www.huffingtonpost.com/todd-phillips/congress-election-results_b_2114947.html.

3. www.cnn.com/2015/09/13/politics/barack-obama-religion-christian-misperceptions.

4. www.electionstudies.org/studypages/anes_timeseries_2016/anes_timeseries_2016_userguidecodebook.pdf.

5. www.washingtonpost.com/archive/politics/2003/11/28/bush-surprises-troops-in-iraq/39bd2362-b6d9-40b4-bb05-5befaa24dccf/?utm_term=.7654fcbdaf03.

6. Ibid.

7. Jeffrey E. Cohen, "The Presidency and the Mass Media," in George C. Edwards and William G. Howell (eds.), *The Oxford Handbook of the American Presidency*, New York: Oxford University Press, 2009, p. 254; David L. Paletz, *The Media in American Politics: Contents and Consequences*, New York, NY: Longman, 1998, p. 240.

8. Matthew Eshbaugh-Soha and Jeffrey S. Peake, *Breaking Through the Noise: Presidential Leadership, Public Opinion, and the News Media*, Stanford, CA: Stanford University Press, 2011, p. 16; Martha Joynt Kumar, *Managing the President's Message: The White House Communication Operation*, Baltimore, MD: Johns Hopkins University Press, 2007.

9. Cohen, pp. 256–257.

10. https://cmpa.gmu.edu/study-obamas-media-coverage-sours.

11. Cohen, p. 265.

12. https://shorensteincenter.org/news-coverage-donald-trumps-first-100-days

13. Herbert J. Gans, *Deciding What's News*, New York: Pantheon, 1979.

14. Farnsworth, p. 57.

15. Nancy Beck Young, "The Presidency and the Press," in Nancy Beck Young [ed.] *Encyclopedia of the U.S. Presidency*, New York, NY: Facts on File, 2013, p. 155.

16. Young, p. 149.

17. Farnsworth, p. 2.

18. Roderick Hart, *The Sound of Leadership*, Chicago, IL: University of Chicago Press, 1987, pp. 193 and 198.

19. https://shorensteincenter.org/news-coverage-donald-trumps-first-100-days.

20. William Clinton, press conference, May 7, 1993, Washington, DC.

21. Michael Baruch Grossman and Martha Joynt Kumar, *Portraying the President: The White House and the News Media*, Baltimore, MD: Johns Hopkins University Press, 1981, p. 316.

22. Petula Dvorak, "Why Blocking Facebook Critics Could Leave Us 'Dumb and Silent,'" *Washington Post*, August 4, 2017, p. B1.

23. Young, p. 150.

24. Steven Levingston, "The Communicators," *Washington Post Magazine*, May 21, 2017, p. 34.

25. Tom Rosenstiel, *The Beat Goes On: President Clinton's First Year with the Media*, New York, NY: The Twentieth Century Fund, 1994, 1998, p. xx.

26. Jeffrey E. Cohen, *The Presidency in the Era of 24-Hour News*, Princeton, NJ: Princeton University Press, 2008, p. 38.

27. Author's interview.

28. Quoted in J. Anthony Lukas, "The White House Press 'Club'," *New York Times Magazine*, May 15, 1977, p. 67.

29. Matthew Kerbel, Dom Bonafede, Martha Joynt Kumar, and John L. Moore, "The President and the News Media," in Michael Nelson (ed.), *Guide to the Presidency*, Washington, DC: CQ Press, 2008, p. 983.

30. Ibid.

31. Howard Kurtz, *Spin Cycle: Inside the Clinton Propaganda Machine*, New York, NY: The Free Press, 1998, p. 288.

32. Cohen, 2008, p. 14.

33. Samuel Kernell, *Going Public: New Strategies of Presidential Leadership*, Washington, DC: Congressional Quarterly Press, 1997, p. 96.

34. www.poynter.org/news/today-media-history-mr-dooley-job-newspaper-comfort-afflicted-and-afflict-comfortable.

35. Quoted in Gary Abernathy, "Will the Media's Anti-Trump Fever Ever Break?" *Washington Post*, October 17, 2017, p. A21.

36. www.aim.org/don-irvine-blog/harvard-study-media-coverage-of-trumps-first-100-days-overwhelmingly-negative.

37. https://cmpa.gmu.edu/media-boost-obama-bash-his-policies.

38. Margaret Sullivan, "Scott Pelly is showing his bias for the truth," *Washington Post*, March 26, 2017, p. C1.

39. www.politico.com/magazine/story/2017/04/28/poll-trump-white-house-press-corps-journalists-215051.

40. http://nypost.com/2017/04/28/more-voters-trust-trump-than-the-political-media-poll/.

41. www.forbes.com/sites/markjoyella/2017/02/26/more-than-half-of-americans-think-the-media-is-too-tough-on-trump/#289333ba1a64.

42. www.monmouth.edu/polling-institute/reports/MonmouthPoll_US_032917.

43. Kernell, pp. 94–96.

44. https://cmpa.gmu.edu/study-obamas-media-coverage-sours.

45. Michael Nelson, "Why the Media Love Presidents and Presidents Hate the Media," *Virginia Quarterly Review*, Vol. 76, No. 2, 2000.

46. http://cmpa.gmu.edu/obamas-media-image-compared-to-what.

47. https://shorensteincenter.org/news-coverage-donald-trumps-first-100-days.

48. Cohen, 2009, p. 265.

49. John Mueller, "Presidential Popularity from Truman to Johnson," *American Political Science Review*, Vol. 64 (1970).

50. Quoted in Ben Fritz, Bryan Keefer, and Brendan Nyhan, *All the President's Spin: George W. Bush, the Media and the Truth*, New York, NY: Touchstone, 2004, p. 48.

51. Bartholomew H. Sparrow, "Who Speaks for the People? The President, the Press, and Public Opinion in the United States," *Presidential Studies Quarterly*, Vol. 38, No. 4, 2008, p. 589.

52. http://content.time.com/time/specials/packages/article/0,28804,1870938_1870943_1870945,00.html.

53. Mark Crispin Miller, *The Bush Dyslexicon*, New York, NY: W.W. Norton, 2002.

54. Margaret Sullivan, "The media's report card for the first 100 days," *Washington Post*, May 1, 2017, p. C1.

55. www.bravotv.com/blogs/obama-favorite-food-and-surprising-dishes-us-presidents-loved-hated-clinton-bush-lincoln.

56. Kumar, p. 289.

57. Ibid.

58. Brendan Nyhan, "Scandal Potential: How Political Context and News Congestion Affect the President's Vulnerability to Media Scandal," *British Journal of Political Science*, Vol. 25, 2014, p. 457.

59. https://shorensteincenter.org/news-coverage-donald-trumps-first-100-days.

60. See Anthony Broh, "Horse-Race Journalism: Reporting the Polls in the 1976 Presidential Election," *Public Opinion Quarterly*, Vol. 44, No. 4, 1980, pp. 514–529.

61. http://abcnews.go.com/print?id=9659064, See also, Brendan Doherty, *The Rise of the President's Permanent Campaign*, Lawrence, KS: University of Kansas Press, p. 120.

62. Newseum, "President and the Press" conference, Session 3, pp. 2 and 14, available at www.newseum.org/2017/04/12/diverse-opinions-spark-conversation-at-the-president-and-the-press.

63. Grossman and Kumar, p. 307.

64. Nelson, p. 255.

65. James Hohmann, "Trump Team Taking Credit for Successes on Obama's Watch," *Washington Post*, March 13, 2017, p. A 15.

66. Quoted in David McCullough, *Truman*, New York, NY: Simon and Schuster, 1993.

67. Ari Fleischer, *Taking Heat: The President, The Press, and My Years in the White House*, New York, NY: HarperCollins, 2005, p. 155.

68. Fleischer, p. 244.

69. Ibid., pp. 237–238.

70. Rosenstiel, pp. xix–xx.

71. James Fallows, "The Presidency and the Press," in Michael Nelson (ed.), *The Presidency and the Political System*, Washington, DC: CQ Press, 1988, p. 295.

72. www.nytimes.com/2017/02/04/opinion/sunday/why-nobody-cares-the-president-is-lying.html.

73. Newseum, Session 6, p. 2.

74. Marlin Fitzwater, *Call the Briefing*, New York, NY: Times Books, 1995, p. 87.

75. www.cnn.com/2017/08/18/politics/steve-bannon-white-house/index.html.

76. Doherty, p. 161.

77. Thomas Cronin and Eugene Genovese, *The Paradoxes of the American Presidency*, New York, NY: Oxford University Press, 1998, p. 4.

78. David Niven, "An Interesting Bias: Lessons from an Academic Year as a Reporter," *PS*, April 2012, p. 35.

79. Ibid., p. 39.

80. See Stephen Frantzich, *O.O.P.S.: Observing Our Politicians Stumble*, Santa Barbara, CA: Praeger, 2012.

81. Abby Philip, "From Little Tweets Can Grow Great Firestorms," *Washington Post*, July 23, 2017, p. A4.

82. www.usatoday.com/story/news/politics/2017/01/24/fact-check-inauguration-crowd-size/96984496.

83. www.nytimes.com/2017/05/25/us/politics/trump-push-aside-leader-montenegro-nato-summit.html?_r=0.

84. Kurtz, p. 186.

85. Fallows, p. 302.

86. *Slate*, www.slate.com/articles/news_and_politics/bushisms/2009/01/ws_greatest_hits.html. For video clips, see www.slate.com/articles/news_and_politics/bushisms/2009/01/ws_greatest_hits.html.

87. Joseph R. Hayden, *A Dubya in the Headlights*, Lanham, MD: Lexington Books, 2009, pp. 41–43.

88. Quoted in Martha Joynt Kumar, *Managing the President's Message: The White House Communication Operation*, Baltimore, MD: Johns Hopkins University Press, 2007, p. 77.

89. www.youtube.com/watch?v=EwtkorQKGFE.

90. Farnsworth, pp. 74–75.

91. Hart, p. 111.

92. Cohen, 2008, pp. 60 and 63.

93. Thomas Patterson, *Doing Well and Doing Good: How Soft News and Critical Journalism are Shrinking the News Audience and Weakening Democracy—And What News Outlets Can Do About It*, Cambridge, MA: Joan Shorenstein Center for Press, Politics and Public Policy, 2000.

94. http://nypost.com/2017/08/29/melania-wears-her-heels-to-harvey-hellzone.

95. www.buzzfeed.com/daveodegard/the-favorite-books-of-all-44-presidents-of-the-united-states?utm_term=.bind6OAWPN#.vmAegoNvJa.

96. www.nytimes.com/2017/01/25/us/politics/president-trump-white-house.html?_r=0.

97. Jenna Johnson, "For Trump, Ghosts of Presidents Past," *Washington Post*, May 4, 2017, p. A4.

98. Cohen, 2008, p. 49.

99. Ibid., p. 50.

100. https://shorensteincenter.org/wp-content/uploads/2017/05/Combating-Fake-News-Agenda-for-Research-1.pdf.

101. A 2002 Pew Research Center poll reported in Fleischer, 2005, p. 99.

102. www.gallup.com/poll/195542/americans-trust-mass-media-sinks-new-low.aspx.

103. www.journalism.org/2016/07/07/the-modern-news-consumer.

104. www.journalism.org/2017/01/18/trump-clinton-voters-divided-in-their-main-source-for-election-news.

105. www.people-press.org/2017/07/10/sharp-partisan-divisions-in-views-of-national-institutions/.

106. http://maristpoll.marist.edu/wp-content/misc/usapolls/us170621_PBS_NPR/NPR_PBS%20NewsHour_Marist%20Poll_National%20Nature%20of%20the%20Sample%20and%20Tables_Democracy_Trust_July%202017.pdf#page=3.

107. Ibid.

108. www.americanpressinstitute.org/publications/reports/survey-research/partisanship-attitudes-about-news.

109. https://poll.qu.edu/national/release-detail?ReleaseID=2461.

110. www.pollingreport.com/obama_ad13.htm.

111. www.forbes.com/sites/markjoyella/2017/02/26/more-than-half-of-americans-think-the-media-is-too-tough-on-trump/#289333ba1a64.

112. https://morningconsult.com/2017/04/28/political-media-earns-poor-marks-americans.

113. Cohen, 2008, p. 1.

114. www.journalism.org/2016/07/07/the-modern-news-consumer.

115. Martha Joynt Kumar, *Managing the President's Message: The White House Communication Operation*, Baltimore, MD: Johns Hopkins University Press, 2007, p. 197.

116. Cohen, 2009, p. 275.

117. www.journalism.org/2017/01/18/trump-clinton-voters-divided-in-their-main-source-for-election-news.

118. Cohen, 2009, p. 276.

119. Cohen, 2009, p. 255.

Chapter 3

Covering the White House

Today, the White House beat is considered a "prestige" job," although journalists were not permanently assigned to the White House until the late 1800s.[1] The route to the White House is varied, but a large number of White House correspondents come off the campaign trail after covering the winning presidential candidate. This may color their reporting since, if "their" candidate wins, their White House job prospects look brighter. Editors and television bureau chiefs often put their more experienced reporters at the White House, "even though it's a heavily controlled and sometimes too-cozy environment with very little news to sniff out. Plus, the schedule is such that you can have children and maintain healthy personal relationships while covering the White House."[2]

In 1896, William W. Price of the *Washington Star* became the first permanent correspondent based at the White House. He was literally an "outsider." His technique was simple. He stood outside the White House gates and interviewed people coming and going. It turned out to be very interesting to his editors and readers. In 1898, the existence of a White House beat was validated when William McKinley invited reporters into the White House, giving them space to write and conduct interviews.[3]

Observing the current White House press corps one might be surprised that until Franklin Roosevelt took office "correspondents evolved from an amorphous collection of visiting editors, reporters on temporary assignment, and disguised job seekers to a stable community of professional journalists."[4]

Franklin Roosevelt (FDR) arrived on the scene as journalism became more professional. Unlike his cousin Teddy, FDR did not pick favorites among the press but rather facilitated competition. Journalists began to recognize that fairness and openness were best for them both individually and collectively. The bywords of the FDR approach were "hard news, openly conveyed."[5]

FDR used cordiality and charm to influence and disarm. He often suggested to reporters how they might write a particular story. He let the reporters on the White House beat off the hook for negative stories, suggesting they must have been the result of their editors.[6] FDR largely eschewed one-on-one interviews after a barrage of criticism from other journalists when he carried out one with a *New York Times* reporter. Reporters whose tenure spanned a number of presidencies look back at the Roosevelt model with appreciation.[7]

Who Covers the President?

Although virtually any reporter can write about the president, we think of the White House press corps as those who have regular access and cover the president's activities on an ongoing basis. The right to attend White House briefings is limited to those holding official press passes. Prior to September 11, 2001, that number had grown to over 1,700. Given increased security considerations, that number was reduced to less than 800 and limited to those covering the White House on a regular basis. The first requirement to get a White House press pass is a congressional pass. The congressional press pass requires working for an independent news organization with a Washington bureau and living or working in or around Washington. Second, to get a press pass, one must have a letter from

Photo 3.1 Laura Bush Tours the Cramped White House Press Offices

Source: AP photo/Pablo Martinez Monsivais

the bureau chief of one's organization assuring that you will cover the White House on a regular basis. Other reporters can apply for one-day passes to cover special events, such as press conferences.[8] About seventy journalists cover the White House beat on a daily basis.[9] The briefing room usually used by the press secretary—and much less frequently by the president—only has forty-nine seats for reporters.[10] The regular participants in the White House briefing process (see Chapter 4) are dominated by the major news outlets. In recent years, they have been joined by online outlets.

Demographically the White House press corps matches the overall bias in the media in general. Journalists are predominantly male (72% for newspapers versus 49% in the general population) and white (83% versus 63% in the general population). White House correspondent, as is true for the media in general, remains a dominantly male occupation. As of 2017, only 35% of the correspondents are female.[11] This figure, however, is up from 28% during the Obama administration.[12] In earlier years, the lack of black journalists in the White House press corps resulted from the nature of publications they represented. The rules for admission to briefings and press conferences stipulated they would only be open to reporters covering the White House on a daily basis. Most of the black publications for which African-American reporters worked were weeklies thus freezing them out of access. African-American reporters did not gain formal access to White House news conferences until 1944.[13]

New media outlets and online media staffs tend to be much more representative of the U.S. population than their predecessors. Despite the imbalance in the White House press corps, the trend is toward a pool of journalists that more and more looks like the population to which they are speaking.[14]

Serving as a White House Reporter

Life as a White House correspondent offers a variety of challenges along with great opportunities. What happens behind the scenes often belies what the public sees or reads. Few ambitious reporters would not be tempted by an offer to report from the White House.

Life in the Fish Bowl

The image of the White House press interacting directly and freely with the president belies reality. As the president strides out to the Rose Garden microphones,

> the press corps [is] funneled by guards to a position at the back of the garden, squeezed in between bleachers for TV cameras. The press also [faces] an

additional obstacle: a moat of several dozen White House staffers standing directly in front of them creating a 30–40 foot barrier. For reporters taking notes it [is] almost impossible to see the President.[15]

Members of the media have limited access to key players in the White House. "Unlike reporters who cover Congress, White House Reporters can't walk the halls and bump into good sources for news. Instead, they are housed in cramped work spaces, waiting for their phones to ring with the returned calls they are hoping for."[16] While far from commodious, the working area for the media was enhanced in 1969 when Richard Nixon had the White House swimming pool covered over to create a press briefing room that now has forty-nine seats and a series of small cubicles from which reporters work. The cramped quarters of the White House press led one reporter to complain that the working conditions "were worse than in the average small-town city hall."[17]

Another press secretary admits that White House correspondents are managed and controlled by the president's schedule, which controls their lunch and leaving times. They might be big names on television or in the newspaper, but at the White House they are thwarted by presidential minions just out of college who tell them to "wait here" or "go over there."[18] "The press corps is an unwanted appendage . . . a problem to be managed, a block of people to be moved around like a checker."[19]

The White House journalists' job is very competitive. "All reporters live in fear of getting scooped . . . when you are covering something else and you get beat, no one knows it. When you're covering the White House and you get beat, your editor calls you at home."[20] Being stationed at the White House may grant professional status, but the daily grind of putting out a story is both challenging and degrading. Journalists are treated more like pests than vital players in a democracy. On many issues the media speaks with a very similar voice. "Pack journalism" reflects the fact that members of the media interact with each other, and, despite inherent competition, often share information and perspectives. White House counselor Kellyanne Conway argues that it is not so much that "familiarity breed[s] contempt" but rather "familiarity breeds content."[21]

Despite their prestige with the public, reporters have to go "hat in hand" to beg information, often from White House staff failing to match the reporter's education and experience. The media seek unique stories and perspectives. They want exclusives and are frustrated with being part of the pack. They want scoops and insights. Journalists get frustrated when White House staff members speak only in "the official tone of voice."[22] On the whole, the White House press corps is a rather unruly crowd, jockeying for position to get good pictures or a random question at a White House photo op. While the White House dress code is rather formal, the press corps troops into the Oval Office in "blue jeans, sandals and all manner of garb."[23]

The White House press corps has an insatiable desire for information. As Marlin Fitzwater observed, it "gathers every morning like a pride of lions. It snarls, and growls, sleeps and creeps, and occasionally loves, but it always stays hungry."[24] The White House press staff has a number of tools to "kill the messenger." Freezing out certain publications or reporters from press conferences, pool assignments or interviews deprives them of the meat and potatoes of their jobs—information. On the other side of the coin, White House operatives are not above leaking important information to reporters known for favoring the administration, offering them interviews allowing them to ask questions during press briefings[25] and other means of "coddling the messenger."

Much of the job of the individual White House correspondent is a "body watch" (see later discussion). No reporter wants to miss the big story of a presidential assassination, illness, or even tripping down the stairs. Presidents are covered 24/7 and the media are frustrated when they lack access. Much of the job is simply showing up and being there for the disaster. Just like Milton's army, "They also serve who only stand and wait."[26] The White House press pass "provides the privilege to wait—wait for a briefing; wait to see the president; wait until a press conferences is called; wait to see the press secretary; wait to see senior officials; wait to have phone calls returned."[27]

In an attempt to make covering the president more fair and humane, the press secretary has the option of putting the "lid" on, guaranteeing that there will be no newsworthy items coming out of the White House for a designated period. This allows reporters to go to lunch or home in the evening. In the event of unexpected events, the press secretary is expected to contact reporters and get them back to the White House for a briefing or press release.

White House correspondents put up with the negative parts of the job by recognizing that it's "an institutional ticket. The guy who gets to the White House goes on to some bigger job" such as an editor, columnist or television news anchor. Now-famous names such as Dan Rather, Leslie Stahl, Sam Donaldson, and Chris Wallace all served their time in the White House "trenches."

Into the Pool

Often it is not practical to have the entire contingent of reporters gather in such places as the Oval Office or Air Force One. In these cases a set of "pool" reporters is chosen by the White House Correspondents Association to represent the various types of media (print, radio, television).[28] Pool reporters are expected to be "honest brokers," bringing back to their colleagues the full, unvarnished report of the event. Pool reports emphasize providing "color," describing the events in human terms.[29] The press office distributes transcripts of the pool reporter's observations. Since the pool rotates through the various media groups, there is motivation to get the story right. That said, being part of the pool grants some advantages. One picks up facial expressions and details such as who else was in attendance that the pool reporter can follow up with later.

Both the press office and White House correspondents facilitate the "body watch," remaining on the ready 24/7 for a presidential assassination, major illness, or personal gaffe. The press office needs to be ready to calm the nation, serve the president's interests, and provide the media with needed information. The media want to make sure they do not miss a story covered by their competition. Modern presidents can't simply slip out of the White House like Harry Truman did for a daily walk.[30] Each time a president leaves the White House he is accompanied by members of the press staff and a group of pool reporters. It is rare, and seemingly inappropriate, for a president to avoid such an entourage. Journalists feel they deserve full disclosure of the president's location, activities and companions. President Trump has failed to play by the traditional rules, ditching the press pool to go out to dinner or play golf. The Trump White House also refuses to disclose his golfing partners or even when he is playing.[31]

When the president gets sick, the nation's heart skips a beat. There seems to be an almost insatiable desire among the press and the public for a diagnosis and prognosis of even the most minor ailments. When George H.W. Bush collapsed in Japan after contracting the flu, his press secretary, Marlin Fitzwater, explained that his "first responsibility was to let the world know the president's condition."[32]

Pools have not been without controversy. During the Obama administration, frustration grew among journalists over the press office's requirement that pool reporters submit their reports to the White House before they were distributed via email. The press office claimed that this was an attempt to improve accuracy, while journalists saw it as a method of control and even censorship. In reaction, the press corps began distributing pool reports directly to their membership.[33] While competition among the news media in the White House is often the norm, they can at times bind together to make a point. When the Obama White House threatened to keep Fox News out of events, their case was championed by Jake Tapper of ABC with the support of the other major networks. "Strength in numbers worked. The White House relented and included Fox News."[34] Typically pools are made up of mainstream media having independent editorial control. Early in the Trump administration some observers questioned the inclusion of *The Signal*, the news service sponsored by the conservative Heritage Foundation. While no one questioned the actual pool report, some felt that a line had been crossed enhancing the position and access of the partisan press.[35]

The terrorist attack of September 11, 2001, revealed in an indirect way the importance of media pools in the eyes of the White House itself. As the enormity of the event began to unfold it was decided that the president would have to get airborne on Air Force One with a smaller contingent of accompanying passengers. Rather than simply dropping all the media, the pool was cut to five, while the rest of the media and the deleted White House staff were left behind.[36]

Negotiating the News

Political officials often get into a process of negotiating newsworthiness with the media.[37] They try to convince reporters to run particular positive stories, to refrain from publishing specific negative stories, or to select negative stories about their opponents.

A negotiation of newsworthiness is especially obvious when it comes to scandals. Scandals "are a 'co-production' of the press and the opposition party."[38] The media works on the assumption that scandal sells, while the opposition party "has strong incentives to create scandal in order to discredit the president or damage his political standing."[39] Once a scandal story emerges in one outlet, their competitors rush to provide their own expanded coverage. Even if relatively scant evidence initially comes out, both the media and the opposition party have a stake in keeping the drumbeat of scandal in the news until stronger evidence of wrongdoing emerges. Although the American principle of 'innocent until proven guilty" stands as an ideal, the very fact that a president is charged with misconduct may be enough to harm his presidency. Even if the charges are proven to be demonstrably false, the harm might be done. As one executive branch victim of a potential scandal put it after he was proven innocent, "What office do I go to get my reputation back?"[40]

Throughout history media fascination with scandal drove many presidential stories, but the breadth of the Watergate scandal and its conclusion with Richard Nixon leaving office helped make scandal and conflict prime fodder for presidential reporting. A number of political figures fed the two junior reporters (Bob Woodward and Carl Bernstein of the *Washington Post*) information suggesting how it could move the story along. Their scooping of more senior and better-positioned White House reporters left an indelible mark. Emerging as public heroes, having their exploits championed in a movie (*All the President's Men*), receiving a Pulitzer Prize, and securing their future careers because of their coverage only added insult to injury. Taking a more investigative role, reporters began to look for scandals suggested by political insiders to pursue.

President Trump and his staff became part of the negotiating process, meeting with the author of a proposed article and passing along the word of the White House interest in having it published. In an attempt to counter the story that Russia had help candidate Trump's cause by publishing internal Democratic National Committee information to WikiLeaks, the president's staff encouraged the publication of an article by Fox News that the leaks were really done by a DNC staffer later found murdered, allegedly at the hands of the Clinton campaign. Even though Fox withdrew the story after a week, the damage had been done. Other members of the media and political leaders such as former Speaker Newt Gingrich kept the alleged story of a young staffer disgusted with DNC corruption going.[41]

A variant of the negotiation of newsworthiness occurs when a journalist alerts the White House to upcoming stories and attempts to force them into a response they did not want to give. The White House press staff takes late-night calls from journalists and tries to "correct" impending stories or to threaten that running the story would lead to significant embarrassment.[42] Clinton's press secretary commented rather sanctimoniously that all his staff was doing was to "protect people from getting a bunch of bad stories . . . by aggressive[ly] responding to fake, fallacious, damaging and politically motivated attacks on the president."[43]

Friends, Enemies, or Competitors?

The line between journalists and the government has not always been distinct. President Andrew Jackson surrounded himself with his so-called "kitchen cabinet," made up of journalists.[44] President Kennedy attempted to gather useful information and co-opt members of the media by consulting with them on policy issues. Numerous journalists have joined the administrations of their day, usually taking positions in the press office. Ben Bradlee, editor of the *Washington Post*, remembered that "some of [Kennedy's] best friends . . . were in fact reporters."[45]

Presidents have a number of "goodies" they can hand out to reward supportive behavior and dampen criticism. For journalists, invitations to state dinners and exclusive interviews allow the aura of the office and the charm of the president to show through.

Lyndon Johnson attempted to treat journalists as associates whom he could buy with fast drives through his Texas ranch and trinkets from Air Force One. He was amazed when stories about his erratic driving became news and reporters he had befriended wrote critical stories.[46] Like some other presidents, President Johnson was not above attempting to use back channels to affect his coverage. He would promise to put in a "good word" for a reporter to their boss if they cooperated, or complain to their boss about negative stories. The effectiveness of these tactics was diminished by the fact that White House reporters tend to be senior and secure, so their jobs were not on the line.[47]

President Clinton was also seen as relatively naïve about the press; "he thought that if you were nice to reporters, they would be nice to you." He felt betrayed "when some journalist whom he had been courting wrote a tough piece. . . . [He] did not understand that it was nothing personal, just part of the game."[48]

The White House press corps has moved a long way from its protection of previous presidents to an almost insatiable pursuit of personal details. Reporters protected Franklin Roosevelt by not writing about or showing pictures of his physical limitations due to polio. It is almost impossible to find a picture of him showing his wheelchair. President Kennedy's sexual exploits were no considered news since "[i]n those days, the possibility of a presidential affair, while titillating, was not considered 'news' by the mainstream press."[49]

All presidents develop an adversarial relationship with the media over time. Even President Obama and his staff came in line for criticism as "cocky, controlling, punitive and in many ways the least transparent of staffs."[50] In 2014, thirty-eight news organizations sent a letter to the Obama administration protesting its obstruction of journalists. Among their complaints were the blackballing of certain reporters, delaying interviews until deadlines had passed and preventing staff from talking with journalists.[51]

Joe Scarborough, journalist and former Trump supporter and friend, found himself on the wrong end of President Trump's wrath. After he, his cohost, and their program, *Morning Joe*, were condemned by Trump, Scarborough pointed out that Trump "always thinks that if he is nice to you and invites you to lunch or dinner that somehow you're going to give him favorable coverage. And it always ends the same, where somehow he is shocked."[52] On numerous occasions, President Trump declared the media as not only his enemy but also the enemy of the American people.[53] Humor serves as a seemingly safe envelope for the truth. When retired general and later White House chief of staff, John Kelly, presented President Trump with a ceremonial saber at the U.S. Coast Guard graduation he offered the suggestion "use this on the press, sir."[54] While clearly a joke, it fit closely with the acrimonious "duel" between Trump and the media.

The media recognize the gulf between themselves and President Trump. Based on a survey by Politico, White House correspondents are less happy with the Trump administration than with the Obama administration. On a scale of 1 (friendly) to 10 (hostile), Obama and his staff rated 5.3 and Trump came in at 7.2. Sixty-eight percent of the surveyed journalists thought that Trump was the most openly anti-press president in history. Much of the frustration with the Trump administration revolved around honesty. Sixty-three percent of the correspondents felt they had been lied to by Trump or his staff.[55] President Trump's attacks on the media created a backlash in the form of expanded fact-checking by the media of his supposed misrepresentations.[56] The list of alleged untruths and misrepresentations by the Trump White House is long and remembered. The media like assertions that can be easily checked for their factual basis. When Donald Trump asserted that his victory in the Electoral College was the largest since Ronald Reagan, reporters were quick to point out that he won fewer Electoral College votes than Bill Clinton, George W. Bush, or Barack Obama.[57]

The vast majority of Americans are dissatisfied with the relationship between President Trump and the media. Eighty-three percent feel that the relationship is generally "unhealthy" and 73% feels that the relationship is "getting in the way of American access to important political news."[58] Republicans are somewhat less likely to see the relationship as unhealthy than are Democrats. This may be explained by the fact that Republicans seem to revel in Trump's facing up to the media. The relationship between the media and the president has received extensive coverage and over 90% of Americans say they are aware of it.[59]

Wise presidents and their staffs would be smart to remember the journalists' admonition that "in the conflict between the president and the media the media are not the enemy, but we are not your friend, either."[60]

Conclusion

White House correspondents hold one of the more prestigious positions in the media, but must operate in a less than commodious setting. Concerned about missing an important story, correspondents spend considerable time waiting for opportunities to interact with the president and his staff. Working together with press pools make the constant monitoring of the president possible. The news emerges from a process in which the players attempt to influence each other in negotiating newsworthiness. The relationship between the president and the media has become more strained in recent years, a condition recognized by all the players.

Notes

1. Matthew Kerbel, Dom Bonafede, Martha Joynt Kumar, and John L. Moore, "The President and the News Media," in Michael Nelson (ed.) *Guide to the Presidency*, Washington, DC: CQ Press, 2008, p. 943.

2. https://shorensteincenter.org/wp-content/uploads/2013/08/d80_hamby.pdf.

3. Nelson W. Dale, *Who Speaks for the President?* Syracuse, NY: Syracuse University Press, 1998, p. 78.

4. Samuel Kernell, *Going Public: New Strategies of Presidential Leadership*, Washington, DC: Congressional Quarterly Press, 1997, p. 69.

5. Kernell, p. 78.

6. Ibid., p. 80.

7. Ibid., p. 81.

8. Kerbel et al., p. 976.

9. Marlin Fitzwater, *Call the Briefing*, New York, NY: Times Books, 1995, p. 306.

10. Martha Joynt Kumar, *Managing the President's Message: The White House Communication Operation*, Baltimore, MD: Johns Hopkins University Press, 2007, p. 142.

11. www.politico.com/magazine/story/2017/04/28/poll-trump-white-house-press-corps-journalists-215051.

12. www.politico.com/magazine/story/2015/04/white-house-correspondents-survey.

13. Dale, p. 78.

14. www.washingtonpost.com/lifestyle/style/white-house-press-corps-of-largely-white-faces/2013/07/25/d8fdacec-f556-11e2-9434-60440856fadf_story.html?utm_term=.58013a139079; Matthew Kerbel, Dom Bonafede, Martha Joynt Kumar, and John L. Moore, "The President and the News Media," in Michael Nelson (ed.) *Guide to the Presidency*, Washington, DC: CQ Press, 2008, p. 976; www.washingtonpost.com/lifestyle/style/white-house-press-corps-of-largely-white-faces/2013/07/25/d8fdacec-f556-11e2-9434-60440856fadf_story.html?utm_term=.58013a139079.

15. Louise Sweeney, "Sam Donaldson, Town Crier of the White House Press Corps," *Christian Science Monitor*, April 16, 1987.

16. Ari Fleischer, *Taking Heat: The President, The Press, and My Years in the White House*, New York, NY: HarperCollins, 2005, p. x.

17. Howard Kurtz, *Spin Cycle: Inside the Clinton Propaganda Machine*, New York, NY: The Free Press, 1998, p. 13.

18. Fitzwater, p. 80.

19. Ibid., p. 81.

20. Kurtz, p. 57.

21. Newseum, "President and the Press" conference, Session 5, p. 4, available at www.newseum.org/2017/04/12/diverse-opinions-spark-conversation-at-the-president-and-the-press/

22. Michael Lewis, quoted in Joseph R. Haden, *A Dubya in the Headlights*, Lanham, MD: Lexington, 2009, p. 55.

23. Fitzwater, p. 262.

24. Ibid., p. 3.

25. Stephen Farnsworth, *Spinner in Chief: How Presidents Sell Their Policies and Themselves*, Boulder, CO: Paradigm, 2009, pp. 36–37.

26. www.brainyquote.com/quotes/quotes/j/johnmilton122739.html.

27. Kerbel et al., p. 976.

28. Kumar, p. 19.

29. Kerbel et al., p. 977.

30. www.trumanroadtrip.com/articles/article/6829750/120407.htm.

31. James Hoffman, "Secretive White House is unapologetic about keeping information from the public," *Washington Post*, April 18, 2017, p. A13.

32. Fitzwater, p. 301.

33. Paul Farhi, "New ripple in White House pool reports," *Washington Post*, October 15, 2014, available at www.highbeam.com/doc/1P2-37292114.html.

34. Margaret Sullivan, "Fox News Will Defend the Media—Sometimes," *Washington Post*, August 14, 2017, p. C3; www.foxnews.com/opinion/2009/10/23/lloyd-green-fox-news-white-house-attack-hunter-thompson-gibbs.html.

35. Paul Farhi, "Press Pool No Longer Just for Mainstream," *Washington Post*, March 11, 2017, p. C1.

36. Fleischer, p. 145.

37. www.umsl.edu/~fogartyb/Fogarty_Negotiation_of_Newsworthiness.pdf.

38. Brendan Nyhan, "Scandal Potential: How Political Context and News Congestion Affect the President's Vulnerability to Media Scandal," *British Journal of Political Science*, Vol. 25 (2014), p. 438.

39. Ibid.

40. Labor Secretary Ray Donovan, quoted in www.nytimes.com/1987/05/26/nyregion/donovan-cleared-of-fraud-charges-by-jury-in-bronx.html?pagewanted=all.

41. Margaret Sullivan, "You Don't Have to Believe Everything in That Seth Rich Lawsuit. What's Been Confirmed Is Bad Enough," *Washington Post*, August 1, 2017, p. C1.

42. Kurtz, pp. 94–95.

43. Quoted in Kurtz, p. 101.

44. Kerbel, et. al, p. 942.

45. Quoted in Steven Levingston, "The Communicators," *Washington Post Magazine*. May 21, 2017, p. 34.

46. https://books.google.com/books?isbn=1135880204, P. 237.

47. Michael Baruch Grossman and Martha Joynt Kumar, *Portraying the President: The White House and the News Media*, Baltimore, MD: Johns Hopkins University Press, 1981, p. 210.

48. Tom Rosenstiel, *The Beat Goes On: President Clinton's First Year with the Media*, New York, NY: The Twentieth Century Fund, 1994, pp. 25–26.

49. Marvin Kalb, *One Scandalous Story*, New York, NY: Free Press, 2001, pp. 5–6.

50. Alexis Simedinger, quoted in Paul Farhi, "Spicer's Apology Tour, and Friends in High Places May Save His Job," *Washington Post*, April 13, 2017, p. C. 2.

51. www.theatlantic.com/politics/archive/2014/08/nixons-revenge-his-media-strategy-triumphs-40-years-after-resignation/375274.

52. Monica Hess, "Lovebirds Joe and Mika All Atwitter about Trump," *Washington Post*, July 14, 2017, p. C1.

53. www.nytimes.com/2017/02/17/business/trump-calls-the-news-media-the-enemy-of-the-people.html.

54. Quoted in Margaret Sullivan, "Kelly May Need a Sword to Cut through Mendacity," *Washington Post*, August 7, 2017, p. C1.

55. www.politico.com/magazine/story/2017/04/28/poll-trump-white-house-press-corps-journalists-215051.

56. See www.washingtonpost.com/news/fact-checker/?utm_term=.93a95894eadd; www.politifact.com/personalities/donald-trump/#.

57. Peter Baker, "'I'm Not Ranting and Raving,' Trump Rants in Wild Presser," *Toronto Star*, February 17, 2017, p. A1.

58. www.journalism.org/2017/04/04/most-say-tensions-between-trump-administration-and-news-media-hinder-access-to-political-news.

59. Ibid.

60. www.politico.com/magazine/story/2016/04/2016-white-house-press-corps-reporters-media-survey-poll-politics-213849.

CHAPTER 4

THE WHITE HOUSE PR MACHINE

To a large degree, the White House is one large public relations organization designed to promote one brand (the president) and one product (the president's policy preferences). The job of the White House communications staff is to "ensure positive news coverage and to mitigate the harm of negative stories through what is generally referred to as 'spin control'."[1] Concern about media coverage is omnipresent in the White House. "Although presidents have long worried about how they are portrayed by reporters, today's hyperactive executives have turned what was once merely an area of White House concern into an overriding obsession."[2] As one press secretary put it,

> just about everybody who has any serious, consequential role at the White House, from the chief of staff on down, has to be mindful of, cognizant of playing a role in how we are going to communicate, how are we going to present our message, how we are going to put our best argument forward. . . . The modern presidency revolves around this question of how you use or how you penetrate the filter of the press to go directly to the American people, which is your ultimate source of political strength.[3]

Long-term White House correspondent Helen Thomas offered a more cynical evaluation, stating "Every day they work on a story of the day and how to shape it. . . . They don't believe in the right to know but people's right to know some things at some times."[4]

Presidents do not arrive in the Oval Office as blank slates. They are experienced politicians who have just come victoriously through a strategically successful battle. Ex-candidates "carry their campaign into the Oval [Office]."[5] Media strategies that outside observers, presidential staff, and the president himself saw as effective in the campaign are likely to be continued once in office. "Campaigning is not the presidency, but it's definitely prologue."[6] The campaign serves as a rehearsal for actions once in office. Anyone watching the 2016 campaign should not be surprised at President Trump's actions toward the media. He dealt with negative coverage by creating a blacklist of a half-dozen news organizations that were banned from receiving media credentials establishing a strategy he would carry with him to the White House. During campaign rallies, he also regularly encouraged his supporters to boo journalists and demonized the mainstream media.[7]

As president Donald Trump kept up the attacks on the media and tried to freeze out certain disfavored outlets, such as CNN, by not giving their reporters the ability to ask questions. From the onset of his administration, the President Trump ordered his press secretary, Sean Spicer, "to conduct his first press briefing as a frothing attack dog."[8] He bragged to his supporters that they were the "last line of defense against the media's hit jobs."[9] As one publication editorialized,

> the White House should never be the arbiter of which media outlets are right and wrong, fair and unfair, acceptable and unacceptable. That goes against the grain of the Constitution, which establishes the press as the people's check on the government; if we lose that, we lose democracy.[10]

Without direct access to the president, White House reporters are severely handicapped in playing their intended role.

Organizing for Action

The White House communications operation has to perform four functions to be effective. "It advocates for the president and his policies, explains the president's actions and thinking, defends him against critics and coordinates presidential publicity."[11] Communications operations take on, or perhaps lead, the character of the rest of the administration. "Communications operations reflect the president they serve. The White House staff is not a complement to a president but a reflection of him."[12] Democrats such as Bill Clinton tended to emphasize flexibility and adaptability. Republicans such as George W. Bush opted for structure and control.[13] At least part of this can be explained by the backgrounds of presidents and their staffs. Coming from a corporate background, Republicans value hierarchy and chain of command. Democratic presidents create organizations in which they serve as the focal point, with a large number of staff reporting directly to them.[14] President Trump began his administration with a loose organization chart, but over time tightened the lines of authority.

For much of the nation's history relations with the media and the commitment of presidential staff to press relations was a second thought. President William McKinley gave George B. Cortelyou the task of dealing with the media in terms of providing information and reporting back press coverage among his other duties.[15] The growth of the total White House staff facilitated the ability to designate more of them for media relations. When Franklin Roosevelt entered office in 1933, the White House staff numbered thirty-five. It has grown to over 400, with about 25% directly carrying out press-related tasks.[16] President Trump has opted for a somewhat smaller staff (377), but pays them more than the larger (472) Obama total.[17]

No matter the White House structure, "[a]lmost all of the White House senior staff are concerned in one way or another with presidential publicity."[18] President Clinton's press secretary Mike McCurry points out the "I'd say 25–30 percent of the paid White House Staff devotes at least two-thirds of its time to communicating and shaping the storyline."[19] A significant amount of staff time is spent "talking to the press, plotting press strategy, or reviewing how their latest efforts had played in the press."[20] On the media side, presidents tend to be judged more and more by their effectiveness in dealing with the media as opposed to the impact of their efforts on solving problems.

The Office of Communications

When it comes to formal responsibilities in dealing with the media, two White House offices stand out. While a clearly designated White House press secretary has been around since President Herbert Hoover's term (see following discussion), the Office of Communications was not created until 1969 under Richard Nixon. From the outside, it may look like having a communications staff with a director and a press secretary and his or her staff means considerable duplication. In reality their jobs are quite different. Under President Clinton, George Stephanopoulos attempted to fill both positions but it ended up angering the press, which had become accustomed to direct access to the press secretary, a condition not amenable to a director of communications.[21] Early on in the Trump administration, Sean Spicer tried to play both roles, but was overwhelmed with the duties.[22]

The pressure on the Director on Communications is intense. Turnover is relatively frequent. As opposed to the press secretary, communications directors work behind the scenes and are comparatively unknown outside of the White House community. They increasingly bring with them public relations more than journalistic experience (see Table 4.1).

The communications director position encompasses a broad purview both in terms of tasks and time. The communications director deals with the long-term strategy of providing information to the entire range of media and coordinating the media outreach beyond the White House press corps. The Office of Communications also attempts to synchronize the president's message from within the White House and among the broader executive branch. The press secretary, on the other hand, is on the daily operational firing line, providing information about emerging issues. As one long-time White House communications observer

Table 4.1 Modern Communications Directors

Name	President	Tenure	Most Relevant Previous Work Experience
George Stephanopoulos	Clinton	1993	Political consultant
Mark Gearan	Clinton	1993–1995	Campaign worker
Don Baer	Clinton	1995–1997	Media lawyer/ journalist
Ann Lewis	Clinton	1997–1999	Congressional staffer/ interest group activist
Loretta Ucelli	Clinton	1999–2001	Journalist
Karen Hughes	G.W. Bush	2001	Journalist/campaign worker
Dan Bartlett	G.W. Bush	2001–2005	Campaign worker
Nicolle Wallace	G.W. Bush	2005–2006	Journalist/campaign worker
Kevin Sullivan	G.W. Bush	2006–2009	Public relations
Ellen Moran	Obama	2009	Interests group activist
Anita Dunn	Obama	2009	Congressional staffer/campaign worker
Dan Pfeiffer	Obama	2009–2013	Government spokesperson/ campaign worker
Jen Psaki	Obama	2015–2017	Campaign press secretary
Sean Spicer	Trump	2017	Congressional and party information aide
Anthony Scaramucci	Trump	2017	Financier
Hope Hicks	Trump	2017–2018	Public relations consultant

Sources: Matthew Kerbel, Dom Bonafede, Marth Joynt Kumar, and John L. Moore, "The President and the News Media," in Michael Nelson (ed.), Guide to the Presidency, Washington, DC: CQ Press, 2008, p. 959; Dale W. Nelson, Who Speaks for the President? Syracuse, NY: Syracuse University Press, 1998; updated by the author

put it, "The press secretary and the communications director each have more tasks than he or she can accomplish. It is not possible for one person to successfully undertake both jobs."[23]

The director of communications usually operates behind the scenes, leaving the press secretary to serve as the public face of the administration. That does not always work. Anthony Scaramucci's short term as White House communications director for President Trump arose out of two fatal errors on his part. In the first place, he showed considerable ignorance about what "off the record" means. He launched a profane attack on other members of President Trump's staff, without having an agreement as to whether he could be quoted. About all the White House press office could say was that his words were "colorful."[24] Second, he broke the cardinal rule for a press spokesperson: don't become part of the story. The press spokesperson is charged with making the president look good, not to grab headlines, either positive or negative.

President Trump turned to long-term aide and loyalist Hope Hicks as his next director of communications. After less than six months, she resigned after telling a congressional committee that her position required telling "white lies."

The pressure on the media operations has increased in recent years as media have changed. To a large degree, what a president gives affects what he receives. Presidents vary in their attentiveness to the news media. Presidents Ford and Carter "failed to appreciate the importance of courting the press." Early images of Ford literally and figuratively "stumbling" were impossible to overcome.[25] President Carter tended to keep the media at arm's length. Presidents who feed the media with reasonably relevant material from which to fashion a story are more likely to have their story told. Early on, President Clinton and his staff failed to fill reporters' "days and nights with a continuous flood of press releases, briefings, and interesting stories about the president . . . his family, appointments and policies."[26] The twenty-four-hour news cycle places heavy pressure on the White House communications operations. In many ways, the term "twenty-four-hour news cycle," underestimates the need for timeliness. The news cycle has in reality shrunk to minutes.[27] The White House is faced with the insatiable demand for information on an hourly basis as they attempt to "feed the beast."[28] The demand is not only for information but for new information to keep the journalists' stories fresh enough to sell them to their editors. The need to provide information on a constant basis requires the press office to establish rotations where everyone serves as a "duty officer" for some period of the day or night.[29]

Avoiding the media is not a real option for modern presidents. They increasingly focus some of their staff resources to help meet the media's needs, even when they feel coverage is unfair or inappropriate.

The Press Secretary

Serving as a presidential press secretary is a high-pressure and high-visibility job. Errors may have significant consequences since what one says represents the president's thinking. Dealing with the day-to-day demands of the media requires full-time effort.[30]

The Role of the Press Secretary

The presidential press secretary is the first line of defense for the president, fielding questions and deflecting jabs. The White House briefing room is unintentionally symbolic with its fire alarm over the door since press secretaries spend the much of their time preventing, controlling public relations "fires." Farnsworth[31] likens the press secretary to a "first responder to a crisis, sort of like a fire fighting crew. . . . Like firefighters entering a burning building, a press secretary has to be careful where he or she steps." Disclosing all the available information could make future decisions more difficult. The press secretary is more interested in putting out the "fire" than solving the long-term problem that caused it.

In a classic case of standing "between a rock and a hard place," the press secretary stands between opposing forces, explaining, cajoling, and sometimes pushing both sides toward a better understanding of each other."[32] The press secretary serves as a mediator between the media and the rest of the White House staff. He or she is often put in a difficult position of both advocating for the president and serving as an advocate for the press.[33] Neither side trusts the press secretary completely, suspecting that their loyalty is to their adversary. Too much catering to the media by the press secretary may well not serve the president well. Too much insulation of the president from the journalists undermines the role of the press.[34]

The White House wants favorable coverage and the media wants a good story. The two goals are often not compatible. The press secretary operates "squarely at the intersection of news and propaganda, in the white-hot glare of the media spotlight, the buffer between self-serving administration officials and a cynical pack of reporters."[35]

Presidential press secretaries recognize their role as point persons for the president. If they ever forget, they need to remember that briefings take place in the James Brady Briefing Room, named after Ronald Reagan's press secretary, who both figuratively and literally "took a bullet" for the president. Press secretaries like Ari Fleishman described the phenomenon in his memoir as "Taking Heat."[36] On leaving his position, he deadpanned, "I really want to unwind, do something more relaxing, like dismantling live nuclear warheads."[37]

Who Are the Press Secretaries?

Since the inception of the position under Herbert Hoover, the job of press secretary has been the most consistently filled position in the White House.[38] Press secretaries do not represent the same mold. Some have come directly from journalism. Others came from public affairs offices in Congress, the party organizations or bureaucracy. More recently, the emergence of the "permanent campaign," which posits the blurring of the line between campaigning and governing,[39] has led to press secretaries with political campaign experience.[40] The primary criterion for appointment is loyalty to the president who placed them in the position (see Table 4.2).

The Daily Grind

Working in the White House press office is not for the fainthearted or physically weak. The hours are long and the pressure intense. In recent presidencies the press secretary's pattern has been relatively consistent. The press secretary is expected to brief the White House senior staff at their early-morning meeting. He or she

Table 4.2 Modern Press Secretaries

Name	President	Tenure	Most Relevant Previous Work Experience
Marlin Fitzwater	Reagan/ G.H.W. Bush	1987–1993	Government press spokesperson
George Stephanopoulos	Clinton	1993	Political consultant
Dee Dee Myers	Clinton	1993–1994	Political analyst/campaign worker
Mike McCurry	Clinton	1994–1998	Congressional press aide/ PR consultant
Joe Lockart	Clinton	1998–2000	Television reporter
Jake Siewert	Clinton	2000–2001	Communications director, Democratic Governors Association
Ari Fleischer	G.W. Bush	2001–2003	Congressional staffer/party worker
Scott McClellan	G.W. Bush	2003–2006	Campaign staff member
Tony Snow	G.W. Bush	2006–2007	Journalist
Dana Perino	G.W. Bush	2007–2009	Journalist/ congressional staffer/government spokesperson
Robert Gibbs	Obama	2009–2011	Congressional staffer/campaign communications director
Jay Carney	Obama	2011–2014	Journalist
John Earnest	Obama	2014–2017	Communications director
Sean Spicer	Trump	2017	National party spokesperson
Sarah Huckabee Sanders	Trump	2017–	Campaign consultant

Sources: Nelson W. Dale, *Who Speaks for the President?*, Syracuse, NY: Syracuse University Press, 1998; updated by the author

prepares for this with briefing books from staff containing copies of relevant news stories, transcripts of the network news, and trending stories on the Internet. At the press office staff meeting, the press secretary solicits views from fellow staff members as to how to respond to the press on issues within their purview. As an observer at many presidential meetings, the press secretary receives direct input on the president's views.[41]

After early staff meetings focusing on the key issues and activities of the day, the press secretary meets in his office for the informal "gaggle" outlining the president's schedule and answering questions on hot topics (see later discussion). The gaggle serves two important purposes. It provides reporters with information and gives the press secretary some idea of the issues that will come up at the more formal early afternoon press briefing. The timing of the afternoon press briefing is a leftover from the time when the press secretary's primary goal was to get the president on the evening news. Much of the rest of the day is filled with answering telephone calls, emails, and individual inquiries from reporters. The press secretary's day does not usually finish up until well after dinner time, with a meeting designed to assess the successes and failures of the day's initiatives[42] (see Box 4.1).

Box 4.1
A "Typical" Day for the White House Press Secretary

Given the role of the press secretary putting out fires, there are few truly typical days. In general though the following events occur on a regular basis:

7:00–8:00	Meeting with the White House chief of staff, communications director and other top staff. Designed to make decisions and plan the media efforts of the day.
8:00–8:30	Senior staff meeting: Used to inform key staff members of the plans for the day and their responsibilities.
8:30–9:00	Communications meeting: A strategy meeting in which the staff is informed of the message of the day and who is responsible for doing what.
9:00–9:30	Meeting with Press Office staff: Informing the staff about what went on at the previous meetings and what would be expected of them.
9:30–9:45	The gaggle: An informal session with the thirty or so permanent White House reporters to provide them with the president's schedule, the message of the day, and reactions to developing news stories.
9:45–10:00	Post-gaggle meeting: Assignment session with the press office staff to assess reporters' interests and what might come up at the formal press briefing.
10:00–11:00	Meeting with the president: Planning a strategy with the presidents for upcoming events.
11:00–12:00	Conference call with key public information officers in agencies such as the State and Defense Departments, the CIA, the joint chiefs of staff. Designed to inform participants on key public affairs issues.
1:00–2:00	Formal press briefing: a thirty- to sixty-minute session in which the press secretary makes announcements and answers questions from journalists (see later discussion).
3:00–6:00	Afternoon telephone calls and one-on-one interviews: a time to answer specific questions from the media not covered in the formal briefing.
6:00–?	A closed-door session with the press office staff to assess the day's events and begin to think about the whole routine beginning again in about twelve hours.

Source: Adapted from Martha Joynt Kumar, *Managing the President's Message: The White House Communication Operation*, Baltimore, MD: Johns Hopkins University Press, 2007.

The media always want more access to presidents and their spokespersons. Despite White House correspondents' claim of secrecy and lack of accessibility, Trump press secretary Sarah Huckabee Sanders argued to the *Washington Post* correspondent that reporters walk in and out of her office freely asking questions. She asserted that a *Washington Post* reporter was "the eighth one in the last 10 minutes" to visit her the previous day.[43]

From the outside it often looks like White House news development is a top-down process, with key decision-makers "in the know" and the media trying to pry out as much information as possible. As one press secretary saw it, though,

> The press sometimes sees things on the ground that people at the top don't get briefed on until later. The push of my job was to answer reporters' questions as quickly as possible. The pull of my job was to make reporters wait for answers until events settled so I didn't say anything that turned out to be wrong.[44]

Press Secretary Strategies

Press secretaries walk a fine line. If it becomes clear that they have not been telling the truth, they lose credibility (see Box 4.2). Truth is a precious commodity in politics. " [T]he job of the White House press secretary isn't to *say* everything you know to be true, but whatever you *say* had better be true."[45]

At times press secretaries are intentionally shielded from information so that they can honestly say "I don't know about that." Even when they know something they can offer a vague response. It is important that they do "*not* make news before the President."[46] There is always tension in the White House over how much information the press secretary should have. A fully informed press secretary reduces his or her deniability. An "I don't know" might well shut off an embarrassing line of questioning more effectively than an "I know, but won't tell you."[47] Not all press secretaries demand or are allowed to be in the information loop. Some press secretaries have been adamant about remaining in the loop for key decisions. Marlin Fitzwater, having the distinction of serving two presidents (Reagan and George H.W. Bush), demanded the right to sit in on any meeting he needed to do his job. He threatened resignation if access was not allowed.[48]

Bill Clinton's press secretary, Dee Dee Myers, was kept in the dark about many issues and not even given the office occupied by her predecessors. Aware of this, journalists perceived her as uninformed and of less use.[49] On the other end of the scale, President George W. Bush made clear his view of Press Secretary Karen Hughes by saying, "I don't want any important decision made without her in the room."[50] Whatever the case, in order to do their jobs, press secretaries and their staffs need adequate "heads up" information (see Box 4.3). Effective press secretaries have credibility with the media and enough background on the issues to present the president's views well. The media shows great interest in how close

Box 4.2
The Political Body Count

Sean Spicer's tenure as White House press secretary clearly started off on the wrong foot. Just one day after the inauguration Spicer reflected Donald Trump's fondness for superlatives by asserting that the inaugural "was the largest audience to ever witness an inauguration—period—both in person and around the globe." Photographic comparisons with President Obama's first inauguration seemed to tell another story. Spicer spent much of his time, effort, and credibility in trying to convince the media and the public of the truth of his statements. The *Washington Post's* Fact Checker column gave Spicer's comments its worst grade: Four Pinocchios.[51] Even the conservative *Washington Times* asserted that the crowd size had been exaggerated by the White House.[52] Not only did Spicer fall short on content, but also in demeanor. As one journalist put it, Spicer "came in, shouted at everybody and refused to take questions."[53]

Photo 4.1 President Trump's 2017 Inaugural Crowd

Source: U.S. Park Service

Photo 4.2 President Obama's 2013 Inaugural Crowd

Source: U.S. Park Service

Box 4.3
Ready, Fire, Aim

Not all communications decisions are fully vetted through the communications organization, often with negative results. President Trump's firing of FBI director James Comey came as a surprise to most of his communication aides, leading to frustration and a mad scrambling to try to get ahead of the story and frame it in the most positive manner. Over the next few days the alleged timeline and nature of the firing changed, leaving the White House looking like it was misrepresenting the facts and motivation. It became clear that "Trump's team did not have a full-fledged communications strategy for how to announce and then explain the decision." Many staff members learned about the firing through news alerts on their phones after the fact.[54] One White House staff member admitted that "this is probably the most egregious example of press and communications incompetence since we've been here. . . . It was an absolute disaster."[55] Commenting on the failure to work with the communications staff, Newt Gingrich commented, "You can't be the quarterback of the team if the rest of the team is not in the huddle. . . . The president has to learn to go a couple of steps slower so that everyone can organize around him."[56]

Communications staff members often felt out of the loop, failing to receive the information they needed to craft an effective message. They lacked the time for consistent message development but were blamed for the failure by both Trump and his inner circle of family and aides. As it was described, Trump makes decisions "on impulse and emotion" and either avoids or rejects the advice of staff aides, especially those in the communications realm. "Trump is in some ways like a pilot opting to fly a plane through heavy turbulence, then blaming the flight attendants when the passengers get jittery."[57]

The firing became entwined in the investigation into the Trump campaign relations with Russia which Comey was directing. The first story line was that Comey was fired for mishandling an earlier investigation of Hillary Clinton's emails, and that Trump was acting on the advice of his Justice Department appointees. Later Trump argued that he had made the decision earlier and that Comey had lost the confidence of the FBI and was not doing a good job.[58]

President Trump's frustration boiled over during the following days. In a tweet, the president argued that:

> The Fake Media is working overtime today! As a very active president with lots of things happening, it is not possible for my surrogates to stand at podium with perfect accuracy! Maybe the best thing to do would be to cancel all future "press briefings" and hand out written responses for the sake of accuracy?[59]

> The new story line pursued by the press questioned whether Trump was threatening Comey and raised the issue of whether conversations in the Oval Office were taped. In a press conference, White House press secretary Sean Spicer refused to answer questions about the possible taping.

a press secretary is to the president. Press secretaries who work closely with the president and meet with him daily have more credibility than those kept at arm's length.[60]

Unlike other White House officials, who tend to speak on background without attribution, the press secretary is the public voice of the president. His or her briefings are on the record. There is a tacit understanding between effective press secretaries and the media that they won't lie and won't cover up. At the same time, it is recognized that the press secretary will try to report negative information in the most positive light possible. As one press secretary put it, "It's the toughest job in the country because the president has me to explain what he says and I don't have anyone to explain what I say."[61]

Few press secretaries would pass the courtroom criteria of "telling the truth, the whole truth and nothing but the truth." Press secretaries learn that lying is not a good strategy. There are too many ways of getting caught and losing one's credibility and that of the president. On the other hand, full and immediate disclosure may not be the correct strategy. A noncommittal "no comment," a dribbling out the truth slowly, or an "I'll look into the issue" may buy the necessary time to frame a more complete and accurate answer.[62]

There have been a number of clear misrepresentations by the White House. Woodrow Wilson's press secretary misled the media about the president's stroke and Eisenhower's heart attack was initially described as a digestive upset. Ron Nessen, Richard Nixon's press secretary, made numerous untrue statements about the Watergate break-in, only to declare them "inoperative" later. Such shifting led to being "accused of the dreaded sin of flip-flopping."[63] Just prior to the attempt to rescue U.S. hostages in Iran, Jimmy Carter's press secretary wrote off a possible rescue as nonsensical, while Ronald Reagan's spokesman declared an invasion of Grenada to rescue U.S. citizens as "preposterous" on the same day it was about to occur.[64] Bill Clinton, himself, misled the American public about his relationship with Monica Lewinsky, while George W. Bush and his staff maintained a charade about the existence and ease of confirming Iran's weapons of mass destruction.

Press secretaries and journalists take stock of each other on a personal basis. It soon becomes clear as to which press secretaries will be honest and reasonable and who will fall short. Press secretaries also evaluate journalists in terms of who would be reasonable and tell the story straight. When reasonable rapport is established, the White House can help guide the journalist to telling a more accurate story.[65]

Without such rapport, journalists may view all White House "help" as simply an attempt to get out the story the White House wants.

An analysis of the early Clinton White House, with much broader applicability, suggested some lessons for press secretaries:

1.   Return telephone calls in a timely manner to meet journalists' deadlines.
2.   While some spin is expected, unrelenting and excessive spin undermines credibility.
3.   The best way of ameliorating a mistake is to admit it (see Boxes 4.4 and 4.5).
4.   Avoid viewing the press as nothing but a necessary, but dangerous and infuriating institution.[66]

Box 4.4
Bombing Out

Presidential press secretaries are like all public relations specialists: they can do little for their boss if they lack credibility. While selective dissemination of information remains a valid and useful strategy, outright lying remains counter-productive in the long run.[67] "No experienced spokesperson in his right mind would advocate dissembling, particularly if there were the slightest chance of being exposed."[68] Since every word and assertion of the White House press secretary gets parsed, checked, and evaluated, he or she must remain extremely careful. Clinton's press secretary Mike McCurry warned, "Look, my personal views don't count. I'm here to represent the thinking, the actions, the decisions of the president."[69] He found it to be an effective strategy to have the media take out their frustrations on him, rather than on the president.[70]

As the public face of the president, every word of the press secretary is combed for both intentional and unintentional meaning. They are not sup-posed to generate news about themselves or their views. President Trump's former press secretary, Sean Spicer, learned that the hard way.

Analogies can be useful mechanisms for increasing understanding, but they must be correct and applicable. In answering a question at the daily press briefing, Spicer commented on Syrian President Bashar Assad's use of chemical weapons by saying "You had someone as despicable as Hitler who didn't even sink to using chemical weapons."[71] Reminded of the Holocaust by reporters at the briefing, Spicer tried to correct his statement by saying that "he was not using gas on his own people the same way." The explosive reaction of the legacy media, social media, and Jewish groups forced Spicer to go on an "apology tour" to the major news outlets to "tamp down some of the outrage about his gaffe."[72]

Box 4.5
How Do I Get Out of This Mess?

As in many aspects of life, one reaps what one sows. The White House press corps often "reaches a consensus about an individual,"[73] making it hard for them to escape the evaluation of the journalistic pack. George H.W. Bush's chief of staff, John Sununu, "offended one person after another with his bellicose personality and belligerent meetings."[74] Other political players who had been "trampled" by Sununu "were only too happy to use the press to even the score."[75] When the press discovered that he had been using presidential aircraft for private purposes there was no reservoir of goodwill among the media to protect him. It was clear that the "press loves this kind of 'waste and abuse' story because it is easy to understand, it's highly symbolic, and it offends the American people."[76] Sununu refused to cooperate with the media or apologize and was forced to resign.

Reminiscent of Mr. Sununu's travel problems, Tom Price, President Trump's Secretary of Health and Human Services, got into trouble for questionable travel expenditures. He was forced to resign after the media picked up the story.[77]

High-level presidential appointees need to take heed of the three basic rules for dealing with a story about misbehavior:

1. Come clean. It's all going to come out anyway. Do it fast and all at one time.
2. Make restitution. The public will never forgive you as long as you keep the booty.
3. Most importantly, give the press their pound of flesh. It is an absolutely nonnegotiable demand for ending a public controversy.[78]

The Revolving Door

The job of press secretary is a high-pressure position. Serving as the face of the administration in front of a critical media leads to burnout. It is a "pressure-cooker assignment."[79] Ari Fleischer, President George W. Bush's press secretary, called it the "most grinding and grueling job I could ever imagine holding . . . sometimes, no matter what you do, you get in trouble for it."[80] President Clinton and President Barack Obama utilized three press secretaries each. President George W. Bush called on the service of four press secretaries during his eight years in office.

American politics lacks the tradition of resignation in protest. Most press secretaries have followed the borrowed and paraphrased dictum of "my president, right or wrong, but my president." One major exception was J.F. terHorst, who served Gerald Ford. Only a month after his appointment, terHorst disagreed with Ford on the pardoning of Richard Nixon over the cover-up of the Watergate break-in. He felt not only that the decision was wrong but that he had not been informed about it in advance. TerHorst went public, explaining that "I cannot in good conscience support [the] decision to pardon former President Nixon even before he has been charged with the commission of any crime. . . . As your spokesman, I do not know how I could credibly defend that action."[81]

The revolving door entrances and exits of White House press secretaries should not generate too much pity for those forced to leave. "For most press secretaries, the job opens the door to a lifetime of sinecures: lucrative speaking circuits, punditry gigs . . . and book deals."[82]

Most departures are handled with rationales about "the good of the team" or "personal reasons." Individuals shown the door seldom publicize their complaints. They leave praising the president and declaring that it was "an honor to serve." The departure of Sean Spicer as press secretary after six months and Anthony Scaramucci as White House communications director after ten days followed this pattern. Spicer implicitly took responsibility for President Trump's rocky relationship with the media, even though insiders claim he resigned because of Scaramucci's appointment. Scaramucci shot himself in the foot by giving an obscenity-laced interview to a reporter.[83]

Maintaining Focus

The presidential task is immense and there is little guidance as to the issues and procedures on which to focus. The federal government has been likened to a large mountain of different colored blobs of Jell-O in a warm room. Each blob represents a different policy realm. The blobs melt together to some degree, showing that policies in one realm affect those in another. The task for the president lies in determining which blobs to attempt to move in his preferred policy direction. Too broad a target almost guarantees failure. Wise presidents focus their efforts on a relatively few policy areas, announcing policy initiatives and touting successes. Focusing on the "issue of the day" or "issue of the week" sends important signals to the public and other decision-makers. While a focused president can have significant effect on drawing attention to a few issues, the pressure needs to be kept on. If the president's focus moves on to another policy area the impact on a particular blob of Jell-O declines and it reforms much like it was before the president's involvement.[84]

In a well-run media operation, key participants get their stories straight so as to maintain credibility. The White House communications team attempts to stay on message, portraying positive plans and accomplishments while downplaying mistakes and failures. Journalists often have their own agenda of what they want to know. In this tug-of-war, each side compromises. The preferred White House message is news that deserves to be reported. On the other hand, sticking solely to the message may well lead journalists to believe that the White House is stonewalling and making the journalists jobs more difficult.[85]

President Obama received considerable criticism for his contradictions on national security and foreign policy.[86] While Obama's contradictions occurred over the long term, early in his term President Trump fell victim to contradictory stories occurring in close proximity. When explaining the firing of FBI director James Comey, White House staff and Vice President Pence asserted that the president was acting on the advice of the deputy attorney general. A few days later, President Trump declared that he had made up his mind about the firing before getting the advice.[87] Initially claiming that he had not shared sensitive information with the Russians, the next day Trump and his spokespersons claimed that a president has the right to determine what is classified and what is not. By not getting their stories straight, the image of a White House in disarray grew (see Box 4.3). President Trump has had relatively little success in controlling both his own and the political messages of his supporters. His staff members "are relatively reticent to comment publicly or privately about the administration's position. . . . [In] part they worry that Trump will almost immediately undercut them with his own words or tweets."[88]

White House Briefings

Journalists demand accessibility to the press secretary and he or she recognizes that it must be given. On a typical day, the press secretary gives two briefings, answers calls from reporters, and allows reporters to stop by his or her office to explain policies or presidential actions. Into this schedule, the press secretary must fit meetings with the senior White House staff and consultations with the president. The primary constant is the set of press briefings.

The Gaggle

By ten in the morning, the press secretary is ready to meet with the "gaggle," an informal, nontelevised meeting in the press secretary's office. The gaggle heavily represents wire service reporters who are attempting to get the White House response to overnight developments.[89] As George W. Bush's press secretary, Ari Fleischer, described it,

> Thirty or forty reporters, notebooks and tape recorders in hand, would cram into my office to hear me walk through the President's schedule, and then fired

away, asking questions about whatever the controversy du jour was. . . . It lasted only fifteen minutes, and then it took another five minutes to shoo the last reporter out since almost every one of them had "just one more question."[90]

Picture a group of geese squawking and pecking around a target and you will get a feel for the morning "gaggle" involving the press secretary and the thirty or so full-time members of the White House media group. These informal sessions began in the Reagan White House, replacing the full-fledged morning briefing. During the gaggle, the press secretary attempts to promote the message of the day and respond to questions emanating from overnight news reports. The importance of the gaggle has increased with the continuous demands of cable news and online outlets. They need stories earlier in the day than was the case when the White House focused on satisfying the needs of the network evening news programs.[91] The gaggle has been called the "road map for the day."[92] It provides reporters leads as to the stories they should pursue. The ground rules of the gaggle generally require journalists to shut off their cameras and use their tape recorders only to check accuracy, not to broadcast the voice of the press secretary.

The gaggle serves a second purpose, giving the White House press office a heads up as to what the media are interested in. Often reporters preview the questions they plan to ask at the formal press briefing later in the day. Since the gaggle is not televised live, it is a lower-risk "warning system" of what issues need to be addressed.[93]

Traditionally open to the entire press corps, the Trump White House has shown its dissatisfaction with some major outlets such as CNN, the *New York Times*, and *Politico*, barring them from some if its gaggles.[94] A spokesperson for the *New York Times* complained,

Nothing like this has ever happened at the White House in our long history of covering multiple administrations of different parties. We strongly protest the exclusion of the *New York Times* and other news organizations. Free media access to a transparent government is obviously of crucial national interest.[95]

The "Daily" Afternoon Press Briefing

The formal afternoon briefing is a much higher stakes game than the morning gaggle. Often televised live, it not only goes out in real time but also serves as the basis for segments on the evening news. Internet feeds use the content of the briefing for immediate updates. Recognizing the high visibility, reporters push hard to get answers to tough questions. It has long been a "contest between reporters skilled in ferreting and officials adept at straddling."[96]

White House press conferences have tended to be dominated by the major news outlets. Facing increased criticism from these sources, President Trump's press secretary, Sean Spicer, intentionally called more frequently on reporters from conservative outlets. He also had monitors installed in the briefing room so that live questions could be beamed over Skype from news organizations outside the Beltway.[97] Spicer proclaimed that the "Skype seats" would open up the process to "a diverse group of journalists from around the country, who may not have the convenience for funding to travel to Washington."[98] Other journalists were less happy about sharing the mike with those individuals outside Washington. They pointed out that three-quarters of the Skype questions came from individuals in states that Trump won in 2016 and that a number of the questioners had questionable credentials as journalists. Most of those allowed to ask questions via Skype are Trump supporters with contempt for the existing participants and had been recruited by the White House.[99]

White House briefings follow a variety of protocols the by which the press secretary must abide. Most briefings begin with an opening statement by the press secretary who tries to set the agenda and preempt questions whose answers might be embarrassing if asked in another way. Reporters are expected to wait until called on, and not "hog" the mike. During the Reagan administration, the policy of allowing follow-up questions helped journalists fill out the information they needed. For television reporters, follow-ups meant more time on the air. For the press secretary, follow-up questions are "always easy because your mind is already working on the subject."[100] By tradition, the "dean" of the White House press corps—the senior correspondent—closes off the questioning with a "thank you."[101]

Participation in the afternoon press briefings is limited by the size of the briefing room. With only forty-nine seats, only a limited number of outlets get accommodated. The major news outlets are well represented. In recent years they have been challenged by pressure from more ideological publications. With the arrival of the Trump administration a number of more conservative news outlets such as One American News (OAN) and the *Daily Mail*, a British newspaper, received one of the coveted seats for the daily briefings.[102] Among the many cable networks, OAN:

> has become a reliably sympathetic voice of the [Trump] administration's goals and actions. The network is known for only interviewing conservative lawmakers and experts. Despite its relatively small audience, OAN has been favored by the White House press office, granting their reporter an inordinate number of the highly sought after questions during the daily press briefings.[103]

While decisions on the allotment of briefing room seats is done by the White House Correspondents' Association, they apparently took into account the Trump administration's desire for more diversity (see Figure 4.1). The placement of an outlet's seat makes a difference, since press secretaries are more likely to call on those in the front rows, while at the same time favoring outlets that agree with the president's positions. The Trump White House expanded the pool of White

PODIUM

NBC	FOX News	CBS News	Associated Press	ABC News	Reuters	CNN
Wall Street Journal	CBS Radio	Bloomberg	NPR	Washington Post	New York Times	USA Today
AFP	AP Radio	McClatchy	American Urban Radio Networks	Politico	Tribune	ABC Radio
MSNBC	Foreign Pool	Washington Times	The Hill	Fox News Radio	Voice of America	National Journal
Bloomberg BNA	TIME	Sirius XM	Regionals	Christian Science Monitor/ New York Post	RealClearPolitics	Al Jazeera/PBS
Washington Examiner	Yahoo News	Salem Radio Network	Newsmax	Daily Mail	Huffington Post/ N.Y. Daily News	Westwood One
Talk Radio News Service/Univision	Dallas Morning News	Boston Globe/ Roll Call	CBN	BBC/OAN	BuzzFeed/ Daily Beast	Financial Times/Guardian

Figure 4.1 White House Briefing Room Seating Chart (2017)

Source: www.washingtonexaminer.com/here-is-the-new-white-house-press-briefing-seating-chart/article/2627600

House correspondents and directed questions to more conservative outlets, frustrating the more traditional set of players.[104]

Recent press secretaries have allowed television cameras into the sessions, with clips from these sessions playing a prominent role on evening news programs. Not all participants find televised briefings desirable. Ari Fleisher, a former press secretary, explained that the daily briefing:

> has become a TV show and lost its value as a serious briefing. . . . I used to try to figure what my bite was and deliver with a little hand movement and look to the middle of the room so my eyes were up. It becomes a stage that you can act on.[105]

In cutting back televised briefings the Trump White House press staff argued that reducing the number of televised press briefings was designed to "thwart reporters who are trying 'to become YouTube stars' by asking 'some snarky questions.'"[106]

The Trump administration's frustration with the media can be seen in how they handled press briefings. As the disconnect with the media grew, the White House responded by cutting the number of press briefings, delegating the duty to others or by holding some briefings off camera.[107] The "daily" White House press briefing soon became a misnomer. During the first 100 days of the Trump administration, press secretary Sean Spicer held only fifty-three formal press briefings and informal untelevised "gaggles" where reporters could ask questions. The pace slowed even more over time. Press briefings also became more brief over time. Early sessions often lasted over an hour, with those in the later period often less than fifteen minutes.[108] To add insult to injury, press briefings often started late, keeping journalists waiting.[109]

The mechanics of the press briefing favors the press secretary. Every day when the press secretary arrives, he or she determines with an opening statement as to what the news will be for that day. That said, reporters help set the tone of the briefing through the questions they ask. With the memory of charges that the media were too accommodating to presidents on issues such as Watergate, Clinton's character, and weapons of mass destruction in Iraq, contemporary reporters vie with each other to ask the toughest questions possible.

Journalists often ask "gotcha" questions designed to force an embarrassing response. For example, in March 1999 the UPI radio correspondents asked Bill Clinton's press secretary whether there would be a press conference on April 30. A bit flustered, the press secretary indicated that such events were not scheduled that far out and inquired about the reason for the question. The reporter shot back that April 30 would mark the one-year anniversary of the last press conference. The tactic worked. Clinton held a press conference a few weeks later.[110]

Gotcha questions are designed for more than a way to get sensitive information or to force presidential action. White House reporters realize that by asking a tough question there is more chance they will receive on the air on the evening news—not a bad thing for their careers.[111]

The White House staff often grates at the tone and nature of questioning. After the media badgering her with repeated questions about the connection of the Trump campaign with Russia, then deputy press secretary Sarah Huckabee Sanders struck out at the reporters, likening them to young children. She commented, "I'm kind of looking around for my kids because I feel like, with toddlers, you get to answer the same question over and over."[112]

Like the gaggle, the afternoon press briefing serves another purpose for the White House. If the media are asking questions about an action or topic, it is a signal that it is of interest to the public. Getting a feel for what is on the minds of the press alerts staff that the matter deserves attention. Reporter's questions "often short-circuit the official channels of bureaucracy, and tiers of staff advisors that insulate a President from the real world."[113]

Even the media recognize the challenge of facing the press. While showing little sympathy in their questioning, White House reporters recognize the difficulties in carrying out the briefings. As one reporter put it, "People who go out there and dance on that high wire every day and do not fall off are remarkable. It's a rough job, coming out here and standing before thirty or forty people [whose] job it is to pick at what you say."[114]

A few unguarded words in a press briefing can set off a chain reaction. When press secretary Marlin Fitzwater commented on Ronald Reagan's meeting with the Soviet leadership, saying that "This is not a summit or session to be taken lightly between old friends. This is a summit between old enemies; you could hear the 'gotcha' buttons going off all over the room." The transcript of the session spread around the world in seconds and news stories placed Fitzwater's sentiments in the president's mouth, giving the Soviets ammunition to use in the future.[115] Sean Spicer saw the same thing happening when he made comments about the Holocaust.

If there is tension between the media and the White House, it first appears in the relationship between reporters and the press secretary. No one expects the contemporary relationship between the press secretary and the media to be cozy and cordial. "Confrontational" and "conflictual" better describe the strained connection. With a bit of gallows humor, a ceremonial flak jacket is passed down from one press secretary to the next.[116]

Conclusion

The White House marshals significant resources to deal with the media. The Office of Communications looks after long-term and broad concerns, while the press secretary serves on the daily firing line interfacing with the media through individual and collective press briefings. The press secretary speaks for the president and seeks to make sure that the White House speaks with one voice on key issues. Briefings have become more contentious in recent years, with both sides attempting to control and direct them.

Notes

1. Jeffrey E. Cohen, "The Presidency and the Mass Media," in George C. Edwards and William G. Howell (eds.), *The Oxford Handbook of the American Presidency*, New York: Oxford University Press, 2009, p. 254; David Paletz, *The Media in American Politics: Contents and Consequences*, New York, NY: Longman, 1998, p. 263.

2. Stephen Farnsworth, *Spinner in Chief: How Presidents Sell Their Policies and Themselves*, Boulder, CO: Paradigm, 2009, p. 2.

3. Mike McCurry, quoted in Martha Joynt Kumar, *Managing the President's Message: The White House Communication Operation*, Baltimore, MD: Johns Hopkins University Press, 2007, pp. 5–6.

4. Ibid., p. 201.

5. www.politico.com/magazine/story/2016/04/2016-white-house-press-corps-reporters-media-survey-poll-politics-213849.

6. Ibid.

7. Kathleen Parker, "When Push Comes to Shove," *Washington Post*, May 28, 2017, p. A21.

8. Philip Elliot, "White House: Chaos Theory," *Time*, February 27, 2017, p. 37.

9. Kurtis Lee, "Other Presidents Have Battled the Press. But Never Like Trump," *Los Angeles Times*, February 19, 2017, p A8.

10. *San Bernardino Sun* editorial, "Trump's War with the Media Divides Nation," March 5, 2017, p. A21.

11. Kumar, p. 6.

12. Ibid., p. 286.

13. Ibid., p. 71.

14. Ibid., p. 136.

15. Nelson W. Dale, *Who Speaks for the President?*, Syracuse, NY: Syracuse University Press, 1998, p. 13.

16. www.quora.com/How-many-employees-does-the-White-House-have.

17. www.npr.org/2017/06/30/535069910/trump-white-house-staff-payroll-nearly-36-million-and-top-heavy.

18. Matthew Kerbel, Dom Bonafede, Martha Joynt Kumar, and John L. Moore, "The President and the News Media," in Michael Nelson (ed.), *Guide to the Presidency*, Washington, DC: CQ Press, p. 958.

19. Quoted in Matthew Eshbaugh-Soha and Jeffrey S. Peake, *Breaking Through the Noise: Presidential Leadership. Public Opinion and the News Media*, Stanford, CA: Stanford University Press, 2011, p. 7.

20. Tom Rosenstiel, *The Beat Goes On: President Clinton's First Year with the Media*, New York, NY: The Twentieth Century Fund, 1994, p. xxiv.

21. Marlin Fitzwater, *Call the Briefing*, New York, NY: Times Books, 1995, p. 239.

22. John Wagner, "Trump Hires Mike Dubke as White House Communications Director," *Washington Post*, February 19, 2017, p. A8.

23. Kumar, p. 131.

24. Margaret Sullivan, "For Scaramucci, F Is for Foolhardy," *Washington Post*, July 29, 2017 and www.washingtontimes.com/news/2017/jul/31/anthony-scaramucci-removed-as-white-house-communic.

25. David Paletz, *The Media in American Politics: Contents and Consequences*, New York, NY: Longman, 1998, p. 246.

26. Ibid., p. 251.

27. Kerbel, et al., p. 983.

28. See Kenneth Walsh, *Feeding the Beast: The White House Versus the Press*, New York, NY: Random House, 1996.

29. Kumar, p. 197.

30. Kumar, p. 51.

31. Farnsworth, p. 17.

32. Fitzwater, p. 4.

33. Newseum, "President and the Press" conference, Session 2, p. 4, available at www.newseum.org/2017/04/12/diverse-opinions-spark-conversation-at-the-president-and-the-press.

34. Ari Fleischer, *Taking Heat: The President, The Press, and My Years in the White House*, New York, NY: HarperCollins, 2005, p. 177.

35. Rosenstiel, p. 15.

36. Fleischer.

37. Fleischer, p. 353.

38. Kumar, p. 186.

39. See Sidney Blumenthal, *The Permanent Campaign*, New York, NY: Simon and Schuster, 1982 and Brendan Doherty, *The Rise of the President's Permanent Campaign*, Lawrence, KS: University of Kansas Press, 2012.

40. Kumar, p. 192.

41. Fleischer, p. 37.

42. Newseum, Session 3, p. 3.

43. Philip Rucker and Ed O'Keefe, "Secrecy Is a Hallmark of Trump Administration," *Washington Post*, June 20, 2017, p. A18.

44. Fleischer, p. 161.

45. Fleischer, p. 246.

46. Fleischer, p. 155.

47. Ted Gup, "Working in a Wartime Capital," *Columbia Journalism Review*, September/October 2002, p. 10. Available online at www.cjr.org/year.02/5/gup.asp.

48. Fitzwater, p. 144.

49. Kerbel et al., p. 961.

50. Ibid., p. 968.

51. Margaret Sullivan, "Spicer's Exit Was Long Overdue," *Washington Post*, July 22, 2017, p. C1.

52. www.foxnews.com/us/2017/01/21/fact-check-trump-overstates-crowd-size-at-inaugural.html.

53. Newseum, "President and the Press" conference, Session 4, p. 2, available at www.newseum.org/2017/04/12/diverse-opinions-spark-conversation-at-the-president-and-the-press.

54. Philip Rucker, Ashley Parker, Sari Horwitz, and Robert Costa, "Comey Sought More Resources for Russia," *Washington Post*, May 11, 2017, p. A6.

55. Ibid.

56. Ibid.

57. Philip Rucker, "Comey's Ouster Embodies the Dysfunction Trump Leads," *Washington Post*, May 13, 20-17, p. A1.

58. www.washingtonpost.com/news/post-politics/wp/2017/05/10/as-trump-fired-comey-his-staff-scrambled-to-explain-why/?utm_term=.7b95b0bcb9a8.

59. www.bostonglobe.com/news/politics/2017/05/12/president-trump-says-perfect-accuracy-from-surrogates-isn-possible/RbebGodEA4DVwBcOcn296I/story.html; www.nytimes.com/2017/05/12/us/politics/trump-threatens-retaliation-against-comey-warns-he-may-cancel-press-briefings.html.

60. Kumar, p. 208.

61. Ibid., p. 179.

62. Ibid., p. 48.

63. Rosenstiel, p. 2.

64. Ibid., p. xxi.

65. Kumar, pp. 211–212.

66. Rosenstiel, p. 10.

67. Joseph R. Hayden, *A Dubya in the Headlights*, Lanham, MD: Lexington Books, 2009, p. 227.

68. Ibid.

69. Quoted in Howard Kurtz, *Spin Cycle: Inside the Clinton Propaganda Machine*, New York, NY: The Free Press, 1998, p. xv.

70. Ibid., p. 68.

71. Noah Bierman, "Spicer Apologizes for 'Blunder' on Holocaust," *Capital Gazette*, April 13, 2017, p. A2.

72. Paul Farhi, "Spicer's Apology Tour, and Friends in High Places May Save His Job," *Washington Post*, April 13, 2017, p. C1.

73. Marlin Fitzwater, *Call the Briefing*, New York, NY: Times Books, 1995, p. 176.

74. Ibid.

75. Matthew Kerbel, Dom Bonafede, Martha Joynt Kumar, and John L. Moore, "The President and the News Media," in Michael Nelson (ed.), *Guide to the Presidency*, Washington, DC: CQ Press, 2008, p. 940, p, 980.

76. Fitzwater, p. 177.

77. www.politico.com/story/2017/09/29/price-has-resigned-as-health-and-human-services-secretary-243315.

78. Fitzwater, p. 177.

79. Joseph R. Hayden, *A Dubya in the Headlights*, Lanham, MD: Lexington Books, 2009, p. 55.

80. Fleischer, pp. ix, 9.

81. Bruce Weber, "J.F. terHorst, Ford Press Secretary, Dies at 87," *New York Times*, August 1, 2010.

82. Ben Terris, "He Landed a Dream Job in Washington, but at a Price," *Washington Post*, July 22, 2017, p. C1.

83. Paul Farhi, "It Was an Honor to Serve, Mr. President, and to Reset Your Totally Clean Slate. . ." *Washington Post*, August 1, 2017, p. C2; Philip Rucker, Abby Phillip, Robert

Costa, and Ashley Parker, "Priebus Out in Major White House Shake-Up," *Washington Post*, July 29, 2017, p. A1.

84. Based on author's interview with a White House staff member.

85. Kumar, p. 49.

86. www.theatlantic.com/international/archive/2013/09/obamas-many-contradictions-on-foreign-policy/279479.

87. www.nbcnews.com/politics/first-read/white-house-s-explanation-firing-comey-crumbles-n758306.

88. Abby Phillip and Robert Costa, "Republicans Waiting for Trump to Use That Bully Pulpit," *Washington Post*, July 15, 2017, A4.

89. Kerbel et al., p. 977.

90. Fleischer, p. 37.

91. Kumar, p. 224.

92. Ibid., p. 228.

93. Ibid., p. 229.

94. www.washingtonpost.com/news/the-fix/wp/2017/02/24/white-house-blocks-cnn-new-york-times-from-press-briefing-hours-after-trump-slams-media/?utm_term=.63a4629eb841.

95. https://twitter.com/NYTeileen/status/835213474464677888/photo/1?ref_src=twsrc%5Etfw&ref_url=https%3A%2F%2Fwww.washingtonpost.com%2Fnews%2Fthe-fix%2Fwp%2F2017%2F02%2F24%2Fwhite-house-blocks-cnn-new-york-times-from-press-briefing-hours-after-trump-slams-media%.

96. Leo Rosten, *The Washington Correspondents*, New York, NY: Harcourt Brace, 1937, p. 65.

97. Renae Merle, Damian Paletta, and Heather Long, "Scaramucci is cut from same cloth as his new boss," *Washington Post*, July 22, 2017, p. A5.

98. "White House to Have 4 'Skype Seats' in Its Press Briefing Room," *Kashmir Images*, January 25, 2017.

99. www.usatoday.com/story/news/politics/2017/07/05/sean-spicers-white-house-press-briefings-every-skype-question/419484001; Paul Farhi, "Few Journalists in 'Skype Seat' at White House Press Briefings," *Washington Post*, April 12, 2017, p. C1.

100. Fitzwater, p. 119.

101. Ibid., p. 105.

102. http://thehill.com/homenews/media/340323-conservative-media-outlets-gain-seats-in-white-house-briefing-room.

103. Marc Fisher, "One America (Hint: It's the Boss's)," *Washington Post*, July 6, 2017, p. C1.

104. www.politico.com/magazine/story/2017/04/28/poll-trump-white-house-press-corps-journalists-215051.

105. Newseum, Session 2, p. 12.

106. Paul Farhi, "No Action from Media on White House Restrictions," *Washington Post*, June 27, 2017, p. C1.

107. Ashley Parker and Sean Rucker, "Embattled Spicer May Be Moving Backstage," *Washington Post*, June 20, 2017, p. A18.

108. Paul Farhi, "Spicer and the Great Unknown," *Washington Post*, June 14, 2017, p. C1.

109. Karen Heller and Kristine Phillips, "Reporter Says 'I'd Had Enough' Bullying," Washington *Post*, June 9, 2017, p. C1.

110. Kumar, p. 258.

111. Howard Kurtz, *Spin Cycle: Inside the Clinton Propaganda Machine*, New York, NY: The Free Press, 1998, p. 283.

112. Quoted in Farhi, "Spicer and. . .," p. C3.

113. Kerbel et al., p. 971.

114. Quoted in Kumar, 2007, p. 240.

115. Fitzwater, pp. 135, 143.

116. David Nakamura, "Spicer Was Caught in the Crossfire from the Start," *Washington Post*, July 22, 2017, p. A1.

CHAPTER 5

DELIVERING THE PRESIDENT'S MESSAGE

When it comes of media strategy, the "modern president now spends much of his time trying to out-think the media."[1] The White House seeks to use the media for its own benefit, promoting positive stories and defending against negative ones.

Some Public Relations Strategies

Presidents and their staffs take a page out of the public relations textbook and create events and initiatives around which the media can weave stories with positive impact for the president.

Timing

Traditionally the timing of news was critical, with positive stories from the White House promulgated at a time to meet newspaper or television network deadlines. On the other hand, negative stories were delayed until after critical deadlines or when they would have to compete with other stories. In was no surprise that Richard Nixon fired Watergate Special Prosecutor Archibald Cox in an event dubbed the "Saturday Night Massacre." By holding off the unpopular firing until after the Sunday morning newspaper deadlines and at a time when the viewership of the next morning's new programs was light, the spread of the story was dampened. Reporters would not have time to write their stories or get comments from opponents.[2] In September 1974, President Gerald Ford again used a Sunday to announce the pardon of Richard Nixon, but with a twist. Not only was there less time for reporters to react, but the pardon story had to compete with dare-devil Evel Knieval's attempt to jump the Snake River Canyon on a motorcycle. Some forty years later, when President Trump fired FBI director James Comey, the twenty-four-hour news cycle reduced the opportunity for strategic timing. Cable news networks were able to cover the story as a news flash, and then follow up with successive waves of stories as more details arrived. The changed news environment did not dissuade the Trump White House from trying to play the timing game. For a number of presidencies voluntary disclosure of official White House visitors gave journalists leads on possible stories. In suspending that procedure so sensitive to the hearts of journalists, the White House waited until the afternoon of Good Friday to dump the news about Comey.[3] The same attempt to downplay controversial news came into play when President Trump pardoned controversial Arizona ex-sheriff Joe Arpaio, who had been convicted of contempt for racially profiling possible illegal aliens. Trump held off the official announcement until 8 p.m. on a Friday evening as the major news outlets were focusing most of their attention on the impending arrival of Hurricane Harvey.[4]

News stories generally have limited "shelf life." Possible news fails to pass the journalists' test for becoming news if it is not new. A president trying to peddle old issues or widely covered solutions will find the White House stories superseded by other events. Riding the wave of a developing story increases the likelihood of presidential coverage. Marshal McLuhan argued that "instant information creates involvement."[5] The timeliness of presidential communications enhances their impact.

Repetition

Presidential communications staffs realize that the only way to make sure their messages gets through is by using repetition, a strategy journalists dislike. Journalists seek the new and different, while the White House wants strives to push its desired message. One effective method involves giving a few select reporters "heads-up" information about upcoming decisions. They will then write a story which implies their well-connected status in the White House. Other reporters will quickly jump on the story to avoid being scooped.[6] Just as Senator Joseph McCarthy (R-WI) used the strategy of holding a press conference to announce tidbits of the following day's press conference, the White House is able to stretch a one-day story into two or more. The White House attempts to stretch out the impact of its efforts by using "rolling" announcements. They announce the existence of upcoming policy initiatives in the hopes of encouraging initial stories. They then make detailed announcements about the content of the policy. These efforts are followed by presidents and their surrogates making follow-up speeches to generate more stories.[7]

Sound Bites

We live in the age of sound bite political communication on television and short headlines on the Internet. Where politicians once had about 40 seconds to express themselves on television news programs, that figure has dropped to less than eight seconds. It probably took you about eight seconds to read the last two sentences. The empirical research to back up the length of sound bites has focused on communication during election campaigns[8] but the practice applies equally to the non-election period. Recognizing the penchant for short bursts of information, presidents plan sound bites in hopes that the media will pick them up. If one scans newscasts from the various networks on a particular night, there is a great deal of overlap as to which sound bites are chosen for inclusion. The same sound bites also show up in headlines of printed and Web-based stories. White House media staffs gauge their success by their ability to get their preferred sound bite in the news. During his first foreign trip, President Trump offered a simple message about terrorists to Arab leaders: "drive them out." His plea to disavow the radical Islamists from their mosques and communities was reported hundreds of times on national networks and local stations.[9]

Barack Obama gave the media particular trouble in the era of sound bite journalism. Journalists felt that it was impossible for him to "speak in simple declarative sentences. He simply [did] not do sound bites."[10] President Obama relished long and detailed answers, much like the law professor he once was. Responding to one question about the Baltimore riots, his answer was almost 2000 words long.[11]

Given the short attention span of both the media and the public, presidents have given in to simplifying their message and focusing on "sellable" policies rather than on the most important issues facing the nation. For the modern media market, the White House has learned that it can play to the cameras by "keeping it simple, keeping it lively, and keeping it focused on the short-term payoff."[12]

Redirection

At times, fiction matches reality. Presidents in trouble with the public or the media may redirect public attention by engaging in military action or foreign policy activism, as portrayed in the movie *Wag the Dog*. The term comes from the idea that irrelevant factors, the "tail" (the desire for positive news coverage), could be causing the wagging rather than vice versa.[13] While presidents won't admit such a strategy, the correlation is high enough to make coincidence unlikely. As far back as the earliest days of our country, John Jay argued that "monarchs will often make war when their nations are to get nothing by it."[14] Support for military action "is viewed as inherently nonpartisan and skepticism as partisan."[15] Both the media and the public tend to "rally around the flag"[16] during times of national crisis, especially when it deals with foreign affairs. Presidents realize this tendency and may use a "wag the dog" strategy of allowing the pursuit of public support to drive foreign policy decisions and divert attention from other failings.

When the Clinton–Lewinsky scandal was at its height, President Clinton took a trip to China and pushed the scandal off the front pages. President George W. Bush was accused of shifting his military focus from Afghanistan to Iraq as his public support declined.[17] He saw his media approval soar after the attacks of 9/11, paving the way for a military buildup that also received significant media support.

When President Trump tweeted an unverified message that his offices had been bugged by the Obama administration, it helped push a competing story about the Russians helping Trump win the election off the front pages. As the charges of questionable contacts by Trump campaign officials continued, President Trump reversed his opposition to U.S. involvement in the Syrian conflict and engaged the U.S. more directly in that conflict.[18] His sending fifty-nine missiles at a Syrian airfield had the media of most stripes falling over itself with praise. The news media "seem to get bored with their own narrative," welcoming this chance "to switch it up" and tell a different story.[19] During the week of the Syrian attack, Trump's coverage in the media "improved" from 80% negative to "only" 70% negative.[20]

Similarly, with the looming threat from North Korea and the disastrous hurricane in Puerto Rico, President Trump decided to attack the NFL athletes who took a knee rather than standing for the national anthem. "The spat over sports wasn't just a diversion, but a move straight from Trump's political playbook. Confronted with crises, he creates new ones, picking fights that stir up his supporters and enrage his opponents."[21] The media reacted by covering the battle over free speech and patriotism extensively, leaving less room for the other issues.

Leaking

Leaking is common in government. Individuals lacking easy access to the media not wanting to be identified as a source may be able to get their message out unofficially. Reporters are quite willing to protect such individuals by only referring to them as "a White House source." The most famous leaker was Mark Felt, better known as "Deep Throat." His cooperation with Bob Woodward and Carl Bernstein helped lead to Richard Nixon's downfall in the Watergate scandal. Most leaking is more benign, yet it remains frustrating to presidents. Presidents come out strongly against leaking, except in those cases where they and their staffs intentionally feed the press a story.[22] At times leaking comes from the top echelon of the White House in order to plant a story or launch a trial balloon, leading to the assertion that "the ship of state is the only vessel that leaks from the top."[23] Some leaks are designed to affect the internal politics of the White House, with the leaker attempting to get his or her point of view out to the public and hope-fully affect his or her policy or career position. Some leaks come from "whistle-blowers" attempting to bring attention to undesirable behavior. In other cases, leakers attempt to demean those who oppose them within the White House. Presidents and their communications staffs attempt to limit unauthorized leaks.[24]

There is a certain excitement to the idea of a leak. The image of a clandestine meeting, secret phone call or a sheaf of papers anonymously slipped under a journalist's door add drama. While many legitimate stories have been broken by a leak, the very fact that they are anonymous makes it difficult to tell the degree of truth they contain. Previous press secretaries raised their own concerns about leaks, arguing that anonymous "background" sources within the White House should not be used since the "American people should know who is speaking for the administration and hold sources accountable for the information they share."[25] This shutting off of leaks could make the job of the press secretary easier but would stifle information flow.

At times, leaks are part of a communications strategy. President Reagan's top staff leaked a proposal to tax home mortgage interest. After a maelstrom of criticism, Reagan himself stepped in on his white horse to counter this by saying, "in case there's still any doubt, I want you to know we will preserve that part of the American dream . . . that deduction, that symbolizes, I think, that American dream."[26]

There is a difference between leaking classified material and descriptions of political strategy, internal White House conflict, or evaluations of other political players. Most journalists hesitate to use classified material. An issue develops when the categories overlap. After being selected as national security advisor by President Trump, it was leaked that classified intercepts contradicted Michael Flynn's claim that he had not been in contact with the Russians. At a time when the Trump's strategy was to show an effective and smooth transition, the leak made his nomination vetting look weak and Flynn was forced to step down.

Defenders of leaking to the media admit that there are certain national security secrets that must be protected, but that much of the material leaked from the White House fails to meet that criterion. According to an executive order signed by President Obama, prosecutors can only bring charges against leakers or journalists when the leak involves classified and other national security material. There is no violation when the material involves the disclosure of illegal or embarrassing material. Supporters of whistle blowing assert that "Whistleblowers are the nation's first line of defense against fraud, waste, abuse and illegality within the federal government."[27]

Supporters of leaking even classified information argue that the "biggest and most important stories of recent years wouldn't have been done without classified leaks."[28] They point at stories such as the Watergate cover-up, the *Pentagon Papers*, the U.S. government's widespread surveillance of its own citizens and the expansion of America's drone warfare. Such supporters of leaks assert that

"We need journalism to break through government secrecy and inform citizens. Punishing reporters has no place in a country that calls itself a democracy."[29]

Although it may look from the outside like a well-organized machine, efficiently promoting the president's interests, the White House is more like a series of tribes trying to get the attention of the ultimate leader. For the first six months of the Trump administration, clear lines of communication and authority were hard to determine. Aides could be seen "loitering in clumps of five or six outside the Oval Office and trying to catch the President's eye." With the arrival of General John Kelly as chief of staff, aides were encouraged to operate from their offices and work out their differences before approaching the president. In response, some of the aides turned to television knowing that it would be "an excellent way to attract the President's attention."[30] This often means leaking self-serving information to the media.

Each year, Reporters Without Borders ranks countries in terms of their support for freedom of the press. For 2017, the U.S. ranked forty-third out of 180 nations, down a few places from recent years. Part of the ranking emanates from the president's relation with the media and attempts to stifle leakers. Despite promising one of the most open administrations ever, President Obama's legacy led the evaluators to comment that:

> It bears repeating that [Obama] left behind a flimsy legacy for press freedom and access to information. . . . The Obama administration waged a war on whistleblowers who leaked information about its activities, leading to the pursuit of more leakers than [every] previous administration combined.[31]

Members of the media described the Obama White House as "one of the most closed-off presidential administrations in recent memory."[32]

Reporters like leaks as much as presidents tend to despise them. To members of the journalistic community, government leakers are heroes, calling them the "nameless government officials who risked their jobs and their freedom to get the truth out."[33] Leaks carry with them a sense of excitement and the potential for breaking a story independent of their colleagues and the official White House line. In covering Barack Obama, White House correspondents felt that "there were no leaks, no revelations from sources. This White House controls the news frustratingly well."[34] Despite early aggressiveness toward leakers, no journalists were successfully prosecuted under the Obama administration, but prosecutors did subpoena records and secretly obtained telephone records of reporters.[35] The fear of prosecution may well have had a chilling effect, discouraging leakers and dissuading journalists from using leaked material. Evaluating his first few months in office, the analysts pointed out that "Donald Trump's repeated diatribes against the Fourth Estate and its representatives—accusing them of being 'among the most dishonest human beings on earth' and of deliberately spreading 'fake' news—compromise a long U.S. tradition of defending freedom of expression."[36] (See Chapter 7.)

President Trump takes a very different approach to leaks than did candidate Trump. During the campaign he encouraged Russian hackers to try to obtain information on Hillary Clinton's emails.[37] As a candidate, Trump even exclaimed "I love WikiLeaks," since their revelations were causing damage to his opponent.[38] As president, Trump disavowed the legitimacy of the leaks coming out of his administration, saying "It is my opinion that many of the leaks coming out of the White House are fabricated lies made up by the Fake-News media."[39] President Trump's disdain for leakers carried over to his staff. His former press secretary, Sean Spicer, went to far as to order random phone checks of White House staff members to identify the sources of leaks.[40]

Leaks from the White House are both pervasive and, by definition, secret. All presidents have disliked leaks from within their organization and tried to track them down. But, as Marlin Fitzwater sees it, "Most leaks are never discovered, and most don't matter anyway."[41] If the leaker can't be found, presidents may punish the journalists who use them by not calling on them during press conferences or granting them interviews.

While there is some temptation to write off leaks as idle gossip or unverified assertions, there is always some degree to truth in the information included in a leak. Wise press secretaries recognize that they should "never discount leaks or rumor, or information tips. Never make a total denial. There is always an element of truth in their [the media's] questions."[42]

Controlling the Visual Image

The old dictum that "a picture is worth a thousand words" has been taken to heart by the White House. The first official White House photographer was appointed by Lyndon Johnson. Today virtually every official action of the president is captured by the official photographer and distributed both to the media and via the White House website.[43]

While Washington is a city of words, visual images often convey more content than does verbiage. Images provide both substantive content and triggers to emotions. The White House recognizes the power of the visual and structures events to take the visual message into account. Ronald Reagan's press secretary, Larry Speakes, argued that they learned to think "like a television producer. . . . We knew very quickly that the rule was no pictures, no television piece, no matter how important our news was."[44] Michael Deaver, a key Reagan staff member, argued, "Turn off the sound on the television, and that's how people are going to decide whether you won the day or lost the day: the quality of the picture."[45] Under Deaver's tutelage, "[t]he entire Reagan administration was a made-for-TV enterprise, a daily staging of visuals for all the networks; all activity came to a halt when the 6:30 newscasts came on."[46]

In designing a political event, it is more important how they "seem" than how they actually are. Perception creates a new reality. Presidential advance teams scope out favorable venues which create the context for an event. National defense speeches tend to be given on military bases with the accoutrements of the military fully visible. Labor issues are confronted on shop floors with manufacturing equipment in sight. Television serves to personalize presidents, with the setting often using the trappings of power as visuals, reinforcing the president's power and authority. A president speaking from the Oval Office carries with him a certain amount of weight as viewers remember previous important pronouncements from that setting. A president standing at the focal point of the House of Representatives, high on a platform, leaves little doubt as to who is controlling the situation. Flags, crowd demographics, and other symbols enhance the president's image, which is then broadcast to millions by television.

What is heard from a president often depends on *where* it is said. Settings reinforce messages by attaching symbolic meaning. The symbolism of location was not lost on Lyndon Johnson, who refused to carry out a press conference in the same auditorium as John Kennedy. Instead, his first press conference was held at his Texas ranch, with a bale of hay serving as a podium, to avoid the comparison with Kennedy.[47] Ronald Reagan and his staff were masters at creating dramatic settings. On a visit to New York to discuss liberty at the hundredth anniversary

Photo 5.1 President Obama Using the Full Array of White House Symbols
Source: AP Photo/Molly Riley

of the symbolic Statue of Liberty, President Reagan stood without a coat and in an open-collared shirt with the statue prominently in the background. In a speech on freedom and oppression, President Reagan was positioned looking over the buffer zone between North and South Korea.

In another attempt to utilize a favorable setting, President George W. Bush's staff created a dramatic image for a speech about homeland security. Standing at the foot of Mt. Rushmore, they allowed camera angles made him look like the fifth president on the granite monument.

It is not only the White House that attempts to use symbolic settings for their endeavors. Television news consumers have become accustomed to reporters telling their stories with the White House as a backdrop. Presidents such as George H.W. Bush rejected requests, arguing that it reduced the dignity of the White House.[48]

The backdrops for presidential events have become an art form designed to communicate a subliminal message. By creating the raw material for a positive visual, the president may be able to overcome the critical media. An evocative setting may be enough to send a clear message. Modern White Houses create "wallpaper" with powerful messages related to the speech at hand. Looking over the president's shoulder, the audience, especially on television, sees a phrase reinforcing the key desired takeaway from the speech. The George W. Bush

Photo 5.2 President George W. Bush Uses Mount Rushmore as a Symbolic Setting
Source: AP Photo/Ken Lambert

BOX 5.1
Primp for Victory

President George W. Bush went to the U.S. Naval Academy to express his appreciation and support of the military. The audience was guaranteed to be a safe one, and, if there was any danger of demonstrations or inappropriate questions, the midshipmen had been warned against such behavior. Rather than reserving the best seats for the highest-ranking and presumably most safe students, they were directed to sit toward the middle of the auditorium, just in front of the press stand. Journalists seeking midshipmen response would get the responses of these most "responsible" representatives of the brigade. A small contingent of photojournalists was allowed to take pictures from a low angle on the floor in front of the podium, thus guaranteeing "power shots" of President Bush. In order to avoid the embarrassment of empty seats, black cloth was used to cover the seldom used seats behind the podium. The event was coordinated with the release of *National Strategy for Victory in Iraq*, a document designed as the White House strategy to win the war. If anyone missed Bush's spoken message of hope, they could not miss the large "wallpaper" banners surrounding him proclaiming "Plan for Victory." The banners had been created by the White House, flown in from California and erected overnight by workers on overtime. While scrupulously planned by the White

Photo 5.3 President George W. Bush and the "Plan for Victory" Wallpaper
Source: U.S. Naval Academy Archives

House, the media had the last say. The headlines about the event varied dramatically across sources.

The *Washington Post* balanced a neutral lead with a countervailing view: "Bush Presents Plan to Win Iraq War: Pelosi Says More Democrats Backing Call to Bring U.S. Troops Home Now."[49] Fox News headlined its online coverage with the title "America will not run." CBS followed with "Bush urges patience on Iraq," with MSNBC asserting "Bush foes on offensive over Iraq policy."

Since many readers simply skim newspapers and web sites, headlines can be very important in creating a mind set through which stories are interpreted. A president's supporters are more likely to hang on positive headlines, while opponents take negative summaries as gospel truth.

administration even created a special lectern with a narrow base to expand the portion of the background visible to the public.[50] When the George W. Bush White House realized that the background of boxes at a Missouri trucking plant said "Made in China," they had volunteers use stickers to rechristen them as "Made in the U.S.A." to fit the message of the speech[51] (see Box 5.1).

The audience becomes a critical "prop" for a presidential speech. Every attempt is made to bring in a supportive audience with a broad demographic mix and no hecklers. The setting is designed to send a message. Appearing before members of the military offers a "safe" venue. Security on military bases helps assure that no "undesirables" will be in the crowd. Additionally a sea of uniforms behind the president projects patriotism and dedication.[52] For all events, the president's advance team tries to make sure that the visible crowd is not only well-behaved but also evocative of the policy realm under discussion. Presidents attempt to compensate for weaknesses among certain group in the population by having individuals within camera range belie generalizations. For example, Republicans make sure there are some black faces in the crowd that surrounds them. The nature of the crowd assembled depends on the issue to be discussed. In a made-for-television bill signing ceremony, President Trump announced his support for the coal industry with an executive order allowing for increased mining with a crowd of mine workers in hard hats standing behind him.[53]

The White House takes advantage of some unexpected settings to promote its policies. President Trump stood in front of the Air Force Academy football team to present the Commander in Chief football trophy and incongruously commented on his health care plan.[54] Recent presidents have used visits to military installations, with the troops in the background, as locations for national defense–related speeches. In such cases, the people in the picture serve as props for a larger cause. "Military base visits are like gold to the White House public relations staffers."[55]

Photo 5.4 President Trump with a Favorable Audience Backdrop

Source: AP Photo/Mark Humphrey

Military audiences are polite to presidents and can be held accountable for any untoward actions. The crowds are generally briefed ahead of time and warned not to embarrass their commander in chief. The presence of the well-respected military uniforms leads to the "hope that the good feelings directed at those in the politician's company will rub off."[56]

The nature of the invited crowd depends on the White House goal. Personal experiences with my students verify that perspective. Presidents are quite sensitive about the audiences to which they speak. They want a rousing welcome, a positive response to applause lines, and the avoidance of hecklers. Many "public" events featuring the president require tickets that are distributed to likely supporters. President George W. Bush's staff created "rally squads" to stand between protestors and news cameras shouting "USA! USA!"

Presidents dress for the occasion. Most of the time this means a suit and tie. Knowing that many of his campaign rallies would be outside, then candidate Donald Trump wore a baseball hat to protect his prized hair. When he became president the hat had to go and he had to face crowds in windy environments with his hairdo waving in the breeze.[57] Other changes to the appropriate "costume" are carefully planned. Appearing at Ground Zero after the 9/11 attacks, George W. Bush opted for an informal jacket and no tie as he talked to the rescue workers. In order to promote energy savings, Jimmy Carter gave a speech from the White House wearing a cardigan sweater.

Presidents attempt to walk a fine line between trying to be seen as extraordinary leaders capable of almost extra-human accomplishment and regular folks with the ability to empathize with average citizens. The arrival of radio and then, even more so, television helped to humanize the president and his family. Pictures seared into the public's awareness of images of presidents include horseback riding (Reagan), stopping in for a burger at McDonalds (Clinton), riding around the ranch (George W. Bush) or playing basketball (Obama). For billionaire Donald Trump, attempting to play the common man card has been more difficult. Few of us lead the lifestyle of five-star resorts and playing golf with celebrities.

There is some temptation to view presidents as actors, fully in charge of their script and stage directions. While they desire such control, presidents, "[l]ike actors in a theater . . . work within a limited space, following scripts and stage directions that are largely *not* of their own making."[58] Events and the expectations of others intrude and presidents are often placed in a reactive role in which they must meet the expectations of other players and the public. The public has become accustomed to some stock story lines. For the president, one of the most common is to portray him in charge of a command center where key decisions are being made.[59] The night of the capture of Osama bin Laden, the White House was quick to send out a picture of President Obama and key advisors monitoring the developments as they were happening.

The distinction between a presidents "direct" communication to the citizenry through speeches and the indirect interpretation of presidential views and actions by the media fails to account for how the media affect any attempt by the president to communicate. "Even live television . . . broadcasts by the president are not totally devoid of media influence, because camera angles and other photographic techniques that journalists use slant all presentation somewhat."[60] Presidents attempt to counter this type of bias by controlling public events. They look for venues sending positive messages, choose favorable audiences, create positive backgrounds and control the placement of cameras.

Using Surrogates

The president cannot be all places at all time. While the president serves as the focal point for any administration, the use of surrogates to spread the White House message is a force multiplier. The perspectives of cabinet members and key policy-makers can reinforce the president's points, as long as they stay on message. The danger lies in surrogates seemingly disagreeing with the intended White House message, or implying a split within the White House. Surrogates are often given talking points that they are expected slip into the conversation, no matter the content of the question. Watching the Sunday morning news programs with the same guest appearing on a number of networks, one is struck by the seemingly rote recitation of rehearsed answers.

Among the most powerful surrogates have been first ladies. Most of them have limited themselves to comments on "safe" issues such as anti-drug campaigns (Nancy Reagan), beautification (Barbara Bush), literacy (Laura Bush), or children's health (Michelle Obama). A few first ladies have taken a more active role in policy development and promotion. Eleanor Roosevelt wrote a widely read newspaper column. Hillary Clinton served as the point person for her husband's attempt to reform health care.

A key goal of presidential communications is message control. Presidents want members of their administration to "talk about what they, [the president] want[s] to talk about . . . [to] get everyone on the same song sheet."[61] While presidents see this as legitimate management of *their* story, members of the media see it as a "'wall' to keep the information among the insiders and out of the hands of reporters."[62]

When presidential surrogates face the media, it looks like a prisoner in a lion's den facing many opponents without protection. In reality, White House staff brief the White House participants with possible questions, preferred responses, and, especially, sound bites that might make the news. One White House communications briefing paper, undoubtedly similar to many others, suggested that George W. Bush's treasury secretary, Paul O'Neill, simply ignore the first question on *Meet the Press* and answer "We must act to ensure our economy recovers and people get back to work."[63]

In setting up interviews, the White House and the media establish ground rules about the topic to be discussed and the usage of the content. The limitations imposed depend on the perceived need of the White House to present their side and the media's desire for the story (see Box 5.2).

As head of the executive branch, the president has the potential for utilizing hundreds of public affairs offices in the bureaucracy to promote his policies. The key challenge lies in getting them to send a consistent message. President Trump received considerable criticism for demanding that bureaucrats in the Environmental Protection Agency stop emailing about their claims of global warming.[64] This certainly was not the first time this contentious issue led to attempts by the White House to squelch the story. During the George W. Bush presidency, scientists at the National Oceanic and Atmospheric Administration (NOAA) were told to remove a statement about 2005 being the warmest year on record. The censorship did not last long, since the Democrats in Congress began spreading the word.[65] In 2017, President Trump forced the Environmental Protection Agency to take down its climate change website since it did not match with his policy perspective on global warming.[66]

At times, the line between journalists and political operatives has been muddied in recent years by individuals who attempt to play both roles simultaneously. Most of us expect journalists to be independent seekers of the truth. During the George W. Bush administration, conservative talk show host Armstrong Williams received

---

BOX 5.2
Interviewing Ground Rules

Members of the White House staff often want to get a story out but don't want to be identified as the source. Journalists and their interview subjects negotiate the conditions under which the interview is conducted. A number of options are possible:

On the record: The information can be used with no caveats, quoting the source by name and position.

President Ford's chief of staff, Donald Rumsfeld, promulgated "Rumsfeld's Rule," that one should "[a]ssume that most everything you say or do will be on the front page of the *Washington Post* the next morning . . . conduct yourself accordingly."[67]

Background: The information can be published but only under conditions negotiated with the source. Generally, sources do not want their names published but will agree to a description of their position. It is permissible to indicate "a senior White House official" as one's source, but not indicate which official. The White House seems to want it both ways, Obama's press secretary, Josh Earnest, criticized the *Washington Post* for using anonymous sources, "[e]ven as the White House insisted its own officials remain anonymous during phone interviews with reporters."[68]

Deep background: The information can be used but without attribution. The source does not want to be identified in any way by name or general position, even on condition of anonymity.

Off the record: This is the most restrictive arrangement. The information gathered in the interview cannot be used for publication. It is designed to help lead the journalist in the right direction with comments such as "You might want to look into" or "you are on the right track."

To add credibility and enhance the story, journalists attempt to interview on the record if possible.[69]

$240,000 to promote the Bush education policy of "No Child Left Behind." One observer described the process as "the best defense as being a good offense."[70] News reports of this and other payments by the Bush administration led to considerable criticism and the suspension of the practice.[71] Mark Serrano served as one of President Trump's fiercest defenders on Fox News, while at the same time his firm had a "communications consulting" contract with the Trump 2020 campaign organization.[72] The potentially confusing relationship was terminated when Fox took him off the air.[73]

Making the Media's Job Easier

The White House recognizes the tight financial constraints under which contemporary journalists operate. With the closing of many Washington bureaus, newspapers and television stations look for ways to cover the president. Presidential press releases have long been mechanisms for trying to frame journalists' stories by selectively feeding them facts and opinions. The hope is that the press release will be used largely verbatim. In the George W. Bush administration, hundreds of video press releases were created to tout administration successes. Each segment showed the president in the most positive political light possible. Made to resemble actual news segments, local stations were even given suggested lead-ins to introduce each story. Local stations lacking a Washington presence often aired them in their entirely, never telling their viewers that they were the creation of the White House.[74] The White House then posted the media "reaction" on its website as evidence of media support for the president.[75] Only later did some of the media react negatively, calling the pieces "propaganda" and "shilling."[76] Both Presidents Obama and Trump continued the practice of providing video clips on the White House website.[77]

Pseudo-Events

The job of the president as outlined by the Constitution and customary practice speaks little of presidential outreach to the public through the media. Suggesting policy solutions, validating legislative decisions, and overseeing the administration of laws could all be done (albeit perhaps with less effectiveness) outside the glare of public exposure. A large number of presidential activities are "pseudo-events,"[78] staged to receive media coverage, as opposed to real events demanded by the presidential role.[79] Most speeches, bill signing ceremonies, presidential trips, and visits to the Oval Office by groups such as the World Series winners or poster children for some dreaded disease all fall into the pseudo-event category. The president has become the "congratulator in chief" and "encourager in chief" through such symbolic events. Pseudo-events share a number of common characteristics. They go beyond the specific constitutional demands on the president and involve careful planning as to the audience, setting, and logistics.

Not all pseudo-events reap the hoped for benefits. With the economy faltering, President George H.W. Bush's staff proposed that he leave Camp David to visit ordinary people in the nearby town of Thurmont, Maryland. This would portray the image of a president interested in ordinary people and their economic hopes and fears. Between the initial planning and the final accomplishment, it was decided that the president should go to a fancy shopping center and buy a pair of socks. The message of a caring president was lost and became an image of the president believing that the economic problems were the fault of the consumers who were not spending enough.[80] Despite careful planning, the White House cannot guarantee which portions of the story the media will take away. The danger is heightened by the media's penchant for controversy (see Box 5.3).

Natural and manmade disasters provide presidents with unique opportunities to show their power and concern, while delayed or ineffective actions loom as potential dangers. Presidents reap rewards from timely action, with the media creating a timetable for what is acceptable. Presidents who hesitate to become engaged after natural or manmade disasters face criticism from the media for not "minding the ship."

Less than six hours after the *Challenger* disaster Ronald Reagan eloquently observed:

> The crew of the space shuttle Challenger honored us by the manner in which they lived their lives. . . . We will never forget them, nor the last time we saw them, this morning, as they prepared for their journey and waved goodbye and 'slipped the surly bonds of earth' to touch the face of God.[81]

Three days later, he went to the NASA Space Center in Houston to express his condolences. Both initiatives garnered him positive media coverage.

President George W. Bush garnered both public and media support when he arrived at Ground Zero after the disaster of 9/11. Dressed in appropriate informal clothes, Bush showed compassion by putting his arm around one of the firemen and spoke comforting words to the rescue workers. The picture of the president with the bullhorn and stories about his presence were very positive.

Images of the president comforting victims and attempting to bring relief represent some of the most abiding stories about every president. After Hurricane Harvey (2017), President Trump realized that he would be judged by the speed of his response. He visited Texas twice in the first ten days after the hurricane to observe the damage and bolster the spirits of victims and first responders. The president repeated his "performance" a few weeks later shortly after Hurricane Maria hit Puerto Rico. His visits were not without their critics, who questioned his decision not to talk to the victims and to focus on the crowd size at his speech.[82] The use of pseudo-events is not a set of isolated incidents, but rather a series of broad-based public relations initiatives promoted and managed by the White House.

Conclusion

The White House operates like a public relations firm, using many of the strategies found in commercial advertising. It attempts to get its story out through propitious

BOX 5.3
Landing Gear

Public relations events often fail to pan out the way planned by the White House. The landing of President George W. Bush on the carrier USS *Abraham Lincoln* seemed like a perfect event. Having set the record for the longest deployment by a nuclear-powered aircraft carrier in history, it would be a chance for the president to express his appreciation for the dedication and sacrifices of the crew. The visit started out well. The ship was positioned in such a way that it looked like it was out to sea, rather than a few miles from the California coast. Bush arrived via Viking fighter aircraft and walked through the adoring crowd of crew members in his jaunty heroic flight suit "costume."[83] It was a public relations dream, but did not last forever.

As Bush changed into more presidential attire to give a speech, the media began to dissect the visit. An initial question arose over why the president arrived by jet rather than the less dangerous helicopter. It was explained that they initially expected the ship to be further out to sea and that the president wanted to experience a deck landing. The next wave of questioning pointed out that the speech delayed the arrival of the *Lincoln* in port and the reunion of the crew with their families. Again the press office had to explain that the *Lincoln* arrived on time. In reality, it could have come in one day earlier given its unexpected progress.

Photo 5.5 President George W. Bush Declares "Mission Accomplished"
Source: AP Photo/J. Scott Applewhite

Perhaps most importantly, the media focused on the banner behind President Bush reading "Mission Accomplished." Originally the White House gave the *Lincoln* crew the "credit" for the banner; only later did they divulge that it had been created by the White House and only hung by the crew.[84] The media also began questioning just what had been "accomplished" since U.S. troops were still in harm's way in the Middle East.

The sensitivity of the media to this clearly public relations visit may well have emerged since it occurred during "sweeps week," when audiences are measured carefully for the purpose of establishing advertising rates. By covering the speech, the networks were forced to bump highly ranked shows off the air.[85]

timing, repetition, sound bites, redirection leaking, and controlling the visual image of the president. The president expands his reach by using surrogates to deliver his message. Much of the presidential media effort goes well beyond the constitutional demands of the president's job, with the White House creating opportunities to reach the public through the media.

Notes

1. Lawrence R. Jacobs and Melanie Burns, "The Second Face of the Public Presidency: Presidential Polling and the Shift from Policy to Personality Polling," *Presidential Studies Quarterly*, Vol. 34 (2004), No. 3, p. 239.

2. George C. Edwards, III, *Governing By Campaigning: The Politics of the Bush Presidency*, New York, NY: Pearson/Longman, 2007, p. 41.

3. James Hoffman, "Secretive White House Is Unapologetic about Keeping Information from the Public," *Washington Post*, April 18, 2017, p. A13.

4. www.cbsnews.com/news/trump-faces-bipartisan-backlash-for-pardoning-sheriff-during-hurricane-harvey.

5. Tony Schwartz, *Media: The Second God*, New York, NY: Anchor, 1983, p. 14.

6. Howard Kurtz, *Spin Cycle: Inside the Clinton Propaganda Machine*, New York, NY: The Free Press, 1998, p. 92.

7. Edwards, p. 37.

8. Stephen Farnsworth, *Spinner in Chief: How Presidents Sell Their Policies and Themselves*, Boulder, CO: Paradigm, 2009, p. 87.

9. www.cnn.com/2017/05/21/politics/trump-muslim-speech-saudi-arabia.

10. www.politico.com/magazine/story/2016/04/2016-white-house-press-corps-reporters-media-survey-poll-politics-213849.

11. www.realclearpolitics.com/articles/2015/08/29/obama_meets_the_press_--_on_his_terms_127907.html

12. Farnsworth, 2009, p. 130.

13. www.usingenglish.com/reference/idioms/wag+the+dog.html.

14. Margaret Sullivan, "Much of the Media Marches to the President's Military Tune," *Washington Post*, April 10, 2017, p. C1).

15. Ibid., p. C3.

16. John Mueller, "Presidential Popularity from Truman to Johnson," *American Political Science Review*. Vol. 64 (1970).

17. Farnsworth, p. 86.

18. www.politico.com/magazine/story/2017/04/why-did-trump-bomb-syria-215001.

19. Ibid.

20. https://shorensteincenter.org/news-coverage-donald-trumps-first-100-days.

21. Alex Altman and Sean Gregory, "Trump's Offensive Playbook," *Time* October 9, 2017, p. 34.

22. Margaret Sullivan, "Trump's Tough Talk on Leaks Is One Thing, His Actions Tell Another Tale," *Washington Post*, February 28, 2017, p. C1.

23. Attributed to James Reston, www.brainyquote.com/quotes/quotes/j/jamesresto 147742.html.

24. https://consortiumnews.com/2017/03/17/the-trumpobama-leak-war.

25. Mike McCurry [Bill Clinton] and Ari Fleischer [G.W. Bush], *Columbia Journalism Review*. Available online at www.cjr.org/covering_trump/white_house_press_corps_trump.php.

26. www.deseretnews.com/article/700200108/Eliminating-the-mother-of-all-tax-deductions.html.

27. Matt Zapotosky and Devlin Barrett, "Leak Probes Have Tripled, Sessions Says," *Washington Post*, August 5, 2017, p. A1.

28. Margaret Sullivan, "His Answer to a Free Press: Jail It," *Washington Post*, May 18, 2017, p. C1.

29. Ibid.; Paul Steiger, quoted in Margaret Sullivan, "Of Course Washington Is Plagued by Leaks. That's a Good Thing," *Washington Post*, June 4, 2017, p. C1.

30. Michael Duffy, "Country First," *Time*, August 21, 2017, p. 28.

31. Paul Farhi, "Index Ranks U.S. 43rd for Freedom of the Press," *Washington Post*, April 26, 2017, p.C1.

32. www.politico.com/magazine/story/2016/04/2016-white-house-press-corps-reporters-media-survey-poll-politics-213849.

33. Dana Milbank, "TV Shows Trump Should Watch Instead of Fox News," *Washington Post*, March 12, 2017, p.A21.

34. www.politico.com/magazine/story/2016/04/2016-white-house-press-corps-reporters-media-survey-poll-politics-213849.

35. Joseph Tanfani, "Feds to Turn Up the Heat on Leaks," *The Capital*, August 5, 1017, p. A2.

36. Ibid.

37. Ibid.

38. Sullivan, "Trump's Tough. . .", p. C3.

39. Laura King, "For Trump, Clouds at Home, Abroad," *The Capital*, May 29, 2017, p. A2.

40. www.politico.com/story/2017/02/sean-spicer-targets-own-staff-in-leak-crackdown-235413.

41. Marlin Fitzwater, *Call the Briefing*, New York, NY: Times Books, 195, p. 249.

42. Ibid., p. 178.

43. Matthew Kerbel, Dom Bonafede, Martha Joynt Kumar, and John L. Moore, "The President and the News Media," in Michael Nelson (ed.), *Guide to the Presidency*, Washington, DC: CQ Press, 2008, p. 965.

44. Quoted in Kerbel et al., p. 978.

45. Quoted in Martha Joynt Kumar, *Managing the President's Message: The White House Communication Operation*, Baltimore, MD: Johns Hopkins University Press, 2007, p. 100.

46. Kurtz, 1998, p. 105.

47. Tom Wicker, "Remembering the Johnson Treatment," *New York Times*, May 5, 2002.

48. Fitzwater, p. 211.

49. Michael A. Fletcher, December 1, 2005, p. A1.

50. Kumar, p. 101; Farnsworth, p. 79.

51. Elizabeth Bumiller, "Keepers of the Bush Image Lift Stagecraft to New Heights," *New York Times*, May 16, 2003, p. A1.

52. Farnsworth, p. 81.

53. http://thehill.com/policy/energy-environment/319938-trump-signs-bill-undoing-obama-coal-mining-rule.

54. http://usa-politicsnews.com/2017/05/02/president-trump-uses-speech-to-air-force-academy-football-team-to-ask-hows-health-care-coming-folks.

55. Farnsworth, p. 81.

56. Ibid.

57. Jenna Johnson and David Nakamua, "Trump to Graduating Cadets, 'Things Are Not Always Fair,'" *Washington Post*, May 15, 2017, p. A14.

58. Jeff Smith, *The Presidents We Imagine*, Madison, WI: University of Wisconsin Press, 2009, p. 248.

59. Ibid. p, 259.

60. Doris Graber, *Mass Media and American Politics*, Washington, DC: CQ Press, 2010, p. 231.

61. Lawrence R. Jacobs, "The Presidency and the Press: The Paradox of the White House Communications War," in Michael Nelson (ed.), *The Presidency and the Political System*, Washington, DC: Congressional Quarterly Press, 2010, p. 238.

62. Ibid.

63. Ben Fritz, Bryan Keefer, and Brendan Nyhan, *All the President's Spin: George W. Bush, the Media and the Truth*, New York, NY: Touchstone, 2004, p. 261.

64. www.washingtonpost.com/news/energy-environment/wp/2017/04/28/epa-website-removes-climate-science-site-from-public-view-after-two-decades/?utm_term=.d1b283012771.

65. Kumar, p. 116.

66. www.washingtonpost.com/news/energy-environment/wp/2017/04/28/epa-website-removes-climate-science-site-from-public-view-after-two-decades/?utm_term=.8299512e1f00.

67. Matthew Kerbel, Dom Bonafede, Martha Joynt Kumar, and John L. Moore, "The President and the News Media," in Michael Nelson (ed.), *Guide to the Presidency*, Washington, DC: CQ Press, 2008, p. 988.

68. www.theatlantic.com/politics/archive/2014/08/nixons-revenge-his-media-strategy-triumphs-40-years-after-resignation/375274.

69. For the Associated Press guidelines, see http://blog.chrislkeller.com/aps-guidelines-for-off-the-record-background.

70. Farnsworth, p. 91.

71. Kumar, pp. 116–117. See also, Jim Drinkard and Mark Memmott, "HHS Said It Paid Columnists for Help," *U.S.A. Today*, January 27, 2005.

72. Paul Farhi and Matea Gold, "Pundit Fails to Disclose Trump Ties," *Washington Post*, July 20, 2017, p. C1.

73. http://theweek.com/speedreads/713149/fox-business-benches-protrump-frequent-guest-over-undisclosed-payments-from-trump-campaign.

74. Farnsworth, p. 91; www.nytimes.com/2005/03/13/politics/under-bush-a-new-age-of-prepackaged-tv-news.html.

75. Joseph R. Hayden, *A Dubya in the Headlights*, Lanham, MD: Lexington Books, 2009, p. 201.

76. Ibid., p. 202.

77. See www.whitehouse.gov/featured-videos.

78. Daniel Boorstein, The *Image: A Guide to Pseudo-events in America*, New York, NY: Atheneum, 1961.

79. Matthew Eshbaugh-Soha and Jeffrey Peake, *Breaking Through the Noise: Presidential Leadership, Public Opinion and the News Media*, Stanford, CA: Stanford University Press, 2011, p. 91.

80. Fitzwater, p. 183.

81. www.washingtonpost.com/news/morning-mix/wp/2016/01/28/how-ronald-reagan-explained-the-challenger-disaster-to-the-world-its-all-part-of-taking-a-chance/?utm_term=.4b03d0cf96a9.

82. www.nydailynews.com/news/politics/president-trump-lady-arrive-texas-harvey-article-1.3452254.

83. Lane Crothers, "'Get Off My Plane: Presidents and the Movies,'" *White House Studies*, Vol. 10, no. 3, p. 12.

84. Stephen Farnsworth, *Spinner in Chief: How Presidents Sell Their Policies and Themselves*, Boulder, CO: Paradigm, 2009, p. 78.

85. Matthew Eshbaugh-Soha and Jeffrey Peake, *Breaking Through the Noise: Presidential Leadership, Public Opinion and the News Media*, Stanford, CA: Stanford University Press, 2011, p. 86.

CHAPTER 6

PRESIDENTIAL MEDIA EVENTS

When it comes to receiving coverage, nothing beats the presences of the president. Journalists yearn to hear and see the president in person, even if they realize the event is created largely to influence how they present their stories.

Press Conferences

The modern era of presidential media relations came with Teddy Roosevelt (1901–1909). He provided the media direct access with one cardinal rule. He retained the right to make off-the-record statements and enforced the rule by banning reporters who broke it.[1] He came to the White House with significant media experience. His career had been built on stories about his fighting corruption while in public office and his heroic actions on San Juan Hill. He "was probably the first president to appreciate the value of public opinion on leading Washington."[2] He cultivated close ties with reporters but maintained significant control. In a set of ground rules which seem quaint today, Roosevelt insisted that any confidential information he gave out must not be reported. In his words, "If you ever hint where you got [the story], I'll say you are a damned liar."[3] Woodrow Wilson carried on Roosevelt's regular meetings with the press.

The experiment of weekly presidential press conferences was dropped after two years since "Wilson considered reporters dullards and they sensed condescension."[4] Violations of the off-the-record rules led to the creation of the White House Correspondents' Association, which both regulated press conference attendance and policed fellow members about attribution rules.[5] The concept of open press conferences challenged the following three presidents. Open questioning was replaced with submission of written questions. Calvin Coolidge even established the rule that the president could not be quoted without permission.[6]

Franklin Roosevelt dispensed with written questions and would allow direct quotes attributed to the president with written authorization. To facilitate exchanges with the press, Roosevelt appointed the first full-time White House press secretary. Journalists finally had what they wanted, "assurance of hard news openly conveyed."[7] Roosevelt held almost 1,000 of these informal press conferences during his four terms in office.[8] Reporters were quite happy with these informal affairs. "He never sent reporters away empty-handed." He always gave them "several laughs and a couple of top-head dispatches in a twenty-minute visit."[9]

Dwight Eisenhower (1953–1961) held relatively few press conferences; with those he did hold leaving reporters shaking their heads in confusion over his syntactical convolutions. His major contribution to the news conference lay in allowing film crews. Film of the press conferences was embargoed for broadcast until later in the day to protect the written press.[10] The networks were far from eager to take up their limited time for news and press conferences were seldom broadcast in full.[11] Reporting of Eisenhower's press conferences was relatively bland. Even when there was conflict, it was glossed over. "The flavor was lacking. So the public was not aroused. It slept easy."[12]

John Kennedy (1961–1963) showed significant television talent during the campaign. The Nixon–Kennedy debates marked him as the first television president. He recognized the intimate relationship between performer and audience member. Seeking to capitalize on his skill, Kennedy began planning for live press conferences even before his inauguration. New cameras and lighting equipment made live coverage more feasible by avoiding the glare.[13]

The announcement of live press conferences did not go down well with print reporters, who saw the initiative as undermining their role as an intermediary.[14] As is often the case, procedural and/or technological changes are viewed through the lens of self-interest. The media are often talked about as one homogeneous group, but in reality each media format has its own rules and interests. Accustomed to serving as the exclusive gatekeepers of information, print journalists felt threatened by John Kennedy's plans to open conferences to live radio and television. *New York Times* correspondent James Reston called the plan "the goofiest idea since the hoola hoop."[15] Other print journalists indicated that television reporters would "ham it up" and "cheapen the press conference."[16] Another compared it to "making love in Carnegie Hall. . . . A mess . . . disorderly, disorganized, almost chaotic."[17] Print reporters pined for private press conferences in which they served a more significant purpose.

Dissatisfaction with televised press conference did not subside fully over time. Almost a decade after Kennedy's first foray, a survey of journalists showed that negative feelings remained.[18] The dispensation of hard news with new information and sustained questioning on issues "gave way to presidential position-taking and evasion." Rather than producing hard news, the press conference seemed more like a cat and mouse game, with reporters preparing "gotcha" questions and presidents attempting to put out political fires and to promote the issue of the day. As Donald Trump's press secretary put it,

> There's so much "gotcha journalism," where the press wants to parse every word to create a story, that we have to be as precise as possible. The news has become about the clip and the segment rather than about understanding issues.[19]

More recent administrations have continued the practice of live coverage, but have reduced the number of formal press conferences. (See later discussion.)

Up until the George H.W. Bush administration (1989–1993), presidents could expect news conferences or speeches to be televised by all the broadcast networks. With the arrival of cable news networks that would broadcast entire news conferences live, the networks had an excuse for skipping their own coverage in order to protect their advertising revenue.[20] As one network executive put it in rebuffing President Clinton's request for a prime-time slot, "Are you crazy? It's sweeps month."[21] During the sweeps period, the size and demographics of a network's audience is calculated and serves as the basis for advertising purchases and rates.

The Press Conference Audience

Press conferences serve as communications links to several audiences. The proximate audience of journalists needs the sessions to write stories for their readers or viewers. Presidents and their surrogates may also be sending signals to members of Congress or executive branch officials, setting goals and methods of implementation. Even more broadly, government officials around the world parse the content of press conferences for issues that may affect their country and its inhabitants. Ultimately the president hopes to use the press conference to impart his views to the general public.

Formal press conferences are held outside the regular briefing room allowing for the attendance of several hundred reporters. The decision as to which media outlets receive White House press credentials is a difficult, but important job. Even with a larger venue, seats are limited making access a cherished commodity. While the legacy media all send representatives, the White House has been responsive to the changing media environment. Recognizing the importance of online newsgathering by an increasingly large segment of the U.S. population, President Obama allowed reporters from online outlets equal access compared with print and television reporters during press conferences.[22]

Photo 6.1 The James Brady Press Briefing Room in the White House
Source: AP Photo/Pablo Martinez Monsivais

Demeanor at the Press Conference

Until recent years, most presidential press conferences were relatively passive affairs with reporters asking polite questions and receiving polite, if incomplete, answers. The norms of the press conference favored a hierarchy of outlets. Major newspaper and television networks received the best seats in the front rows and were called on regularly. In the contemporary press conference, journalists challenge the president with adversarial questions and the topics the president does not want to face. Questioning also demands accountability in which presidents must defend and justify their policies. Gone seem to be the days in which mutual respect and even chumminess ruled the day during press conferences.[23] The occasional rude interchange (see Box 6.1) has been replaced "with questions that are increasingly enterprising, direct, and adversarial toward the president. . . . [A]n attitude of basic trust that was tinged with skepticism, was replaced with an attitude of suspicion in which trust occasionally intervened."[24]

Press conference questions tend to be tougher the longer a president is in office. During the typical "honeymoon" period, the media tends to give the new president the benefit of the doubt as he introduces his appointees and programs. The length of the honeymoon varies with the president, but it appears to be shorter and less robust in recent years.[25] As high and unreachable expectations give way to dashed hopes, more critical questions arise. With more grist for the critical story mill, the stories become less flattering. Presidents react by limiting their press conferences (see later discussion).

BOX 6.1
So's Your Mother

While most of the time the presidents and the media control their disdain for each other, in some cases it breaks through with a vengeance. Dan Rather of CBS and Richard Nixon locked horns a number of times during press conferences. One time, after Rather identified himself, Nixon said, "Are you running for something?" Rather shot back, "No, Mr. President, are you?"[26]

In another incident involving a CBS reporter (Robert Pierpoint) the heated exchange went like this:

PIERPIONT: "Mr. President, you have lambasted the television networks pretty well. . . . What is it about the television coverage of you in these past weeks and months that has so aroused your anger?"
PRESIDENT NIXON: "Don't get the impression that you arouse my anger." [Laughter]
PIERPIONT: "I'm afraid, sir, that I have that impression." [Laughter]
PRESIDENT NIXON: "You see, one can only be angry with those he respects."[27]

President Trump seems to have skipped the early stage of respectful questions and answers. His first full news conference was described as "wild" and "unconventional." Striking out against the press, Trump complained, "Tomorrow they will say 'Donald Trump rants and raves at the press'. I'm not ranting and raving. You're just dishonest people."[28] The session was largely an exercise in media bashing. He spent much of his seventy-seven-minute session criticizing the press coverage he had received. He followed up by calling the media "the enemy of the people" (a characterization borrowed from Richard Nixon.)[29] Observers found a striking similarity with Richard Nixon, who also tried "to make the conduct of the press the issue, instead of the conduct of the president."[30] On the defensive, the media tended to strike out in kind. Observers argue that while acrimonious outbursts might play well on television, they are more "memorable for the heat, if not the light they generate."[31]

Mitigating the Danger

John Kennedy's movement to live televised press conferences was a risk. "His television performances were described as a kind of tightrope act without a net."[32] Few presidents enjoy the pressure of performing effectively at the press conference. They describe the experience in a variety of ways. President Eisenhower complained, "I will mount the usual weekly cross and let [the journalists] drive the nails.[33] At the annual pardoning of the Thanksgiving turkey, George W. Bush commented to the audience, "He looks a little nervous, doesn't he? He probably thinks he's going to have a press conference."[34]

The expectations of an all-knowing president have increased in recent years. During press conferences, presidents are not allowed the luxury of saying "no comment" or "I don't know," as was the case for Harry Truman and Dwight Eisenhower. In an attempt to control these events, presidents have attempted to limit the questioning at each press conference to a single policy area.[35] Contemporary presidents spend time preparing for press conferences convening a "murder board" of staff who try to anticipate the kinds of killer questions the journalists will ask and proposing favorable answers.

In order to reduce some of the risks of a freewheeling press conference, presidents increasingly have used opening statements to help guide the subsequent questioning.[36] While the solo presidential press conference has declined in frequency, joint press conferences with visiting heads of state have served as somewhat of a replacement (see later discussion). These sessions, often held in the Rose Garden, generally turn to questions well beyond the foreign policy topics such a setting might imply.[37]

Once into the press conference, the president has some control over who is allowed to ask questions and in what order. They favor large news organizations, whose wide audiences increase the chances of getting the president's message out to the public and key policy-makers.

When possible, presidents favor reporters who have more sympathy for the president and his programs. At President Trump's first news conference, Breitbart News, a conservative outlet, was given a reserved seat in the front row and its reporter allowed one of the coveted questions. CNN, on the other hand, was denied a question, with President Trump publicly calling their organization "terrible."[38]

Presidential press conferences are not only high stakes events for the president. Reporters are under pressure to get their question asked. They prepare questions that the president can't evade, anticipating questions whose answer will show up in the next day's news and "psyching" themselves up for a contest "like that of a professional athlete before the big game."[39] Reporters recognize the visibility television gives them to both the audience and their bosses. They carefully prepare their questions in an attempt to avoid his or her "moment in the camera's eye by stumbling over a spontaneously phrased question."[40]

Press Conference Frequency

Presidents tend to be risk-averse since their decisions and the public portrayal of them have the potential to affect their policy success, public standing and political careers. One way to avoid embarrassment during press conferences lies in simply not having them. Over time there has been a general decline in the number of press conferences the president holds (see Figure 6.1). President Trump's rocky relationship with the media is seen by the single press conference he held the first nine months in office, placing him at the very low end compared with other presidents. Within each presidential term, there tends to be a slight tendency of decline over time. The danger in not facing the press lies in the fact that the media abhor a vacuum. They have deadlines to meet and careers to make; all require content. If the president fails to meet with reporters on a regular basis, they "will treat other informants as the authentic sources for accounts of his administration."[41]

Although presidents serving during times of divided government and presidents having low popularity tend to subject themselves to fewer press conferences, the preferences of individual presidents are more important in explaining news conference frequency than are contextual factors.[42] Press conferences are risky ventures, with significant potential for generating negative publicity. Modern presidents "have more [frequent] and less confrontational means with which to convey a message publicly."[43] There seems to be a negative correlation between the number of presidential news conferences and major speeches.[44] Presidents increasingly turn to public addresses to spread their message, eschewing the more dangerous press conferences. When a president is doing poorly in terms of public support, a press conference is not the most useful vehicle for bolstering his public standing.

Rather than full-blown interviews (or press conferences), Presidents George W. Bush and Bill Clinton used brief question-and-answer sessions. President Bush

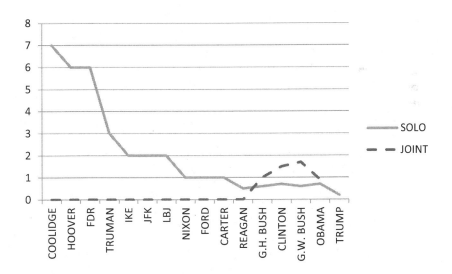

Figure 6.1 Number of Solo and Joint Press Conferences per Month

Source: Data from www.presidency.ucsb.edu/data/newsconferences.php

met with the press 427 times using this format, while Bill Clinton participated in 822 such events.[45]

While the solo press conference has declined in recent years, joint press conferences with world leaders have increased (see Figure 6.1) Such sessions are less risky because of their shorter length and the media's willingness to focus most of their questions on the relationship between the U.S. and the country in question. These events are filled with symbolism. The president and a foreign leader solemnly review the troops. The Marine musicians often provide the ambiance of patriotic music. Government workers are given time off to join other guests to provide an audience backdrop. The entire event is choreographed to provide the best visuals and sound bites for the media. Those in attendance are largely "props" designed to send a desired message.

President Trump has virtually dispensed with traditional press conferences in which a president faces a room full of reporters for an hour or more. What passes for press conferences are "two-by-two" appearances with other world leaders at which a few questions are allowed. At times, Trump has even flouted that custom, stiffing the media after meeting with other leaders.[46]

The decline of formal solo press conferences does not mean a decline in contact with the media. Recent presidents have used smaller gatherings with a pool of reporters to answer a few questions. These sessions have occurred over six times per month.[47] Presidents also subject themselves to one-on-one interviews on a regular basis (see later discussion).

Regional Press Conferences

In an attempt to control information disclosure and avoid the sharp questioning by the White House press corps, presidents use their power to control the audience through which they wish to speak to the public. Regional press conferences with reporters and editors have a number of advantages. By segmenting the audience, the president can "narrowcast his message to a very specific audience."[48] This allows focusing on issues and presenting positions of little interest to the rest of the public. Second, local reporters and televisions stations are hungry for presidential news, especially when having a Washington correspondent is too expensive to bear. Third, local reporters often do not adopt as adversarial an approach to the president as is often evident on the national level.[49]

Running the Gauntlet

As presidents move from one place to another, they often pass members of the media camped out in the hopes of shouting out a question or two (see Box 6.2). These with impromptu, brief question-answer sessions give reporters less time to arm themselves with piercing questions and less material from which to choose as they edit the raw material for broadcast.[50]

Presidents hold a significant number of "grin and greet" sessions in the Oval Office. An honored guest is ushered in for a few minutes with the president. The media is ushered in, ostensibly to get the photo op of the day. Primed with burning questions, reporters try to get a few unguarded words out of the president.

President Clinton was much more open to shouted questions, especially early in his term. As one journalist described it, "If we shouted a question, he'd stop

---

Box 6.2
Drive-By Shouting

President Reagan and his staff turned his helicopter departures from the south lawn of the White House into visual dramas, complete with "costumes" and careful stage directions. If on his way to Camp David, President Reagan would appear in casual clothes appropriate for a weekend of relaxation. Just to show that he would still be on the job, a military aide would stand close to him carrying the nuclear "football," which had the launch codes for weapons. Close at hand was First Lady Nancy Reagan, dressed more like someone going to a wedding and holding the dog in an attempt to soften her controlling "ice queen" reputation.[51]

To set up the best shot, the press pool was located a long distance away on the side of Reagan's bad ear. He would begin walking toward the loud, running helicopter and the reporters would begin to scream questions. Showing his prowess as an actor, Reagan would cup his bad ear, sending the message that he would really like to share all the secrets of the office but just can't hear what the press is interested in. About half way to the helicopter and after having answered no questions, the president would point at his watch implying that he was on a schedule and that the helicopter would take off without him if he stopped for questions. The image was "I would love to tell you all the state secrets, but I am on a schedule and the helicopter will leave without me if I take time to answer your questions." In reality he "owned" the helicopter and could stand there answering questions until hell froze over if he desired.

Recognizing they were beat, the media accepted the fact that all they would get was a picture of President Reagan waving from the door of the helicopter. As the president took off, his communications staff would heave a heavy sigh of relief that Reagan had not made any off-script comments and that the public would be provided with a picture of a vigorous seventy-year-old willing to engage the media but unable to answer their questions through no fault of his own.

and talk. Every time he would run by us on a jog, we'd shout a question and, in between huffs and puffs, he'd give us a one- or two- or three-word answer."[52]

President Trump has shared a number of his views after questions were shouted at him in public. More often he fends off reporters with a series of "thank you"s and a broad smile. President Trump has also invited the media into to portions of a series of working sessions in the Cabinet Room, at which the media are allowed to film and look over the shoulders of members of Congress, foreign leaders or other attendees.

The State of the Union Address

The Constitution (Article II, Section III) requires the president to report to Congress from time to time on the "state of the union" (SOTU). Throughout much of presidential history, presidents submitted their evaluation in writing. Woodrow Wilson revived the practice of presenting the speech in person to Congress. President Johnson moved the speech to prime time.

The SOTU stands out as one of the most visible and choreographed efforts by the White House to present the president and his policy agenda. The made-for-television setting in the House of Representatives is dramatic, with the president speaking from a high podium surrounding by the key leaders of government.

The SOTU is part of a "public relations work plan,"[53] later expanded upon by the president and his surrogates. The media evaluate both the content and context of the speech, counting the number of pauses for applause, reporting the number of times members of Congress stood up (and who refused to stand), and gauging the general mood of the audience. Reporters generally do not like the State of the Union speech. It is typically long and detailed, making it difficult to summarize and report on.[54] Given the complexity of the issues and journalists' perception of disinterest among their audiences, they tend to focus on the "sideshow" more than the content.

Usually presidents can expect complete coverage by the major broadcast and cable news networks. The importance of the speech can be seen by the negotiations the Clinton White House initiated in 1997. Much to the horror of the White House, it looked as if the decision on the O.J. Simpson trial could come down at the same time as the speech. If it were to be announced at the same time as the beginning of the speech, the White House offered to slow down the president's entrance to the chamber to allow the news flash to come through before he began speaking. As it was, the president was forced to share the split screen with coverage of the impending not guilty verdict.[55] Fortunately for Clinton, the final announcement did not come until after his speech was completed.[56]

Unique events such as in 2010 when Representative Joe Wilson (R-SC) yelled out "you lie" when President Obama was talking about health care not covering illegal immigrants, media stories reported the event and President Obama's quick comeback of a subdued and dignified "Not true." Wilson was forced to apologize for his outburst.[57]

The justices of the Supreme Court and members of the joint chiefs of staff usually sit stone faced during the SOTU, not expressing either support or opposition to the president's words. Any break, even slight, garners news coverage. In 2010, President Obama received a silent rebuke from Justice Samuel Alito, who shook his head after Obama criticized the court's ruling in *Citizens United*, which allowed corporations to make campaign contributions. News stories emphasized Republicans who felt that President Obama's attack on the court was "rude," while Democrats saw Alito's reaction as "inappropriate."[58]

Presidents attempt to increase interest in the speech through emotional appeals that aim for the public's "heart" rather than their heads.[59] In order to do this presidents have turned the media fascination with personalities to their benefit by tying policy and philosophical preferences to individual citizen heroes. The practice began in 1982 when Ronald Reagan invited Lenny Skutnik to sit in the first lady's box. The young government worker who had jumped into the Potomac River to save air crash survivors served as a perfect example of using individual initiative rather than waiting for government assistance.[60] Every president since Reagan has used these "Skutnik moments" to tout policy initiatives. Republican presidents tend to single out heroes who have succeeded despite government intervention, while Democrats honor those who have used government programs in creative ways.[61] The media facilitates the strategy by

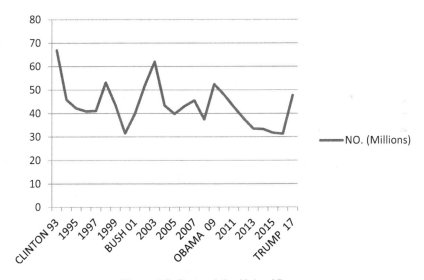

Figure 6.2 State of the Union Viewers

Note: Full years indicate first year of a president's term

Source: Data from www.nielsen.com/us/en/insights/news/2016/31-3-million-viewers-tune-in-to-watch-pres-obamas-state-of-the-union-address.html

speculating on who will be invited to the SOTU and what policy initiative they might represent. Telling a poignant story about an individual affected by a public policy may bring that policy into focus, but may not suggest the best way to solve the general problem.

Despite all the strategic planning, the ability of the SOTU to affect public opinion has increasingly been stymied by the declining size of the television audience (see Figure 6.2). Presidents usually have larger audiences for their first SOTU, when the public is taking their measure. The potential effectiveness of the SOTU speech is reduced to some degree by the fact that the audience overrepresents members of the president's party. By "preaching to the choir," the president may harden their perspectives but it reduces the likelihood of reaching those who oppose him.[62]

General Presidential Speeches

"As presidential press conferences have declined, the number of presidential speeches has increased. Speech-making is the focus of modern presidential governance and is how presidents primarily lead Congress, the media, and the public."[63] The research is not clear about the president's actual ability to gain his policy aspirations through speeches, but presidents act as if ineffective communication dooms their efforts to failure.[64] Presidents "going public"[65] through speeches is not a recent development. Hints at the strategy were evident in earlier presidencies. Teddy Roosevelt described the presidency as the "bully pulpit" and showed little reluctance to use media attention to promote his activist agenda. Woodrow Wilson took on an ambitious whistle-stop initiative to garner media and public support for the League of Nations.[66] What has changed is the volume of presidential speech-making. Presidential speeches have become the preferred method to get the White House message out. Harry Truman gave eighty-eight speeches in a typical year, while Reagan gave 320 and Bill Clinton 550.[67] The primary increases in presidential speeches has occurred in the utilization of "minor" addresses in which the president is talking to a particular group such as veterans, specific government agency employees, or union members. President Clinton averaged a minor address almost every other day he was in office.[68] Presidents Bush, Obama, and Trump continued the heavy speaking schedule.

Presidential addresses carry with them a number of advantages. The president and his staff set the timetable, determine the location, affect the audience make-up, and control the content. Despite some decline in the percentage of the public viewing such events, the news media cover them heavily. Such national addresses help set the public agenda at the beginning of the policy process. The fact that the president is talking about an issue and that the television networks have generally adjusted their schedules to accommodate him imbue presidential speeches with importance.

Staging the Best Outcome

Presidents and their staffs spend a great deal of effort creating the best possible image for an event like a speech with symbolic settings and substantive backdrops. Front-section seats, and those behind the podium, are reserved for the most ardent supporters, who serve as a buffer against possible protestors. President George W. Bush's staff recruited volunteers to sit in the prime seats to drown out protestors.[69] President Trump's staff made presidential speeches seem like campaign rallies, with attendees waving signs in the background. One advisor pointed out that in such a setting "you get to say whatever you want to say, and don't have to take questions."[70]

Radio Addresses

Reminiscent of Franklin Roosevelt's "fireside chats," Ronald Reagan began the practice of weekly radio addresses to the nation for broadcast Saturday afternoons.[71] President George W. Bush added podcasts, while President Obama began doing the events on video. President Trump continued delivering the brief (twenty minutes or so) presentations in a televised format and distributing them via YouTube. A number of media outlets such as C-SPAN and NBC broadcast the addresses in their entirety. While the audience may not be large, it is composed of some of the most interested and politically active segments of the population. Usually recorded on Fridays, transcripts of the talks are given to reporters with an agreement that the content will be embargoed until the actual broadcast. While the immediate audiences are small, presidents recognize that such statements will generate significant media attention.[72]

Going to the Audience

It is clear that modern presidents travel more, give more public addresses, and take a more active role in the public relations of their office.[73] The goal is less to establish direct communications with the public but rather to generate more positive media attention.

"The president who rests his leadership on going public will be tempted to travel frequently, in search of sympathetic audiences and 'presidential' images."[74] Presidential travel has the advantage of fitting a common media narrative: "the popularly elected leader of the country leaves the nation's capital to reach out to his constituents for their support."[75]

Presidential staffs seek out supportive audiences, symbolic settings, and areas where the most political payoff can be gained. Doherty finds that presidential travel decisions have a political flavor with a carry-over from the Electoral College, which directs wise candidates to winnable states with a large number of electoral votes. The media are quick to point out the electoral motivations of travel by sitting presidents.[76] In their strategy of going local, modern presidents "have turned the map of the United States into a kind of political game board, with speeches as tokens and with media coverage the payoffs."[77]

Some of the most iconic images of presidents emerge from their travel. Pictures of President Reagan speaking in front of the Statue of Liberty, George W. Bush standing on top of the rubble of 9/11, and President Obama looking pensively at the Louisiana oil spill all carry with them significant meaning hard to capture in words or sounds.

In his attempt to promote his initiative to privatize social security, President George W. Bush traveled to a half-dozen states where he had beaten John Kerry and "that not coincidentally, were served by a Democratic senator who might be susceptible to voters' demands for the president's plan."[78] President Obama also strategically chose local markets. When dealing with trade legislation, he did interviews with television stations and newspapers in districts represented by a Democrat in Congress who was still uncommitted on the legislation.[79]

During the first few months of his presidency, President Trump enjoyed a "victory lap," visiting states such as Iowa, Ohio, and Pennsylvania crucial to his victory. His goal was clearly to strengthen his support among his base voters and show members of Congress and the public that the support remained.[80] Each event resembled more of a campaign rally than a policy speech.

Presidents and other key players recognize the importance of local media. As one of Bill Clinton's aides put it, "What's not to like, if you're a politician, about cheering crowds and fawning press? It's like force-feeding sugar to an ant."[81] In George W. Bush words,

> I find it's important to get out of town-at least out of the Nation's Capitol—to take my message directly to the people who matter. You see, oftentimes, what I try to say in Washington gets filtered. Sometimes, my words in Washington don't exactly translate directly to the people, so I've found it's best to travel the country.[82]

President Trump's press secretary, Sarah Huckabee Sanders, put a positive spin on presidential travel by pointing out that "anytime the president can talk directly to the American people it is a good thing. It's good for the President and it's good for the American people to be able to get a message directly from him."[83]

As Figure 6.3 shows, presidents have increasingly taken time to travel and made more trips outside of Washington to make their case to the public. In order to compensate for audience inattention and the national media's filtering of the presidential message, presidents turn to the regional and local media for coverage. Local media are generally more willing to cover presidents in the way they desire

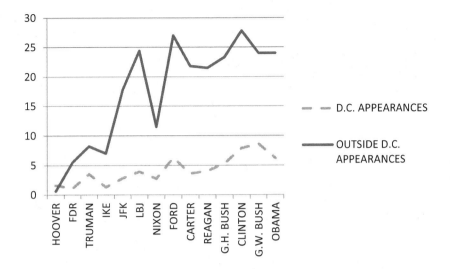

Figure 6.3 Presidential Speeches In and Outside of Washington

Source: Data from Lyn Ragsdale, *Vital Statistics of the Presidency*, Washington, DC: CQ Press, 2014

since they lack the resources to go much beyond the speech itself and can add some local "color" about the event. When a president comes to town, it is big news and almost guaranteed extensive and positive coverage. As one White House staffer put it, a president's reference to a local issue has the impact of "throwing a pebble in a lake" for the national media, but it is "like rolling a boulder into a small pond [making] a very big splash"[84] locally. Such speeches, town meetings and press conferences have all the trappings of "pseudo-events" over which the White House has a great deal of control.[85] Local reporters often lack the expertise and resources to report these events critically, so much of their reporting emphasizes factors such as crowd size, enthusiasm and local responses.

Local media also have a tendency to slant their coverage to match the views of their audiences which may not fit with the opinions of the perceived national audience. As a business, local newspapers are "mindful of audience preferences when reporting the news."[86] A newspaper's endorsement of the president, while a candidate, tends to be related to the amount and tone of subsequent coverage. Not only is local outlet coverage generally more positive[87] but it is trusted more by the public and is its major source of news, especially for Democrats.[88] Good local coverage tends to generate positive national coverage.

Part of the difference between national and local coverage of President Trump results from contemporary realities of news creation. Local stations, low on staff, still want to cover national news. Local stations broadcast segments created by others. Sinclair Broadcast Group owns the largest string of television stations in the country. They hired former Trump campaign aide Boris Epshteyn to present commentaries and then directed stations that these were "must-run" segments. Epshteyn delivered powerful pro-Trump and anti-media messages without revealing his previous connections.[89]

The era of the large nationally televised presidential speeches, and even the generalized press conference, seems to be winding down. Contemporary presidents are not talking to the public less but rather choosing more targeted and local venues, often those overrepresenting their core supporters.

Presidents do not limit themselves to domestic travel. While we are accustomed to presidents traveling abroad and receiving significant media attention, the practice is a relatively new phenomenon. President Theodore Roosevelt was the first president to travel outside the U.S. as president, but his itinerary was scrubbed to only include visits to the American-controlled Canal Zone. President Woodrow Wilson took the first official foreign trip to France in an attempt to create the League of Nations. The number of foreign trips increased with Franklin Roosevelt, with presidents from Truman to Obama taking over 300 trips abroad. Recent presidents have averaged over six trips per year overseas[90] (see Figure 6.4). Most of the time a president travels abroad he takes with him a large media contingent and numerous arrangements are made for press conferences and other interactions with the media. The decision to travel abroad includes a significant political component.

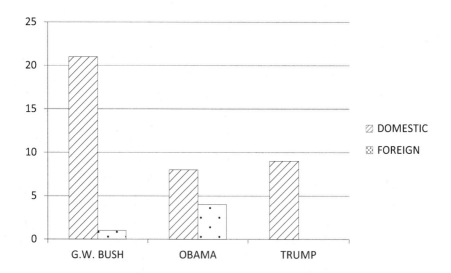

Figure 6.4 Official Trips Outside of Washington during the First 100 Days

Sources: Data from Julie Hirschfeld Davis, "How Trump's Travel Compares with Past Presidents," *New York Times*, April 16, 2017. Updated by the author. See also https://en.wikipedia.org/wiki/list_of_presidential_trips_made_by_donald_trump

Speech Content

Presidential speeches have become "audience driven," with pre-speech polling and focus groups used to determine the content and format of effective messages. Leadership is transformed from showcasing long held presidential values, to a mad rush to get ahead of the audience to meet their preferences. Presidents are pushed to "think of how audience pre-dispositions can be exploited rather than how citizens' needs can be met."[91]

By relying on speeches, presidents retain the ability to control much of what is reported. It is "easy for reporters to become lazy, or to think it presumptuous or unseemly to look behind the presidential staging."[92] Additionally, the focus on what a president says misses an understanding of what is not said. A president's avoidance of certain topics tells a great deal about his priorities and legitimate issues he does not wish to confront.[93] Presidents tend to appeal to the public through the media on popular topics, while avoiding issues and possible solutions that might offend the president's core constituency.

Speeches have become much more than words. Visual backgrounds, music, chanting crowds, and waving signs all help to avoid the "most heinous political crime—being dull."[94] The entirety of what the president says is less important than the sound bite produced and the takeaway image broadcast. The broad line between speech-making and theater no longer exists.[95] The old theater question as to whether something will "play in Peoria" is applied to presidential speeches.[96] Style has become more important than substance.[97] "The eyes of most Americans are constantly fixed on the White House, dazzled by the show jointly produced by the president and the mass media."[98]

The Impact of Presidential Speeches

Both television networks and presidents are strategic actors when it comes to covering presidential addresses. Since presidential speeches are not conducive to commercial breaks, the network covering an address loses advertising revenue. Indirectly, low viewership of a presidential address means a smaller audience to stay with the network after the speech. Since network revenue is based on audience size and composition, presidential speeches are poor programming choices from a business perspective. The television audience is small and made up of older citizens who are less likely to be the target of advertisers given their loyalty to existing purchasing patterns.

During much of the era from World War II to the 1990s all a president had to do was ask for prime-time coverage and it would be granted with little or no question. During the Clinton administration the networks began to regularly rotate coverage of some presidential appearances, allowing regular programming to continue on the other networks. Of Clinton's twenty prime-time addresses, only fourteen were covered by all three broadcast networks.[99]

Recognizing the networks' hesitancy to give up its prime-time audience, clever presidential strategists limit their requests for prime-time coverage to special occasions such as crises or major policy announcements. Presidents attempt to go directly to the public through televised speeches relatively sparingly with an average of about four national speeches per year. Foreign policy tends to be the topic of more speeches than domestic issues.[100] Early in their term presidents are given (or may ask for) more prime-time spots. Presidential speeches have the greatest potential for media coverage when they are rare. A president who goes to the public too often seems much like the little boy who cried wolf. A president can "wear out his welcome [and make] it difficult for citizens to distinguish important from less important issues."[101] Popular presidents are also granted more time exposure than those unpopular with the citizenry.[102] There are limits to how often a president can effectively go to the public for support. The public have lives to live, work to complete, and other interests to satisfy. Too much presidential news devalues subsequent news. When the White House wants the public (and the media) to listen it should not go to them too often or else each new message is lost in the endless chatter. As one former White House communications director put it, it is important to keep "an eye towards preventing the devaluation of presidential currency."[103]

Presidents tend to turn to more speech-making in order to counter negative news and impressions. A poor economy and low presidential approval tend to spawn more speeches. Presidents also tend to ramp up their speaking schedule when running for reelection.[104]

Despite the limitations, nationally televised presidential addresses are still seen as "arguably the best strategy for presidential leadership. ... [M]edia are predisposed to cover the president's national addresses. The public is likely to pay some attention ... at least [to] the news coverage of it."[105] The research is clear. When a president mentions a policy problem or solution in an address, the public reacts by expressing greater concern for that problem or support for the mentioned solution.[106]

Presidential speeches serve as an important way for the president to focus media attention on particular policy areas.[107] Although the impact may be limited in some cases, "media are a central and intervening linkage between the president and public given that the president appears able to indirectly lead the public through the news media."[108] The clearest examples of the president leading the public through the media occur when the president attacks new issues or faces old issues in a new way.[109]

In order to reach the American public (and eventually Congress and the bureaucracy), a president's legislative appeals must be reported by the media. A detailed analysis of presidential legislative appeals indicates that the majority of them received little or no media coverage.[110] Members of the White House press corps chafe at being considered "flacks of the president by only reporting from the president's perspective."[111] A president can increase the likelihood of coverage by speaking at length about the issue, making it the primary focus of his remarks, highlighting the conflict with Congress, and delivering the remarks outside of Washington, DC. New initiatives are also more likely to appeal to the desire for novelty in stories that the media prefers.[112]

The impact of presidential speeches depends on who is listening. Significant media coverage virtually guarantees an influence on the public. A network's decision to air a particular speech live "speaks to its importance and newsworthiness," thus leading to extensive coverage.[113] It is also important to recognize that the smaller audience includes a higher percentage of interested and activist citizens. The "political junkies" magnify their impact by attempting to influence their friends, contacting elected officials, and/or giving campaign contributions.

It is also important to remember that, no matter how skillfully a speech is presented, the media have the final say on how it is interpreted to the public. Presidential speeches do not stand on their own. Rather, their quality is filtered through media expectations. After his slow response to Hurricane Katrina, President George W. Bush returned to New Orleans for a speech described as "perhaps the most important address since launching the War in Iraq in 2003."[114] Despite a strongly worded speech, the media focused on the staging of the speech in Jackson Square. The White House had brought its own lighting and camouflage netting to provide a cozy look. The danger of an adverse crowd reaction was handled by having no crowd. One journalist simply wrote off the speech as like "a motivational speaker regaling an audience of three."[115]

In their role as summarizers and interpreters, the media pick key elements of presidential speeches to correctly or incorrectly encapsulate the entire meaning of the speech (see Box 6.3). President Carter outlined his energy policy using the term the "moral equivalent of war." The media criticized the tepid approach by using the derogatory acronym "meow" to imply the weakness of the policy.[116] In his 2002 State of the Union message, George W. Bush used the phrase the "axis of evil," and it became the short-hand title of the speech, as well as granting the less than extremely articulate president high rankings by the media.[117] Throughout his career, Barack Obama attempted to inspire his audiences with the simple phrase "yes we can," and the media obliged by focusing on these words.[118]

Presidential Interviews

Presidents walk a fine line when they give exclusive interviews to favored reporters. Kennedy expanded the practice even though Franklin Roosevelt had put his "head on the block" by members of the writing press for excluding some of them.[119] The influence of self-interest is revealed by the perspective of James Reston of the *New York Times*. He initially warned President-Elect Kennedy not to generate

Box 6.3
Three "Little" Words

When you are president of the United States, every word you utter is parsed and searched for nuances and hidden meaning. After a violent clash involving white supremacist demonstrators in Charlottesville, VA, over the removal of a statue of confederate general Robert E. Lee, President Trump spoke for the American people and condemned the "hatred, bigotry and violence." His words would be almost universally accepted if he had not tagged on the phrase "on all sides." Immediately his attempt to spread the blame from a marginal group in American society generated an avalanche of negative comments. Reports speculated on the degree to which the president's support from white nationalists permeated his comments.[120] Following two days of controversy after he uttered these words, President Trump was forced to explicitly condemn the Nazi and white supremacist groups.[121] In the kind of reversal that Trump has become famous for, he changed course a day later, blaming both sides for the altercations.[122] This was another example of Trump getting a great deal of coverage but unable to capitalize on it because of his day-to-day contradictions.[123]

In a press event the same week, President Trump warned the leaders of North Korea that should they attempt to use nuclear weapons the U.S. would respond with "fire and fury."[124] The seeming call for military action was repeated twice for emphasis. This warlike warning set off a firestorm of concern on both social and legacy media. Conservative media were more likely to applaud the statement as "about time."[125] He also said that U.S. military resources were "locked and loaded," another set of three words generating a great deal of discussion.[126]

In all three cases, three little words unleashed an avalanche of media interest as they tried to place the comments into broader context for their readers and viewers in the hope of discovering a broader pattern.

the ill-will of exclusives, only to find himself one of the favored few. At that point he changed his view.[127]

One-on-one interviews with reporters almost guarantee distribution to their outlet and often create news covered by others. President Obama was quite fond of this venue, granting over 1,000 such interviews.[128] In comparison, Presidents Bill Clinton and George W. Bush granted only about two-thirds of that number combined.[129] Interviews are critical, since they allow reporters to delve into detail about an issue, not just read a press release or hear a short answer at the press conference. People "interested in presidential policy want answers to the questions reporters will ask, not just what the president wants to say about it."[130] Such sessions with a president have another benefit. The symbolism of the president reaching out to reporters for advice helps co-opt them and soften their criticism.[131]

President Obama found three major reasons for doing so many interviews. In the first place, they allowed him to target particular audiences. Second, the president could set the ground rules on the topics to be covered. Third, the White House gets to choose who will do the interview.[132]

George W. Bush also used focused interview sessions to promote his ideas. In order to reach the "hook and bullet" crowd, the George W. Bush team invited representatives of hunting, fishing, and conservation publications for a roundtable and exclusive interviews with the president.[133]

After recognizing his strong support among conservative talk show hosts, George W. Bush invited fifty to set up on the lawn of the White House. There they broadcast for three days and were given interviews with a large selection of senior staff and cabinet secretaries.[134]

Aware of audience size, President Obama chose to do interviews with the networks carrying the Super Bowl. With an audience of 100 million people, it's hard to imagine a broader distribution of the president's message. Obama even followed the pattern of granting such interviews the year Fox News covered the game.[135]

Despite his public disdain for the media, journalists do report President Trump's willingness to "reach out to reporters, at times directly. . . . I've never experienced that in the five years I covered the Obama administration."[136] It is not that President Trump feels obligated to inform reporters, but rather his outreach is based on the fact the "he feels like it's the only way he can be heard and cut through all the noise."[137] Who he reaches out to is instructive of his strategy. During his first 100 days, six of his eight interviews went to conservative Fox News.[138] When Stephen Bannon served as Trump's chief strategist, Breitbart News became "practically the administration's house organ [resulting] in docile stenography presented as news."[139]

Interviews of any kind are not without their risks. While condemning dishonesty on the part of the White House, reporters and their bosses are not above using misrepresentation to get a story. Producers will promise to abide by ground rules about the length or content of an interview, recognizing that once the interview begins, the interviewer is largely in control.[140] A president's unwillingness to answer a question implies he has something to hide. It is almost unheard of for a president to walk off the set after an offending question. Presidents tend to avoid granting interviews to programs such as CBS's *60 Minutes*, because of its reputation for "gotcha" questions and ambush interviews.[141]

Town Hall Meetings

Presidential town hall meetings present the image of an accessible president facing his fellow citizens.[142] While the format implies interaction with average citizens, the audience is usually carefully screened to avoid embarrassing questions. Such meetings are another arsenal in the president's armory, available when his message is not transmitted through the mainstream media or other formats.[143] Town hall meetings serve as one way to connect with the people. The assumption, as promoted by the White House, is that the citizens involved represent a broad base of the population free to question the president on any pressing issue. Analyzing a George W. Bush town hall, the *Washington Post*:

> learned that the preparations for these town-hall meetings were neither ordinary nor natural. They involved meticulous screening of audience members by the White House's Office of Public Liaison, which then also prepped and rehearsed the participants the night before each event.[144]

President Obama avoided press conferences, where he would have had to "mix it up with the press." Instead, he favored frequent town hall meetings, which allowed members of the public to ask challenging questions about his administration.[145] President Trump has not followed suit.

The President as a Humorist and Target

The White House Correspondents' Association is a yearly "schmoozefest"[146] for politicians, celebrities, and the media. It is similar to the Radio and Television Correspondents' Dinner and one held by the Gridiron Club. At these formal events, open only to select media and their guests, there is usually anticipated that the president will attend and sit through a "roast" in which his shortcomings are publicly displayed in a humorous way.

At these dinners, well-known comedians are given the chance to skewer the president on presumed shortcomings. Presidents attend these black tie events and are on full display at the head table. Trying to show they are good sports who can take a joke, the default position is for the president to smile sparingly and take his lumps. At times, members of the White House staff have walked out in protest when the jokes seemed to cross the line.[147]

Presidents attempt to counter jokes directed at them through their own comedy routines. Telling a joke on oneself embodies a sense of self-confidence. Some presidents, such as Barack Obama, gained kudos by his own stand-up comedy routine (see Box 6.4). He almost seemed to enjoy the joint roasting of the media and himself. "It was Obama's yearly chance to inspire a meme, rip a rival, come off as folksy royalty, [and] remind the public that the media was *not* the enemy."[148]

At the 2004 Radio and Television Correspondents' dinner, President George W. Bush was given a chance to take the stage. Humor can be a risky strategy, especially if few people laugh. That night President Bush became the victim of

Box 6.4
The President as Comedian in Chief

"Performing" at one of the press association dinners, recent presidents took the following approaches:

John F. Kennedy made a joke about appointing his brother as attorney general by saying, "I can't see that it's wrong to give him a little legal experience before he goes out to practice law."[149]

During a time of economic downturn for agriculture, Ronald Reagan exclaimed, "I think we should keep the grain and export the farmers," but the joke did not go down well among the agriculture sector.[150]

Even the first lady gets into the act. Nancy Reagan, known for her extensive wardrobe, did a parody of the song "Secondhand Rose," much to the delight of the president and the 600-person crowd.[151]

George H.W. Bush poked fun at himself by saying, "People say I'm indecisive, but I don't know about that."[152]

In 1995, Hillary Clinton stole the show with a parody of *Forrest Gump* sitting on a bench outside the White House. A year earlier, both the president and the first lady acted out a spoof of the "Harry and Louise" commercials put out by the health industry to attack the Clinton health care plan.[153]

George W. Bush made fun of his search for weapons of mass destruction with a picture of him searching around the Oval Office, to mixed reviews.[154]

Barack Obama faced the "birther" issue about his citizenship by exclaiming, "Of course I love America. If I didn't, I wouldn't have moved from Kenya."[155]

President Trump broke with tradition and declined to attend the 2017 Gridiron dinner, sending his vice president in his stead to field the sharp barbs and initiate his own. Vice President Pence turned his attention to the White House press secretary and indirectly to the media by quipping, "Sean, I really want to apologize that you didn't get served dinner tonight. . . . When the waiter asked you what you wanted for your entree, you shouldn't have said, 'Sit down, I never called on you!'"[156]

"unlaughter," a situation where laughter is expected but does not occur. In the sketch, the president went around the Oval Office looking for weapons of mass destruction. Given the serious consequences of the claim of such weapons, the joke fell flat and became a divisive issue.[157]

President Trump became the first president in thirty-six years not to attend the White House Correspondents' Association dinner, even though he had attended in the past as a guest. In his first few months, "he has developed his own traditions, and it involves relentlessly mocking the media, not laughing with it, not even for a one-night black tie cease-fire."[158] Instead of staying in Washington to face the media, President Trump held a campaign-like rally in Pennsylvania, "the latest iteration of POTUS vs. Beltway."[159] Feeling beleaguered at the 2017 White House Correspondents' Association dinner, First Amendment pins were given out to attendees and the association's president commented, "An attack on any of us is an attack on all of us."[160]

Photo Ops

Normally the communications staff carefully stages photo ops in the Oval Office associated with important meetings between the president and world leaders or individuals of particular achievement. The photographers troop in, along with the official White House photographer, for the beginning of the meeting, and then are ushered out once the serious talk begins. Favorable pictures taken by the White House photographer are posted on the White House website and distributed to the media.

At times, these events fail to portray the desired image. In 2017, the media picked up President Trump's apparent unwillingness to shake hands with German Chancellor Angela Merkel during her visit to the Oval Office.[161] In the midst of the national discussion over the Trump campaign's ties to Russia, the president met with the Russian foreign minister and ambassador in the Oval Office. U.S. photographers were barred, but the White House allowed what they understood to be the foreign minister's official photographer to cover the meeting. It turns out that the photographer also worked for the Russia's Tass news agency. The attempt to downplay the meeting by denying photographic access blew up in the face of the White House. Not only did U.S. news agencies feel slighted, but the Russian pictures were widely spread by the Internet. The fallout of the misguided strategy not only raised questions about media (and public) access but also led to concerns over the security of the Oval Office.[162]

Advertising

In the past presidents and interest groups have largely relied on "free media," provided in news coverage, while eschewing "paid media" in the form of commercials during the non-election period. The Trump administration never relaxed from its campaign mode, creating a Trump 2020 committee and attempting to buy advertising spots almost immediately after the election. At the 100-day mark, Trump's advocates created an ad touting his accomplishments and challenging the alleged "fake news" of the networks. Arguing that the ad itself was false, CNN refused to run it.[163]

Reacting to Media Coverage: The President as Audience in Chief

Recognizing the importance of media coverage, presidents and their staffs carefully monitor what is said about them. Most presidents disdain much of the media coverage they receive, at least in private.

Monitoring the Media

Modern presidents have considerable interest in how they are covered by the media. Starting with the William McKinley administration (1897–1901), the practice of clipping newspaper articles and later summarizing television programs to place in a presidential briefing book was established.[164]

Not all presidents pay the same attention to their media coverage. Many presidents have been sensitive about their portrayal in the news. Lyndon Johnson had three television sets installed in the White House and had an early version of the TV remote created so he could monitor his image on the three major networks. Johnson tended to micromanage White House public relations efforts. Tom Wicker of the *New York Times* remembers calling Lyndon Johnson's press secretary to complain about Johnson's lack of press conferences. Before he knew it, he was connected to Johnson's office for a nonstop monologue about the nature of his coverage. Johnson had been eavesdropping on his own press secretary and took things into his own hands.[165]

Richard Nixon also took great interest in media coverage. Each morning he would read the summary of the news directing his staff how to respond and noting in the margins which reporters and stories he liked and disliked.[166]

Ronald Reagan watched C-SPAN and even called one of their programs. President Clinton, on the other hand, paid little attention to the news, arguing "I make the news; why do I have to read the news."[167] Other presidents such as George W. Bush tried to portray an image of someone who had little concern for what the media was saying about him. "The reality is that he pore[d] over the newspapers each morning."[168]

Arguably the most ardent presidential news "junkie" is Donald Trump. He had a sixty-inch TV installed in the White House and "watches the screen like a coach going over game tape, studying the opposition, plotting next week's plays."[169] At times he watches his press secretary's new conferences, clipping notes mid-briefing about points he wants to get across.[170]

Evaluating Coverage

Democratic and Republican administrations tend to view the media in different ways. "Republicans didn't expect fair treatment and [are] thrilled if you gave them an even break; the Dems secretly believed all journalists were liberal and got all sullen and whiny if you kicked them around."[171]

Most presidents have publicly faced reporters as worthy adversaries just doing their jobs. They followed the classic argument that one should not "pick arguments with anyone who buys ink by the barrel" (or, in contemporary times, anyone who has direct access to the nation's living rooms or smartphones). Until Donald Trump took on the press, public presidential condemnation of the media has been limited—with the exception of Richard Nixon. Behind the scenes, presidential evaluation of the media has been more critical, complaining about the media in private but biting their tongues in public.

There is great temptation for presidents to blame the messenger rather than take responsibility themselves. "The desire to explain one's actions and respond to criticism springs from human nature. Probably every occupant of the White House has at some point blamed press treatment for his troubles in the country."[172] As a president's popularity declines, condemnation of the media tends to increase.

A close advisor of President Clinton explained that Clinton "was contemptuous of reporters. He feels they're a sleazy group of people who lie a lot, who pursue their own agendas, who have a pack mentality, He feels they are a necessary evil."[173] Clinton also complained:

> I really thought my image would not be twisted, and that I would not be turned into a cardboard cutout of myself. . . . I mean, heck, half the time when I see myself on the evening news, I think 'Gosh, if that's all I knew about that guy, I wouldn't be for him either.'"[174]

Donald Trump and his supporters express a great deal of frustration with the media coverage he receives. As Fox News host Sean Hannity put it, "If President Trump could actually cure cancer, make people in wheelchairs walk, give everyone a million dollars, if he could prevent heart attacks or stop car accidents, the media still wouldn't be happy,"[175] President Trump's epithets toward the media are continuous and varied. While some may write off President Trump's battle with the media as "crazy," he well may be crazy like a fox. As long-time news commentator Ted Koppel sees it, it is a:

> win-win position. . . . If the coverage is positive, he pockets it. But if it's negative, he plays it as a battle he is fighting to fend off the apocalypse. And as he benefits from free exposure, he attacks the messengers as dishonest and corrupt.[176]

Much of his criticism of the media falls on receptive ears since his political base is as contemptuous of the media as he is. The origin of Trump's denigration of the media goes back at least as his political campaigns where he found criticism of the media served as a surefire applause line from his base voters.[177] "The more the media attacks him, the more it becomes a self-fulfilling prophesy on the side of Trump supporters who fervently believe the media treat him unfairly."[178] Trump's supporters harbor extremely negative views of the media, with 78% of them believing that the media regularly distribute false stories and 80% believe that the media's false stories are a bigger problem than those misrepresentations committed by Trump.[179] Focusing on alleged media unfairness serves as a perfect distraction from real-world events.

Most presidents "grin and bear it" when confronted with news coverage they do not like (see Box 6.5 for exceptions) and thank their lucky stars when coverage is positive. Cohen[180] asks the question "How receptive would the public be to presidents who also constantly complained about the treatment they receive in the news media"? That question may well get its answer during the Trump administration.

Box 6.5
Among My Worst Enemies

Disparagement of the media has a long history in presidential campaigns and once in office. Among the most direct jabs are the following.

Barry Goldwater's campaign projected the phrase "Don't Trust the Liberal Media" on large screens during the 1964 Republican Convention.[181]

Richard Nixon's vice president, Spiro Agnew, called the media "Nattering nabobs of negativism" who "formed their own 4H Club—the 'hopeless, hysterical hypochondriacs of history.'"[182] He went on to argue that President Nixon was the victim of "a small and unelected elite."[183]

George H.W. Bush's 1992 campaign used bumper stickers proclaiming "Annoy the Media, Re-elect Bush."[184]

President Bill Clinton exploded, "I've fought more damn battles here than any other president in 20 years with the possible exception of Ronald Reagan's first budget and not gotten one damn bit of credit from the knee-jerk liberal press. I am damn sick and tired of it."[185]

President George W. Bush described reporters "as the enemy, engaged in a continual game of ambushes and trap setting."[186]

In one of his most complete condemnations of the media, President Trump tweeted, "The FAKE NEWS media (failing @nytimes, @NBCNews, @ABC, @CBS, @CNN) is not my enemy, it is the enemy of the American People!"

Presidential Reactions to the Media

Many presidents have had problems with the media. Even John Kennedy, who is often held up for his savvy with the media, "had an inexhaustible capacity to take displeasure from what he read . . . and an equally inexhaustible capacity to keep on reading more than anyone else in Washington."[187] Richard Nixon's tumultuous relations with the media led him to threaten his staff, "I want it clearly understood from now on, ever, no reporter from the *Washington Post* is ever to be in the White House. Is that clear?"[188]

Aside from expressions of frustration with the media, presidents have taken clear actions to punish those members of the media in disfavor and to reward those presenting positive stories. Above and beyond granting access to favored reporters, presidents have found other ways to punish and reward. There is no clear correlation between a president's ideology and his treatment of the media. President Kennedy banned some reporters from his press conferences for writing negative stories. At times presidents treat ideological opponents more shabbily than those who agree with them ideologically. President Nixon wiretapped purported liberal reporters' phones and ordered the Internal Revenue Service to harass journalists he disliked.[189] After the *Washington Post* began its stories about Watergate, President "Nixon vowed to 'screw around' with the lucrative TV licenses" of the publication.[190] President Obama allowed the Department of Justice to spy on Fox News reporter James Rosen and subpoenaed months of Associated Press phone records.[191] His administration also spied on Fox News and had to later express regret.[192] Despite the fact that President Obama's policy preferences matched members of the media relatively closely, many members of the media saw his as "the most anti-press administration since the Nixon years."[193] Obama shot back, questioning the media's professional standards, saying, "A job well done is about more than just handing someone a microphone. It is to probe and to question, and to dig deeper, and to demand more. "[194] President Trump, dissatisfied with his coverage, blackballed some reporters from asking questions at press briefings.[195]

On the reward side of the equation, presidents can help their friends in the media. Sinclair Broadcast Group is the largest cable distribution system in the country and strongly supportive of President Trump. The possible payoff for their tilt toward President Trump in its programming can be seen in administration approval of deregulation by the Federal Communications Commission allowing Sinclair to expand its network through the purchase of additional stations.[196]

Not all presidents have seen the adversarial relationship with the media in a negative light. Speaking at the White House Correspondents' Dinner, Ronald Reagan asserted,

> Every president will try to use the press to his best advantage and to avoid those situations that aren't to his advantage. The press can take care of itself quite nicely, and a president should be able to take care of himself as well. I hope my epitaph will be with the White House correspondents—what every president's epitaph should be with the press—is this: "He gave as good as he got." And that I think will make for a healthy press and a healthy presidency.[197]

Other individuals holding the presidential office changed their minds about the role of the media once in office (see Box 6.6).

President George W. Bush had his troubles with the media but retained a healthy respect for their role in a representative democracy. Reacting to President Trump's severe criticism of the media, the former president said:

> We need an independent media to hold people like me to account. . . . Power can be very addictive, and it can be corrosive. And it's important for the media to call to account people who abuse their power, whether it be here or elsewhere.[198]

Box 6.6
It All Depends

Presidents have long been of mixed minds about the media of their day. Prior to taking office, Thomas Jefferson boldly asserted,

> The basis of our government being the opinion of the people, the very first object should be to keep that right: and were it left to me to decided whether we should have a government without newspapers or newspapers without government, I should not hesitate a moment to prefer the latter.

Once in office the reality of press criticism sunk in and Jefferson concluded, "As for what is not true, you will always find abundance in the newspapers" and "Nothing can now be believed which is seen in a newspaper. Truth becomes suspicious by being put into that polluted vehicle."[199]

Another dramatic turnabout occurred to a future president, who stated after the failed U.S.-backed invasion of Cuba:

> The concept of a return to secrecy in peacetime demonstrates a profound misunderstanding of the role of a free press as opposed to that of a controlled press. The plea for secrecy could become a cloak for errors, misjudgments and other failings of government.[200]

Few would attribute these stirring words to Richard Nixon, who would later complain about being "kicked around" by the media[201] and while in office propose making the publication of information about military capability a criminal action.[202]

Where one stands clearly depends of where on sits. Presidents "have long memories of every real or imagined grievance [and] can reel off incident after incident of press errors and distortions and irresponsible reporting."[203]

President Trump's War with the Media

President Trump emerged from the 2016 campaign recognizing that he received more than his share of coverage, and that, although it was heavily negative, it allowed him to win. According to his own staff, Trump follows three basic rules, each of which affects how he deals with the media:

- When you're right, you fight.
- Controversy elevates the message.
- Never apologize.[204]

President Trump clearly operates by picking a fight rather than a flight (see Box 6.7). Part of his approach to countering what he sees as unfair coverage defense involves a "poor me" strategy. In a graduation ceremony at the Coast Guard Academy he stated:

> Look at the way I've been treated lately, especially by the media. . . . No politician in history—and I say this with great surety—has been treated worse or more unfairly. You can't let them get you down. You can't let the critics and the naysayers get in the way of your dreams.[205]

He also turns around criticism on the media. When he found himself dogged by assertions that the Russians had worked to undermine the campaign of Hillary Clinton he struck back. Even after numerous high-level campaign officials eventually admitted meetings with Russian representatives, he claimed they were legitimate or of little consequence. The incidents led to the appointment of a special counsel to determine whether any laws had been broken. Following the adage that the best defense is a good offense, Trump fired back with numerous tweets that investigating these events was "the single greatest witch hunt in American history" and that "with all of the illegal acts that took place in the Clinton administration there was never a special counsel."[206]

"By flouting fact-checkers and making journalists the enemy, [President Trump] is driving home the theme that his turbulent presidency is a struggle to the death with a despised Washington elite.[207] The repercussions of President Trump's condemnation of the media may well spill over to other parts of society. A number of political candidates have been charged with roughing up reporters. A spokesperson for press advocacy group Reporters Without Borders argued, "When you hear people at the highest levels insulting and targeting [journalists], it's not a surprise that other politicians turn these words toward violence. We've reached a new level in this game of war against the media."[208]

BOX 6.7
A Bitter Coffee Break

Little tells more about President Trump's dealing with the media than his battle with *Morning Joe's* Joe Scarborough and his cohost Mika Brzezinski. After giving Trump a great deal of positive attention during the campaign, the couple was invited to Donald Trump's luxurious golf club in Florida. When the two began voicing criticism of Trump after his election, President Trump turned on them calling their show "poorly rated" and characterizing its hosts as "low IQ," "crazy Mika," and "psycho Joe."[209] The initial foray was followed by another gross tweet about Brzezinski's alleged face lift.[210] The battle grew after Scarborough announced that Trump aides promised to kill a negative article about him and his cohost if they would back off their criticism and apologize to the president.[211] In an attempt to put the brouhaha into context, one observer pointed out that Harry Truman received a great deal of negative comments when he criticized the writer of a bad review about his daughter's piano concert. In rather unpresidential terms Truman threatened that the reviewer would need "a new nose and plenty of beefsteak" if they ever met.[212] Trump opponents pointed out that this was simply another case of Trump's low opinion of women. MSNBC tried to capture some of the high ground by saying, "It's a sad day for America when the president spends his time bullying, lying and spewing petty personal attacks instead of doing his job."[213] Many observers felt that the president's personal attacks demeaned the presidency, while his supporters argued "Look, the American people elected a fighter. . . . They knew what they were getting when they voted for Donald Trump."[214]

The Media Reacts

President Trump took out frustration the media to a new level by calling them "the enemy of the American People," "dishonest," and purveyors of "fake news."[215] Reporters countered his disparagements by saying that "words matter, and those kinds of attacks have to be taken seriously."[216] The reporters don't feel they are being thin-skinned whiners. Reporters feel that Trump is "doing real damage to the first Amendment."[217] The White House press corps feels the sting of Trump's perceived animosity. In a 2017 survey, 68% saw him as the most openly anti-press president in U.S. history.[218] The media can be rather sanctimonious at times, viewing any criticism of them as an attack on the First Amendment. While a free press depends on the guarantees of the free speech and free press clauses, it is not out of bounds to criticize the media when it makes mistakes.[219]

Journalists have not sat back and taken President Trump's criticism lightly, with one journalist arguing:

> "We are not the opposition party. . . . Nor is our place to sit down and the world pass by. . . . In our form of government an independent press gathers accurate information and provides it to the citizens. They can take that information, compare it to the Government version of events and then decides what to do about it.[220]

Framing the Trump approach as a "war on the media" reveals how far the presidential media relationship has been degraded.[221] Another journalist pointed out that Trump "dishonors the high office he hold [by] reportedly railing against cable news coverage that he finds insufficiently respectful."[222] Trump supporters would argue that it is the media doing the dishonoring.

With the arrival of the Trump administration and it limitation on press coverage, the *Washington Post* changed its masthead to read "Democracy dies in darkness." Some of the press criticism of President Trump has been brutal. Carl Bernstein, the journalist who helped uncover Watergate, charged that "Donald Trump is demonstrating an authoritarian attitude and inclination that shows no understanding of the role of a free press."[223]

While many of his base voters accept President Trump's claims, established conservative media are also critical. In an editorial commenting on President Trump's honesty with the press, the *Wall Street Journal* "compared the president to a drunk, clinging 'to an empty gin bottle' of fabrication." Trump fired back with his favorite epitaph, calling it "fake media."[224]

Critics of President Trump fear that his war against the media represents a deeper distrust that could threaten basic constitutional freedoms. Comments about putting journalists in jail sent shivers down the spines of these observers.[225]

Conclusion

Presidential efforts to use the media to communicate with the public are not always rewarded. At times the intended message of the White House press operation falls on deaf ears. What seems like an important announcement by the White House is met with a "ho hum," with reporters signaling their disinterest by failing to even take out their notebooks.[226] Lack of effort is likely to be punished with paucity of coverage. The White House public relations "machine" operates like most other individuals and groups desiring coverage, with the exception that coverage of the president is presumed and it is better to manage it rather than fully accept the media's agenda. The president has a vast array of techniques for spreading his message primarily through press conferences, speeches and town meetings. Presidents monitor and react to the coverage they receive, revealing the poisoned relationship between the contemporary media and the president.

Notes

1. Samuel Kernell, *Going Public: New Strategies of Presidential Leadership*, Washington, DC: Congressional Quarterly Press, 1997, p. 74.

2. Ibid.

3. Ibid.

4. Kernell, 1997, p. 75.

5. Ibid., p. 76.

6. Ibid., p. 77.

7. Ibid., p. 79.

8. Ibid.

9. Ibid.

10. Matthew Kerbel, Dom Bonafede, Martha Joynt Kumar and John L. Moore, "The President and the News Media," in Michael Nelson (ed.) *Guide to the Presidency*, Washington, DC: CQ Press, 2008, p. 973.

11. Kernell, 1997, pp. 83–84.

12. Ibid., p. 221.

13. Ibid., p. 974.

14. Kernell, 1997, pp. 85–86.

15. Quoted in Ibid, p. 85.

16. Ibid, p. 87.

17. Quoted in Worth Bingham and Ward. S. Just, "The President and the Press," *Reporter*, Vol. 26, April 9, 1961, pp. 116–117.

18. Jules Whitcover, "Salvaging the Presidential Press Conference," *Columbia Journalism Review*, Vol. 9, Fall, 1970, p. 33.

19. Paul Farhi, "Spicer and the Great Unknown," *Washington Post*, June 14, 2017p. C3.

20. Kerbel et al., p. 972.

21. Quoted in Ibid., p. 984.

22. Danagal Young, "Laughing, Learning or Enlightenment?: Viewing and Avoidance Motivations Behind the Daily Show and Colbert Report," *Journal of Broadcasting and Electronic Media*, Vol. 57, No. 2, 2013, p. 161.

23. Steven Clayman, Marc C. Elliot, John Heritage and Megan K. Becket, "A Watershed in White House Journalism: Explaining the Post-1968 Rise of Aggressive Presidential News," *Political Communications*, Vol. 27, 2010, p. 242.

24. Ibid., p. 230.

25. Bartholomew H. Sparrow, "Who Speaks for the People? The President, the Press, and Public Opinion in the United States," *Presidential Studies Quarterly*, Vol. 38, No. 4, 2008, p. 589.

26. www.youtube.com/watch?v=ZGBLAKq8xwc.

27. www.presidency.ucsb.edu/ws/?pid=4022.

28. Peter Baker, "'I'm Not Ranting and Raving,' Trump Rants in Wild Presser," *Toronto Star*, February 17, 2017, p. A1.

29. Steven Levingston, "The Communicators," *Washington Post Magazine*, May 21, 2017.

30. Michael Grynbaum, "Trump Calls Media the 'Enemy of the People,'" *New York Times*, February 18, 2017, p. A15.

31. Paul Farhi, "A Briefing Room Clash May Be Good TV, but Is It Good Journalism," *Washington Post*, August 4, 2017, p. C3.

32. Steven Levingston, "The Communicators," *Washington Post Magazine*, May 21, 2017, p. 32.

33. Quoted in Martha Joynt Kumar, *Managing the President's Message: The White House Communication Operation*, Baltimore, MD: Johns Hopkins University Press, 2007, p. 253.

34. Ibid.

35. Roderick Hart, *The Sound of Leadership*, Chicago, IL: University of Chicago Press, 1987, p. 147.

36. Kerbel et al., p. 973.

37. Ibid., p. 975.

38. Paul Farhi, "Trump's First News Conference since Election Blasts Usual Suspect," *Washington Post*, January 11, 2017.

39. Robert Pierpoint, *At the White House*, New York, NY: G.P. Putnam's Sons, 1981, pp. 155–156.

40. Kernell, 1997, p. 101.

41. Michael Baruch Grossman and Martha Joynt Kumar, *Portraying the President: The White House and the News Media*, Baltimore, MD: Johns Hopkins University Press, 1981, p. 304.

42. Matthew Eshbaugh-Soha, "Presidential Press Conferences over Time," *American Journal of Political Science*, Vol. 27, No. 2, 2003, p. 353.

43. Ibid., p. 349.

44. Clayman et al., p. 237.

45. www.realclearpolitics.com/articles/2015/08/29/obama_meets_the_press_—_on_his_terms_127907.html.

46. Paul Farhi, "President Trump and the Media from A to Z," *Washington Post*, July 21, 2017, p. C2.

47. Kumar, p. 270.

48. Kernell, 1997, p. 90; Jeff Smith, The *Presidents We Imagine: Two Centuries of White House Fictions on the Page, the Stage, Onscreen and Online*, Madison, WI: University of Wisconsin Press, 2009, p. 270.

49. Kernell, 1997, p. 91.

50. Ibid., p. 92.

51. See Bill O'Reilly and Martin Dugard, *Killing Reagan*, New York, NY: Henry Holt, 2015, p. 189.

52. Mark Knoller quoted in Kumar, p. 35.

53. Kumar, p. 12.

54. Hart, p. 127.

55. Francis X. Clines, 1997, "On Split-Screen Night, Clinton Gets Full Attention of Congress," *New York Times*, February 4; see also George Edwards III, *On Deaf Ears: The Limits of the Bully Pulpit*, New Haven, CT: Yale University Press, 2003, pp. 212–214.

56. Kurtz, pp. 121–122.

57. www.youtube.com/watch?v=Z9Pxf89rDXM.

58. www.washingtonpost.com/wp-dyn/content/article/2010/01/28/AR20100 12802893.html.

59. Stephen Farnsworth, *Spinner in Chief: How Presidents Sell Their Policies and Themselves*, Boulder, CO: Paradigm, 2009, p. 145.

60. David Paletz, *The Media in American Politics: Contents and Consequences*, New York, NY: Longman, 1998, p. 255.

61. Stephen Frantzich, *Honored Guests: Citizen Heroes and the State of the Union*, Lanham, MD: Rowman and Littlefield, 2011, p. 171.

62. George C. Edwards, III, *Governing By Campaigning: The Politics of the Bush Presidency*, New York, NY: Pearson/Longman, 2007, p. 86.

63. Matthew Eshbaugh-Soha, "The Politics of Presidential Speeches," *Congress and the Presidency*, Vol. 27, No. 1, 2010, p. 1.

64. Ibid., p. 3.
65. Kernell, 1997.
66. Farnsworth, p, 9.
67. Kerbel et al., p, 970.
68. Kernell, 1997, p. 115.
69. Farnsworth, p. 79.
70. John Wagner, Robert Cost, and Ashley Parker, "Trump May Retool His Staff," *Washington Post*, May 28, 2017, p. A6.
71. See www.presidency.ucsb.edu/satradio.php?year=2017 for transcripts.
72. Kernell, 1997, p. 107.
73. Ibid., p. 123.
74. Ibid., p. 121.
75. Andrew W. Barrett, "Press Coverage of Legislative Appeals by the President," *Political Research Quarterly*, Vol. 60, no. 4, 2007, p. 657.
76. Brendan Doherty, *The Rise of the President's Permanent Campaign*, Lawrence, KS: University of Kansas Press, 2012, pp. 89–90, 163.
77. Hart, p. 131.
78. Samuel Kernell, *Going Public*, Washington, DC: CQ Press, 2007, p. 223.
79. www.realclearpolitics.com/articles/2015/08/29/obama_meets_the_press_—_on_his_terms_127907.html.
80. www.cincinnati.com/story/news/politics/2017/07/26/trump-taking-victory-lap-ohio/511206001/ and www.npr.org/2017/04/29/526211042/trump-holds-rally-in-pennsylvania-as-journalists-gather-at-annual-d-c-dinner.
81. Matthew Eshbaugh-Soha and Jeffrey Peake, *Breaking Through the Noise: Presidential Leadership, Public Opinion and the News Media*, Stanford, CA: Stanford University Press, 2011, p. 159.
82. Quoted in Matthew Eshbaugh-Soha and Jeffrey S. Peake, "The Presidency and Local Media: Local Newspaper Coverage of George W. Bush," *Presidential Studies Quarterly*, Vol. 38, No. 4, 2008, pp. 611–612.
83. John Wagner and Ashley Parker, "As Going in D.C. Gets Tough, Trump Hits Road," *Washington Post*, June 21, 2017, p. A2.
84. Quoted in Eshbaugh-Soha and Peake, 2011, p. 161.
85. Andrew W. Barrett and Jeffrey S. Peake, "When the President Comes to Town," *American Politics Research*, Vol. 35, No. 1, 2007, p. 6.
86. Ibid., p. 14.
87. Doherty, pp. 92–93.
88. Eshbaugh-Soha and Peake, 2008, pp. 610–613; Barrett and Peake, p. 15; www.journalism.org/2016/07/07/the-modern-news-consumer; www.journalism.org/2017/05/10/democrats-republicans-now-split-on-support-for-watchdog-role.
89. Paul Farhi, "Ex-Trump Surrogate Now Boosts Him on TV," *Washington Post*, June 20, 2017, p. C1.
90. Ammon Cavari and Micah Ables, "Presidential Foreign Travel," paper presented at the 2016 Annual Meeting of the American Political Science Association in Philadelphia, PA., pp. 3–4.
91. Hart, p. 200.
92. Ibid., p. 209.
93. Ibid.
94. Ibid., p. 131.
95. Ibid., p. 132.
96. http://time.com/4675860/donald-trump-fake-news-attacks.
97. Hart, p. 144.
98. Ibid., p. 203.

99. Matthew A. Baum and Samuel Kernell, 1999, "Has Cable Ended the Golden Age of Presidential Television?" *American Political Science Review*, 93 [March], p. 107.

100. Eshbaugh-Soha and Peake, 2011, p. 83.

101. Jeffrey E. Cohen, *The Presidency in the Era of 24-Hour News*, Princeton, NJ: Princeton University Press, 2008, p. 21.

102. Baum and Kernell, p. 109.

103. Quoted in Kernell, 1997, p. 107.

104. Eshbaugh-Soha, "The Politics. . .," pp. 11–12.

105. Eshbaugh-Soha and Peake, 2011, p. 60.

106. Ibid. p. 81.

107. Eshbaugh-Soha and Peake, 2011, p. 108.

108. Ibid., p. 117.

109. Ibid., p. 126.

110. Barrett, p. 655.

111. Ibid., p. 656.

112. Ibid., pp. 662, 664.

113. Eshbaugh-Soha and Peake, 2011, p. 87.

114. Jim VandeHell and Peter Baker, "Bush Pledges Historic Effort to Help Gulf Coast Recovery," *Washington Post*, September 15, 2005, p. A1.

115. Joseph R. Hayden, *A Dubya in the Headlights*, Lanham, MD: Lexington Books, 2009, p. 185.

116. "Energy: Some Action at Last on MEOW," *Time Magazine*, May 1, 1978.

117. www.washingtonpost.com/news/the-fix/wp/2014/01/25/the-4th-best-state-of-the-union-address-axis-of-evil/?utm_term=.08b933d2f0ee.

118. www.washingtonpost.com/news/morning-mix/wp/2017/01/11/obamas-yes-we-can-thank-michelle-for-that/?utm_term=.f2c501d69535.

119. Kernell, 1997, p. 89.

120. Jenna Johnson and John Wagner, "Trump Decries Violence at Rally, but Makes No Mention of White Nationalists," *Washington Post*, April 13, 2017, p. A15.

121. www.washingtonpost.com/news/post-politics/wp/2017/08/14/trump-denounces-kkk-neo-nazis-as-justice-department-launches-civil-rights-probe-into-charlottesville-death/?utm_term=.3a0ac8c6be7a; www.washingtontimes.com/news/2017/aug/14/trump-denounces-white-nationalists-after-violence.

122. www.foxnews.com/politics/2017/08/15/trump-decries-alt-left-in-charlottesville-do-have-any-semblance-guilt.html.

123. http://us.mediatenor.com/en/library/newsletters/1105/trump-not-the-media-drives-negativity-on-his-performance-in-first-months.

124. www.washingtonpost.com/politics/trump-tweets-news-report-citing-anonymous-sources-on-n-korea-movements/2017/08/08/47a9b9c0-7c48-11e7-83c7-5bd5460f0d7e_story.html?utm_term=.90c245edf00e; http://thehill.com/homenews/media/345807-trump-takes-heat-for-fire-and-fury-remarks-on-north-korea.

125. www.washingtontimes.com/news/2017/aug/9/donald-trumps-fury-and-fire-sure-beats-barack-obam.

126. www.washingtontimes.com/news/2017/aug/11/donald-trump-military-locked-and-loaded-for-possib;
www.cnn.com/2017/08/11/politics/trump-locked-and-loaded/index.html.

127. Kernell, 1997, p. 89.

128. https://shorensteincenter.org/news-coverage-donald-trumps-first-100-days.

129. www.realclearpolitics.com/articles/2015/08/29/obama_meets_the_press_-_on_his_terms_127907.html.

130. www.realclearpolitics.com/articles/2015/08/29/obama_meets_the_press_-_on_his_terms_127907.html.

131. Kurtz, 1998, p. 74.

132. www.realclearpolitics.com/articles/2015/08/29/obama_meets_the_press_—_on_his_terms_127907.html.

133. Kumar, p. 78.

134. Ibid., p. 99.

135. www.realclearpolitics.com/articles/2015/08/29/obama_meets_the_press_—_on_his_terms_127907.html.

136. Newseum, "President and the Press" conference, Session 4, p. 6, available at www.newseum.org/2017/04/12/diverse-opinions-spark-conversation-at-the-president-and-the-press/

137. Ibid., Session 4, p. 14.

138. Ibid.

139. Margaret Sullivan, "A Media Game Plan out of the Autocrat's Book," *Washington Post*, March 6, 2017, p. C3.

140. Marlin Fitzwater, *Call the Briefing*, New York, NY: Times Books, 1995, p. 224.

141. Ibid., p. 222.

142. For an example, see http://abcnews.go.com/US/president-obama-urges-police-communities-town-hall-us/story?id=40584530.

143. Tom Rosenstiel, *The Beat Goes On: President Clinton's First Year with the Media*, New York, NY: The Twentieth Century Fund, 1994, p. 17.

144. Hayden, 2009, p. 210.

145. *Washington Post* editorial, "We've Got Some Questions for Mr. Trump," June 19, 2017, p. A20.

146. www.politico.com/magazine/story/2016/04/2016-white-house-press-corps-reporters-media-survey-poll-politics-213849.

147. Klaus Dodds and Philip Kirby, "It's Not a Laughing Matter: Critical Geopolitics, Humour and Unlaughter," *Geopolitics*, Vol. 18, No. 45, 2013, p. 46.

148. Dan Zak, "What's Eating Them?" *Washington Post*, May 1, 2017, p. C1.

149. http://thehill.com/blogs/pundits-blog/media/271900-seriously-the-gridiron-club-dinner-matters.

150. http://articles.chicagotribune.com/1985–04–08/news/8501200542_1_mx-missiles-foreign-aid-farmers.

151. http://newsok.com/article/1978674.

152. www.washingtonpost.com/news/arts-and-entertainment/wp/2016/04/27/the-single-best-joke-told-by-every-president-from-obama-to-washington/?utm_term=.25ee5b170ec5.

153. www.nytimes.com/1995/03/27/us/hillary-gump-a-hit-at-washington-s-gridiron-club-dinner.html.

154. www.theguardian.com/world/2004/mar/26/usa.iraq.

155. http://thehill.com/blogs/pundits-blog/media/271900-seriously-the-gridiron-club-dinner-matters.

156. www.npr.org/2017/03/05/518624553/trump-skips-gridiron-dinner-as-his-staffers-get-roasted.

157. Dodds and Kirby, p. 53.

158. Zak, p. C1.

159. Ibid.

160. http://thehill.com/blogs/pundits-blog/media/331554-media-bemoans-trump-but-didnt-mind-obamas-years-of-stomping-press.

161. www.usatoday.com/story/news/politics/onpolitics/2017/03/17/angela-merkel-donald-trump-handshake/99310398.

162. www.telegraph.co.uk/news/2017/05/11/white-house-misled-russian-photographer-oval-office-amid-security.

163. www.nytimes.com/2017/05/02/business/media/cnn-trump-ad-fake-news.html.

164. Kerbel et al., p. 949.

165. Tom Wicker, "Remembering the Johnson Treatment," *New York Times*, May 5, 2002.

166. www.theatlantic.com/politics/archive/2014/08/nixons-revenge-his-media-strategy-triumphs-40-years-after-resignation/375274.

167. Quoted in Kurtz, 1998, p. 77.

168. Media critic Howard Kurtz, quoted in Kerbel et al., p. 977.

169. Michael Sherer and Zeke J. Miller, "Trump After Hours," *Time*, May 22, 2017, p. 32.

170. Paul Farhi, "Spicer's Apology Tour, and Friends in High Places May Save His Job," *Washington Post*, April 13, 201, p. C1.

171. Kurtz, p. 149.

172. Kernell. 1997, p. 216.

173. Dick Morris, quoted in Rosenstiel, 1998, p. 25.

174. Quoted in Paltez, p. 254.

175. http://thehill.com/homenews/media/347757-hannity-trump-could-cure-cancer-and-the-media-still-wouldnt-like-him.

176. Quoted in www.washingtonpost.com/lifestyle/style/how-trump-attacks-the-media-and-why-that-distorts-reality/2016/07/24/32a456ea-5014–11e6-a7d8–13d06b37f256_story.html?utm_term=.3fb3429b2cbf.

177. Newseum, Session 4, p. 8.

178. Philip Rucker and Ashley Parker, "Trump's War on Media Lets Him Play the Victim," *Washington Post*, July 1, 2017, p. A1.

179. Steven Levingston, "The Communicators," *Washington Post Magazine*, May 21, 2017, pp. 32–33.

180. Jeffrey E. Cohen, "The Presidency and the Mass Media," in George C. Edwards and William G. Howell (eds.), *The Oxford Handbook of the American Presidency*, New York, NY: Oxford University Press, 2009, p. 262.

181. www.washingtonpost.com/lifestyle/style/how-trump-attacks-the-media-and-why-that-distorts-reality/2016/07/24/32a456ea-5014–11e6-a7d8–13d06b37f256_story.html?utm_term=.3fb3429b2cbf.

182. Kurtis Lee, "Presidents vs. the Press, Then and Now," *Los Angeles Times*, February 9, 2017, p A8.

183. www.theatlantic.com/politics/archive/2014/08/nixons-revenge-his-media-strategy-triumphs-40-years-after-resignation/375274.

184. www.nytimes.com/1992/10/28/us/the-1992-campaign-campaign-trail-bush-eases-hammering-of-the-press.html.

185. Quoted in https://shorensteincenter.org/news-coverage-donald-trumps-first-100-days.

186. Joseph R. Hayden, *A Dubya in the Headlights*, Lanham, MD: Lexington Books, 2009, p. 77.

187. www.usatoday.com/story/theoval/2013/10/13/obama-john-kennedy-theodore-sorensen/2975563.

188. http://thefederalist.com/2017/01/24/sorry-journalists-trump-isnt-first-president-threaten-press.

189. www.theatlantic.com/politics/archive/2014/08/nixons-revenge-his-media-strategy-triumphs-40-years-after-resignation/375274.

190. Ibid.

191. http://thehill.com/blogs/pundits-blog/media/331554-media-bemoans-trump-but-didnt-mind-obamas-years-of-stomping-press.

192. Ibid.

193. Ibid.

194. http://fortune.com/2016/03/29/obama-media/.

195. Farhi, "President Trump. . .," p. C1.

196. www.washingtonpost.com/business/economy/a-tv-company-warned-its-viewers-about-the-medias-fake-news-problem-now-its-about-to-take-over-some-of-the-nations-biggest-stations/2017/05/08/dcfc70f0–3416–11e7-b4ee-434b6d506b37_story.

html?utm_term=.8b58751781b5, Farhi, "Ex-Trump. . .," p. C1, and www.truth-out.org/buzzflash/commentary/media-consolidation-accelerates-with-pending-sinclair-acquistion-of-tribune-broadcasting-stations.

197. Lee, 2017, p. A8. See also www.presidency.ucsb.edu/ws/?pid=35717

198. www.forbes.com/sites/markjoyella/2017/02/27/george-w-bush-breaks-with-trump-says-media-indispensable-to-democracy/#573d8dec2e46.

199. Lee, 2017, p. A8.

200. Michael Baruch Grossman and Martha Joynt Kumar, *Portraying the President: The White House and the News Media*, Baltimore, MD: Johns Hopkins University Press, 1981, p. 303.

201. www.youtube.com/watch?v=lo9FlPeKKzA.

202. Ibid.

203. Grossman and Kumar, p. 309.

204. Sherer and Miller, p. 37.

205. Quoted in Jenna Johnson and David Nakamua, "Trump to Graduating Cadets, 'Things Are Not Always Fair,'" *Washington Post*, May 15, 2017, p. A14.

206. Eugene Robinson, "Can Trump Outlast Mueller?" *Washington Post*, May 19, 2017, p. A19.

207. Sam Frizell, Zeke Miller, Pratheek Rebala, and Chris Wilson, "Can Trump Handle the Truth," *Time Magazine* April 3, 2017, p. 37.

208. Quoted in Paul Farhi, "Reporters Say They Are Being Roughed Up. Observers Point to Trump," *Washington Post*, May 26, 2017, p. C1.

209. Jenna Johnson and Abby Phillip, "Trump's Insulting Tweets Criticized," *Washington Post*, June 30, 2017, p. A1.

210. www.washingtontimes.com/news/2017/jun/29/trump-slams-joe-scarborough-mika-brzezinkski-in-tw.

211. David Bauder, "MSNBC hosts fire back amid feud with Trump," *The Capitol*, July 1, 2017, p. A2.

212. Kerbel et. al, p. 972.

213. Paul Farhi, "President's Tweets Are the Latest Salvo in an Ugly War of Words," *Washington Post*, June 20, 2017, p. C2.

214. Johnson and Phillip, p. A12.

215. www.politico.com/magazine/story/2017/04/28/poll-trump-white-house-press-corps-journalists-215051.

216. Newseum, Session 4, p. 7.

217. Ibid.

218. Ibid.

219. Gary Abernathy, "The Media's Martyr Complex," *Washington Post*, July 14, 2017, p. A21.

220. Newseum, Session 7, pp. 5–6.

221. Catherine Rampell, "A War on Independent Voices," *Washington Post*, July 18, 2017, p. A17.

222. Eugene Robinson, "This Country Deserves Better than President Trump," *Washington Post*, July 18, 2017, p. A17.

223. Quoted in Michael M. Grynbaum, "Trump Calls Media the "Enemy of the American People,'" *New York Times*, February 18, 2017, p.!5.

224. http://nordic.businessinsider.com/was-trump-wiretapped-credibility-sean-spicer-wsj-editorial-2017–3.

225. http://thehill.com/homenews/news/333746-press-freedom-group-rips-trump-for-suggesting-comey-jail-reporters; www.nytimes.com/2017/05/17/business/media/trumps-urging-that-comey-jail-reporters-denounced-as-an-act-of-intimidation.html.

226. Scott Shane, "Former Press Secretary Dispels Many Illusions," *New York Times*, January 30, 2017.

CHAPTER 7

OLD BASICS, NEW TECHNOLOGIES

The White House operates like an advertising agency with only one product to sell: the president. In that endeavor the president and the White House staff use traditional public relations strategies and adopt new approaches as they come along. The media have the opportunity to amplify, interpret, or denigrate the president's preferred message.

Establishing the Mandate

Presidents prefer to enter the Oval Office as clear victors who deserve deference. One of the most critical judgment calls made by the media after an election is their definition of the winner's mandate. Newly elected presidents are compared with their predecessors in terms of electoral margin. The larger the margin, the more likely the president and his proposed programs will be seen as legitimate. The ability to lose the popular vote and win the presidency through the Electoral College adds another twist to the media's evaluation. Both George W. Bush and Donald Trump began with a shaky mandate, given their loss of the popular vote. Modern presidents have long spoken of their mandate as justifying policy initiatives (see Box 7.1). Recent presidents have included specific references to their mandate more often than their predecessors.[1] Incorporating comments about one's mandate tends to occur more often during periods of intense partisanship and when presidential popularity has declined.[2] The mandate narrative the White House hopes to implant is "I won this election by taking stands on issues, and now I want to attempt to accomplish them." Reminding reporters of the alleged mandate is a defensive strategy designed to blunt the effect of embarrassing questions during press conferences.[3]

Box 7.1
Mandate Speak

Jimmy Carter, Address to the Nation:

> [W]hen I was running for President, I made a number of commitments. I take them very seriously. I believe they were the reason I was elected. And I want you to know that I intend to carry them out.[4]

Ronald Reagan, first press conference:

> I ran on [the Republican] platform; the people voted for me on that platform. . . . I think it would be very cynical and callous of me to suggest that I'm going to turn away from it.[5]

George W. Bush, Republican National Committee Dinner:

> In 2004, we ran on large issues. . . . We discussed those ideas at every campaign stop, and the American people responded. And now it is our turn to respond and do what they expect.[6]

Barack Obama, press conference:

> I've got one mandate. I've got a mandate to help middle class families and families that are working hard to try to get into the middle class. . . . That's what the American people said.[7]

Donald Trump, Speech to Congress:

> But then the quiet voices became a loud chorus as thousands of citizens now spoke out together, from cities small and large, all across our country. Finally, the chorus became an earthquake, and the people turned out by the tens of millions, and they were all united by one very simple, but crucial demand: that America must put its own citizens first. Because only then can we truly make America great again. Above all else, we will keep our promises to the American people.[8]

The media do not always buy a president's mandate claim, pointing out that the public was ill-informed about the issues, the margin was too small to claim a mandate or that major gaffes led to the winner's opponent losing rather than winner of the election "winning."[9]

The Politics of Spin and Framing

Spinning and framing presidential news are closely related concepts focusing on how a story is presented. "Spin" is the more generalized attempt to turn presidential events and actions into a positive outcome. "Framing" refers to the use of particular terminology or comparisons that will help make the president's position the one preferred.

Spinning

Spin involves putting events and actions in the best possible light. Few would begrudge the president's spokesperson for doing this. President Trump's first press secretary, Sean Spicer, described his job as "amplifying" the successes of the White House.[10] In an attempt to garner the most positive media attention, presidents try to fail silently, "compromise quietly and claim victory boldly."[11] Failures are either ignored or labeled with terms such as a "moral victory." Partial victories are promoted by the White House by implying that "half a loaf is better than none" and that "we are taking steps in the right direction." When things go well, other political actors try to gain their own measure of credit, whether legitimate or not.

While Ralph Waldo Emerson argued that "A foolish consistency is the hobgoblin of little minds, adored by little statesmen and philosophers and divines," he had never had to survive in the political arena. The public and the media expect consistency among politicians, taking them to task for changing positions and explanations. Whether it was George H.W. Bush's shift on his "read my lips, no new taxes" pledge, Donald Trump's changing position on Russian involvement in the 2016 election, or Trump's changing rationale for the firing of FBI director James Comey, the shifts challenged their staffs and undermined their credibility. As one reporter noted, "You can only do so good a job if you are spinning on behalf of a president whose story changes minute to minute."[12]

Effective spinning often involves beating the media at its own game. We live in the age of sound bite journalism where short and quick summaries rule the day. We know empirically that presidential candidates are forced to communicate in an average of seven second clips.[13] Much of the time on television features reporters and anchors framing stories and giving context.[14] Not all of the impetus for sound bites comes from the decisions of journalists. Two can play the sound bite game. As Ari Fleischer put it,

> When I wanted to drive home a point, I tried to think up a one-or two-sentence statement, never longer than several seconds, and I would lean in, hold my right hand up for emphasis, and deliver my line . . . the pithy, short summary or explanation . . . would make it on the air."[15]

It is easy to become cynical about White House attempts to "sell" the president and his priorities. In the long run "it is hard to sell illusions. Good communications operations have to be grounded in solid policies and effective performance . . . if a policy or its implementers are weak or absent, it will be difficult to make it appear otherwise."[16]

Framing

Framing is a more specific form of spinning involving choosing words and concepts to explain actions in a particular way. Both the White House and the media attempt to frame situations. Words matter and their careful choice serves as a key strategy in framing an issue.

The White House Attempt to Frame

Words create labels, and eventually categories, into which we place actions for evaluation. Ronald Reagan was very careful to describe the Nicaraguan Contras as "freedom fighters" rather than "guerrillas" or "terrorists." When President George H.W. Bush was forced to reconsider his "Read my lips, no new taxes" pledge, he attempted to label the compromise with the Democratic Congress as "increased revenues," rather than "raised taxes."[17] Bill Clinton added new ambiguity to words when he made statements like "depending on what the meaning of the word 'is', is" when denying an improper relationship with intern Monica Lewinsky. He later claimed that "I did not have sexual relations with that woman." Later it became clear he had a very restrictive view of what sex included. When the George W. Bush administration first moved troops into Iraq they termed it "liberation," which implied helping the Iraqi people take control of their destiny. After a short period, they began to talk about "regime change," and later "occupation," each of which implied a more active role by the U.S. and less dependence of the Iraqi people.[18] After the 2017 bombing in Manchester, England, President Trump called the perpetrators "losers" rather than "terrorists."[19] President Trump also hesitated to put the label of "domestic terrorist" on the white supremacist driver who plowed into a crowd in Charlottesville, Virginia.[20] Rather than calling conversations among President Trump's staff "arguments" or "disagreements," they were characterized as "robust discussions."[21]

The White House leaves little to chance. Polling and focus groups are not so much used to establish policy positions as to decide the words to use in the message one wants to communicate.[22] In the battle over reform of social security, the George W. Bush White House was careful to avoid talking about "cuts" and rather focused on giving people "choice" and "control." They avoided the term "privatization" when it became clear that the polls showed the public saw such an approach as a cut in benefits.[23]

The Media as Framers

Although presidents have an agenda as to which stories they want covered and how they want themselves covered, "the media independently choose which issues to highlight and how to frame them for their viewers and readers. As a result, the media provide powerful competition for the president and his attempts to structure the choices before the public."[24]

The media try to frame presidents in simple yet dramatic terms. Ronald Reagan was seen as an amiable if not totally engaged and competent president, whose policy views varied significantly from those favored by the media. George H.W. Bush came across as somewhat detached from the real-world life of most Americans. Bill Clinton was viewed as "a slippery, dishonest, cash-obsessed and sex-crazed opportunist."[25] George W. Bush was portrayed as well-meaning but not too bright and easily misguided. President Obama got credit for his rhetorical skills but was seen as less effective in putting his ideas into practice. Donald Trump has had a hard time shaking his reality television star and manipulative business mogul image.

When it comes to policy battles, the media tends to play the role of the great scorekeepers, tallying up wins and losses by the various Washington players. President Trump's inability to legislatively revise and repeal Obamacare during his first six months in office was largely framed as a personal loss by an inexperienced president, an example of the separation of powers at work, and the result of hyper-partisanship. Alternatively, the emphasis of news stories could have been on the nature of the problem, the substance of the bill, the alternatives presented, or the strategies employed by the various players.

The media have been criticized for their emphasis on a framing approach in which presidential events and behaviors are discussed in isolation, leading the American public to miss "the larger causes of and interrelationships among incidents."[26] It is much easier for the media to focus on such episodic things as presidential policy announcements or bill signings than to look into the complexities of policy problems and their potential solutions.

Divining the Truth from the White House

"There is a fundamental difference between spin and deception."[27] Presidents and their spokespersons have the right to present their accomplishments in the most positive light, "but that doesn't give [them] the right to fabricate evidence, distort facts, or cover up exculpatory information."[28] The White House press office crosses the line when it starts "serving up outright falsehoods as facts, with a side of outrage at not being believed."[29] Revealing a realist perspective, former Nixon press secretary Ron Ziegler explained, "it's necessary to fudge sometimes. . . . You have to give political answers. You have to give non-answers. But I never walked out on that podium and lied."[30]

Most modern presidents have misled the American public to some degree, especially when it came to military operations. The Vietnam conflict was pursued with active deception. Body counts were regularly fudged and chances for victory enhanced. The pursuit of unproven weapons of mass destruction undergirded the George W. Bush initiatives in the Second Gulf War.

Despite criticism of the veracity of past presidents, the hue and cry over President Trump's alleged lack of commitment to the truth has been loud and pervasive. President Trump may well be a captive of his own past successes when it comes to telling the truth. As a businessman and deal maker, he espoused the use of "strategic falsehoods, or 'truthful hyperbole' as he preferred to call it."[31]

The media have not been shy about pointing out President Trump's apparent disregard for the truth, going so far as to create lists online of the major alleged misrepresentations. As the *New York Times* put it,

> There is simply no precedent of an American president to spend so much time telling untruths. Every president has shaded the truth or told occasional whoppers. No other president—of either party—has behaved as Trump is behaving. He is trying to create an atmosphere in which reality is irrelevant.[32]

Another set of observers at the Shorenstein Center at Harvard University reinforced this evaluation, saying, "Never in the nation's history has the country had a president with so little fidelity to the facts, so little appreciation for the dignity of the presidential office, and so little understanding of the underpinnings of democracy."[33] After carrying out an exclusive interview with President Trump for *Time Magazine*, the reporter concluded that "the more the conversation continued, the more the binary distinctions between truth and falsehood blurred, the telltale sign of a veteran misleader who knows enough to leave himself an escape route when he tosses a bomb."[34] In the words of former CBS evening news anchor Scott Pelly, "the quickest, most direct way to ruin a democracy is to poison the information. [Trump's] real troubles again today were not with the media, but with the facts."[35] President Trump and his staff assert that he is being held to a higher standard by a media that is biased against him.

The questioning of President Trump's veracity has not come from the media alone. In an uncharacteristic implied criticism of one of his successors, former president George W. Bush bemoaned the "conspiracy theories and outright fabrication" dominating the Trump era.[36]

Not all the blame for false and outrageous statements falls on President Trump. He realizes that the media eschew covering the "normal routine of reason and verification," and rather rush "to examine the President's sensational statements."[37] By playing into media proclivities, Trump sends a message to his core supporters, who believe him more than they believe the media. Trump's electoral coalition and his consistent supporters have little time for the media. "By flouting fact-checkers and making journalists the enemy, he is driving home the theme that his turbulent presidency is a struggle to the death with the despised Washington elite."[38] It seems that the more outrageous the avowal, the more coverage it receives. Television and print reporters virtually trip over each other in covering each new shocking declaration.

Fake News

Journalists have long made mistakes in reporting falsehoods. Rumors and misrepresentations of facts have long been a part of politics (see Box 7.2). As far back as the 1890s, the concept of "fake news" was discussed in the media.[39] Most often, these mistakes are unintentional and corrected as soon as possible. As the "first rough draft of history,"[40] journalists often lack the time to fully confirm all their assertions. Sources lie or tell only part of the story, while gullible or lazy reporters pass them on as facts. Politicians of all political stripes are not beyond stretching the truth for their own benefit, while the media may find it advantageous to make questionable judgments on what to report and how to report it. Fake news comes in a variety of formats:

- Satire: Making fun of political leaders through caricature or, parody of satire may be seen as unfair (see Chapter 8).

Box 7.2
Tale as Old as Time

Fake news is nothing new. Throughout the Revolution and into his presidency, George Washington was dogged by a packet of seven letters supposedly written by him and questioning his commitment to the Revolution, and his pining for reconciliation with Britain. The cleverly written letters in Washington's style were allegedly found in a trunk carried by one of Washington's slaves. Although these so-called "spurious letters" were fake, they were published by many newspapers. The letters bothered him so much that as president he submitted a statement into the public record disavowing the letters and had it sent to all the newspapers that had published the original missiles. Other falsehoods about Washington such his supposed cutting down of a cherry tree and admitting it to his father failed to receive President Washington's commitment to clearing the record.[41]

- Choice: All-news is a selection of reality. Some events are covered and others are lost to history. Choosing those events that make a president look bad may mark them in the president's eyes as "fake news" as opposed to the more "legitimate" positive events. Of course, just reporting the positive events would be just as fake. Journalists' norms and public interest tend to drive the news toward conflict, scandal, and personalities, assuring a nonrandom reporting of events.

- Intentional falsehoods: Intentionally passing on misinformation for partisan or financial benefit is the most egregious form of fake news, especially when the presentation purports to be legitimate. Assuming that "if it looks like news it must be true," might lead one astray. Fake news websites and other venues bolster the beliefs of supporters of a particular political position and/or raise advertising revenue for the originator.

President Trump labels all three categories as fake news, popularizing the idea of "fake news" as an intentional and consistent diet in the current media environment, rampantly affecting both the mainstream media and new entrants into the media mix.

In the strict sense, "fake news" involves transmitting false information under the guise of news with the intent to deceive. "In its purest form, fake news is completely made up, manipulated to resemble credible journalism and attract maximum attention and, with it, advertising revenue."[42]

President Trump subscribes to a much broader definition of fake news. If the story places him in a negative light, he seems to declare it by definition as fake. Early in his presidency when his approval fell below 40%, the president tweeted, "Any negative polls are fake news, just like CNN, ABC, NBC polls in the election. . ."[43] After an unflattering *New York Times* article suggesting that Trump avoids being fully briefed by his staff and spends much of his time watching cable news, the president tweeted, "I call my own shots based on an accumulation of data, and everyone knows it. Some FAKE NEWS media, in order to marginalize, lies."[44] President Trump has taken great pleasure in verified missteps by the media, implying that intentional falsehoods dominate (see Box 7.3). For President Trump, the idea of "fake news" seems to have taken over from charges of liberal bias for conservatives. It is a far more effective criticism and harder to prove than ideological bias. The fact that a number of journalists have been outed for plagiarism in recent years only serves to bolster the more general claim.[45]

Fake news may emerge in the legacy media or in newer social media platforms such as websites and blogs. The number and variety of fake news sources seem to clearly have increased in recent years. The cost of entry into the media world on platforms such as Twitter and Facebook is so low that those sources amenable to the distribution of fake news have little trouble getting their message out. Fake news is particularly sinister since it is often presented in a format that looks like real news and suggests the careful editorial screening we expect from valid news sources.

Box 7.3
Confronting the Fakers

CNN has been one of President Trump's key targets in the media, ferreting out some of his reporters and subjecting them to some of his fiercest criticism. The White House took considerable pleasure in the disclosure of a CNN misstep. After reporting that federal investigators were looking into White House advisor Anthony Scaramucci's ties to a Russian official, they were forced to retract the story based on an anonymous source since it "did not meet CNN's editorial standards.[46] Crowing about his victory over a nemesis, President Trump tweeted "Wow, CNN had to retract a big story of 'Russia' with 3 employees forced to resign. What about all the other phony stories they do? FAKE NEWS."[47]

Lacking editorial review and fact checkers, fake news on the new media spreads without the typical checks found in the legacy media. Fake news sites often fail to identify themselves as such and often adopt names that seem to imply legitimacy such as ABCnews.com.co or WashingtonPost.com.co. These and other sites spread biased for false interpretations of the news.

Social media is the "vector that carries fake news."[48] Fake news often enters the political dialogue through social media and later is picked up and spread by legacy media:

> The tectonic shifts of recent decades in the media ecosystem—most notably the rapid proliferation of online news and political outlets, and especially social media—raise concerns anew about the vulnerability of democratic societies to fake news and other forms of misinformation.[49]

Charges against the media in spreading fake news have tended to take hold, with the evaluation of something as "fake news" being to some degree affected by one's political views. Nearly 60% of the American public believes that traditional media outlets report fake news, with a large percentage of Republicans (79%) and Independents (66%) holding such beliefs. The criticism of websites for presenting fake news is even greater, with a large percentage of respondents believing that the transmission of fake news is intentional.[50] Despite public concern, almost a quarter of Americans (23%) admit to having shared a fake story, with 14% admitting they knew the story was fake before they shared it.[51] At the same time, the public tends to believe that fake news short changes their ability to acquire basic facts about politics and government. In a classic case of generalizations not applying to oneself, Americans tend to believe that they personally can detect fake news, but that is not the case for their friends and neighbors.[52]

The attack associating the media with fake news strikes at the heart of journalism. As one journalist put it, the central idea of journalism is that:

> facts are facts; that they are ascertainable through honest, open-minded and diligent reporting; that truth is attainable by laying fact upon fact, much like the construction of a cathedral; and that truth is not merely in the eye of the beholder.[53]

Presidents and New Media

Presidents are constrained and energized by each new wave of media technologies, with power and prestige going to those who effectively use them. William McKinley seized on national newspapers. Calvin Coolidge used the radio to speak "directly to more people than any other chief executive had addressed in a lifetime."[54] Franklin Roosevelt turned the radio into an effective political tool. John F. Kennedy first used television effectively.[55] Barack Obama turned to the Internet, seeing it as a way to engage and activate individuals to promote policy initiatives. Donald Trump became the first Twitter-centric president. While other presidents used new technologies as they became available, the volume and effectiveness are tied to their use by specific presidents (see Box 7.4).

Presidential adoption of new technology is often more symbolic than pragmatic. Utilization creates the image of the president being "with it" and are often more important than the communications advantages they provide. In discussing Bill Clinton's appearance on cable's MTV, media advisor Mandy Grunwald commented, "What the president said was less important than that he was there, that he was reaching out to these young people."[56] Much of the same could be said about presidents such as Barack Obama who was the first to effectively use Facebook and Twitter.

Technological innovation is far from costless. Technologies may not work in the way intended. A cleverly hijacked or hacked website can do more damage than good. Someone searching www.whitehouse.org rather than www.whitehouse.gov will come upon a site parodying the president. Presidents need the cooperation of other Washington players. Any innovation runs the potential risk of violating established expectation and triggering hostile reactions from other political elites in Washington.[57] Numerous Republican leaders bemoaned President's Trump's extensive use of Twitter to communicate with the media and the public. Senate Majority Leader Mitch McConnell (R-KY) commented, "I've not been a fan of the tweets and the extracurricular comments. I said last week we could do with a little less drama."[58] Others pointed out that President Trump's "twitter-shaming" and "twitter-blaming" tweets were unpresidential and demeaned the office of the presidency.[59] From a pragmatic perspective, President Trump's tweets and the

Box 7.4
Technology and the White House

Presidents have long seen technology as a way of expanding their power and influence by adapting relatively new technologies for political purposes. While seldom among the earliest adopters of technology, the White House has generally been more forward-looking than the other branches of government. Recognizing that information is a power resource, presidents have turned to new technology for both expanding their incoming information resources and improving their ability to communicate with the public more effectively.

Some Technology Milestones[60]

1866: Andrew Johnson installs the White House's first telegraph.

1879: Rutherford B. Hayes installs the first telephone in the White House.

1897: William McKinley becomes the first president to be filmed.

1924: Calvin Coolidge makes the first national presidential radio speech.

1933: Franklin Roosevelt inaugurates his regular "fireside chats" on the radio.

1939: Franklin Roosevelt makes the first presidential television appearance at the New York World's Fair.

1945: Harry Truman allows audio recording of press conferences for later radio broadcast.

1953: Dwight Eisenhower allows filmed recording of press conferences for later television broadcast.

1958: NBC television first broadcasts Dwight Eisenhower in color.

1960: Richard Nixon and John Kennedy participate in the first televised presidential campaign debates (black and white).

1961: John Kennedy initiates live televised news conferences.

1965: Lyndon Johnson installs three television sets in the Oval Office to monitor the three networks.

1977: Jimmy Carter attempts to recreate Roosevelt's fireside chats on television.

1977: Jimmy Carter attends a televised town hall meeting.

1981: Ronald Reagan returns to using radio as a major method of communicating with the public by giving weekly radio addresses.

1981: White House email system installed.

1983: Ronald Reagan makes a call to a C-SPAN call-in program.

1991: George H.W. Bush becomes the first president with a computer terminal in his office but shows little sign of using it.

1993: Bill Clinton publishes his email address, and White House documents are made available on the Internet through a gopher server.

1993: Bill Clinton begins the use of video press conferences.

1994: The Clinton White House establishes a home page on the Web, allowing the transmission of text, sound, pictures, and video.

2005: The George W. Bush White House creates its first Facebook page.

2006: George W. Bush begins the distribution of prepackaged video press releases.

2008: Barack Obama gives up his Blackberry smartphone for fear of national security leaks.

2008: Barack Obama becomes the first president to use Twitter.

2009: Barack Obama holds the first live televised town hall meeting.

2010: Barack Obama becomes the first president to take questions at a town hall meeting via Skype.

2012: Barack Obama answers questions on the social news site Reddit.

2017: Donald Trump expands the personal use of Twitter by a president.

2017: The Trump press office allows remote questioning via Skype during press conferences.

Accessing the Electronic Presidency

Email address: President@Whitehouse.gov.

Web: www.whitehouse.gov.

Twitter: @Whitehouse or @realdonaldtrump.

Contacting the White House: www.whitehouse.gov/contact.

media reaction are seen by some as diminishing the president's focus and distracting all the players from key issues.[61]

New technology allows the discovery and retrieval of contemporary presidential behavior throughout their entire political careers. Reporters were once limited to their memories or hard to use newspaper "morgues" to search for previous comments and policy positions of presidents. Today searching for inconsistencies in a president's statements begins with a LexisNexis search of printed materials, going to archives of websites and tweets, or taking a foray into the world of YouTube (see Box 7.5). It is much harder for a president to say "I never said that," since the quote can be shown to a public that rightfully believes "seeing is believing."

Even the more basic technological applications such as taped conversations, computer memory, and open mikes have tripped up presidents (see Box 7.6). All types of presidential activity are scoured for meaning and missteps.

Despite some hesitation, the White House press operation has had to change with the times in order to remain relevant and satisfy the demands of the media.

BOX 7.5
Tracking the Presidents Online

New technology challenges the definition of a "public record." Increasingly, electronic archives of presidential sites have become available.

Archived websites for recent presidents can be found at www.archives.gov/presidential-libraries/archived-websites.

President Obama's tweets can be found at https://twitter.com/potus44?lang=en.

President Trump's tweets appear at www.trumptwitterarchive.com.

BOX 7.6
New Technology and the Undoing of White House Information Control

New technology is sometimes responsible for a loss of White House control over information, as the following incidents demonstrate.

The Taped Record

Richard Nixon installed a tape-recording system in the Oval Office to capture his presidency for history. When a staff member let it slip to the congressional committee staff investigating the Watergate break-in that tapes of White House meetings existed, the revelation unleashed demands for access. After an appeal to the Supreme Court, the tapes (minus a crucial eighteen-minute section "mistakenly" erased) were the basis for numerous media stories and some of the impeachment charges brought by the House of Representatives. Without such taped evidence, Richard Nixon probably would not have had to resign the presidency.

The Computer's Memory

By the 1980s, paper shredders were customary equipment in many government offices. After an internal investigation had begun into possible illegal activities associated with aiding the Nicaraguan Contras and exchanging arms for hostages, Lieutenant Colonel Oliver North spent many hours in his National Security Council office in the White House shredding sensitive papers that could have linked him and other White House staff to the Iran-Contra affair. The independent White House investigation team (the Tower Commission) thought that it had reached a dead end until someone discovered that North's computerized word processing system had backup file copies for many of the shredded documents. "Computers have an unnerving habit of remembering what you wrote even after you tell them to forget it."[62] The supposedly deleted but simultaneously backed-up records were used by the Tower Commission, Congress, and the courts to assign much of the guilt.[63]

The Open Mikes

We have come to expect presidents to be seasoned performers in public. Public events are carefully scripted and presented to create the most positive image. Yet, some of the same technologies that allow presidents to expand their public relations reach can also be their undoing. While testing his mike for a radio broadcast, Ronald Reagan joked, "My fellow Americans, I'm pleased to tell you today that I've signed legislation that will outlaw Russia forever. We begin bombing in five minutes." The public furor over joking about nuclear war resulted in a negative image of Reagan both in the United States and among foreign leaders.[64]

George H.W. Bush also was tripped up by an open mike. For a number of months, he used the new teleconferencing facility in the White House to hold press conferences with specialized audiences. The image of a freewheeling question-and-answer period implied presidential competence and openness. That the sessions involved planted questions and scripted answers came to light when Bush complained into an open mike after a session, "We lost everything! . . . We've got to get this sorted out." Through the mike, an aide was also heard to say, "They flip-flopped the questions."[65] From that point on, some of the positive impact of these events was diminished.

George W. Bush seemingly failed to learn from his father about open mikes. During the campaign, he made a snide and crude side comment about a top *New York Times* reporter that was picked up by the C-SPAN microphones and became a lead story the next day.[66]

On what should have been a day of celebration and universally good press coverage after the passage of President Obama's health care plan, the stories out of the press conference broadly covered Vice President Biden's whispering into the president's ear that this was a "big f> deal."[67]

One of President Trump's most commented-on tweets, delivered only about four months into his presidency, read, "Despite the constant negative press covfefe." The 12:06 a.m. missive sent journalists to their dictionaries to find the nonexistent word, "covfefe." The incomplete thought without context was probably a typo for which the president meant "coverage." The fact that it stayed up until 5:50 a.m. led to the conclusion that President Trump really did his own tweeting without the filter of staff to check facts, grammar, and language. In the meantime time the tweet broke records for retweets and likes. Nonplussed by the word going viral, President Trump countered with a 6 a.m. tweet saying, "Who can figure out the true meaning of 'covfefe'???" leading to no clarification of the initial tweet. While one might simply rack up the experiences as an example of human error, it runs counter to the normal impression of presidents with complete control over well-crafted messages.[68]

Press releases, once handed out to the media in hard copy, now are distributed electronically, speeding up the process. With the arrival of email and the Internet there is considerable pressure on the White House to provide both "heads up" information and immediate responses. White Houses have responded by creating rapid response teams to provide the president's perspective before the story becomes accepted as conventional wisdom.[69] Neither the White House nor the media are bound by the traditional news cycles of daily newspapers or network news. Prior to the emergence of instant access sites such as YouTube, Twitter, Facebook, and news alerts, the news cycle no longer takes hours or even days to develop. As online stories are shared and moved up on the search rankings, the mainstream media and politicians themselves have little choice but to respond, giving the information wheel another spin. Presidential actions and statements can go "viral" in a matter of minutes, limiting the ability of the White House to control the content and timing of messages. Content is created and distributed constantly electronically.

The White House is not passive about accepting what they see as errors on the part of the media. They counteract incorrect stories with electronic "Setting the Record Straight," or "Myth/Fact" messages.[70] The goal is twofold: The correction may appear in subsequent stories sent out in frequent blogs, and the very fact that reporters are being watched both by the White House and fellow journalists puts reporters on guard encouraging them to check their stories carefully. It is not only fear of looking bad to the White House but the fear of public embarrassment that tempers journalists. They realize that their colleagues are quick to jump on their mistakes. When Dan Rather and CBS broadcast a poorly fact-checked story questioning George W. Bush's National Guard service, the other networks gleefully piled on condemnation of CBS.

The content of presidential news stories, whether truthful of not, mean little if they fail to reach the public. New media technologies have arisen that change the nature of news dissemination.

Purported Advantages and Disadvantages of New Media for the Public

Through the various waves of technological change, some observers have pinned their hopes on new technologies as saviors of democratic citizenry well informed about presidential motives and actions. Radio, then television and the Internet were seen as tools for making enlightened citizenship easier to accomplish. Promoters of more direct democracy laid out an optimistic future where citizens could use the Internet to make policy demands on government and react to government decisions, bypassing the intermediate role of the legacy media in gathering and disseminating necessary information. It is argued that social media systems also expand the ability of messages to reach the less partisan and less ideological members of society who are more susceptible to persuasion. Delivery of presidential messages to these less politically motivated citizens was much more difficult in the past.

The speed and accessibility of new information sources promise some tantalizing opportunities for a better-informed and more engaged public, but promise does not necessarily mean performance. The use of social media to communicate directly with the public and effectively receive their input assumes wisdom on the part of the participating populace, responsiveness on the part of government officials, and the ability to create compromises not reachable by traditional means. These conditions may be hard, or impossible, to achieve.[71]

Other analysts have not seen new technology as a positive "game changer."[72] They see the new technologies as luring citizens away from concern with political news and carrying with them new challenges for informing the public.[73] Even if the public is informed and activated by social media, the fact that the use of applications such as Facebook and Twitter is skewed toward younger and more affluent segments of the population means that the social media "choir" sings with a clear bias.[74]

In the process of "informing" the public, "[s]ocial media systems provide a fertile ground for the spread of misinformation . . . [they] provide a megaphone for anyone who can attract followers."[75] Publication on the Internet potentially lacks the screening by editors. The expectation of immediacy in information provision leads to a race to get the information out first, with cross-checking for accuracy taking a back seat. The referee role of the media in sorting out the integrity of information is undermined when the referee is subject to constant challenges.[76]

Social media also tends to create "echo chambers" in which like-minded people feel comfort in sharing misinformation that does not challenge their predispositions. There is considerable evidence that humans are biased information seekers and "asymmetric updaters"[77] about political issues. They look for affirmation of existing biases rather than challenges to their assumptions.

Purported Advantages and Disadvantages of Social Media for the President

From the president's perspective, social media gives him a tool for spreading his message out more directly without the "interference" of the legacy media. (See Photo 7.1) Social media largely did not come to the scene until the Obama administration. President Obama creatively used social media during the 2008 campaign and brought with him into the White House a mindset supporting its effectiveness. While both former presidents Bill Clinton and George W. Bush engaged in online chats on the Internet, President Obama "was the first to communicate in a live video format, streamed directly from the White House website." The event not only reached the public directly, but also received broader legacy media attention.[78] Such open forums telegraph the message that the president had a "popular touch, command of the facts, and ability to connect with audiences."[79] The Obama White House recognized the danger of embarrassing questions from ordinary citizens, so retained the right to select questions to be answered.[80]

President Obama and his communications team saw the Internet as a giant "megaphone" that would make it possible "to reach . . . a larger audience of people who wouldn't normally pay attention to policy."[81] Obama attempted to change the Internet from a depository of documents and visual images "to an interactive engine that reaches more Americans in more intimate and meaningful

Photo 7.1 President Trump Circumvents the Media

Source: Tribune Media Services/Dana Summers

ways."[82] The Obama website included the ability to search for policy proposals and direct access to YouTube videos in which the president could speak directly to the public without having to go through the filter of the media. Early on, he even talked about broadcasting portions of cabinet meetings.[83] The Obama administration promised to change the Internet from a unidirectional "broadcast" mode emanating from the White House to an interactive approach where they could "make sure that every American voice is heard [and that] the American people [have] a seat at the table, and that we receive the benefit of their feedback."[84] Their use of the Internet would break from the model of "seeing individuals as possible receptacles to be dragged out of their slumber by barrages of requests. Instead, it embraced the web's capacity for building social networks to create a web of communication and engagement."[85] Despite the attractive-sounding goal, the ultimate objective was to improve the public's image of the president and strengthen his political position. By informing and engaging citizens, it was hoped that these involved citizens would put pressure on members of Congress to follow the president's direction. One Democratic strategist saw "millions of Americans ... pounding on them, e-mailing and knocking on district office doors,"[86] promoting the president's message. As the administration progressed, reliance on social media declined, using it much less to actually govern.

Also influenced by his success with social media on the campaign trail, President Trump continued to remain extremely active on social media (particularly Twitter). He regularly used tweets "to marshal a community of support for his policies once in office," as a prime factor in governing[87] (see later discussion). While much of the discussion about the impact of social media emphasizes the impact on the public, social media can also affect elites. After the 2016 election, Donald Trump received hundreds of tweets (mostly from robots) asserting that millions of illegal aliens voted in the election, leading to his loss of the popular vote.[88] This "information" emboldened him to broadly publicize the claim and create a presidential commission on voter suppression and fraud.[89] In general, though, the Trump White House continued the pattern of using social media more as a broadcast tool than an interactive platform.

The availability of social media is a double-edged sword. What is good for the president may also be good for his opponents. Competing websites and messages may well undermine the carefully controlled message the White House is hoping to deliver.[90] Stories reported by independent Internet-based investigators not only have the potential for direct delivery to the public but also virtually demand eventual coverage and circulation by the legacy media. Examples abound. "The dynamics behind the eruption of the Monica Lewinsky scandal represented an important turning point in the White House's ability to manage the press, and in its informational relationship with the American People."[91] Key aspects of President Clinton's sex scandal were broken first on the Internet. The White House effectively fought "fire with fire," using digital media to defend the president.[92] The key conclusion is that presidents cannot ignore these alternative news flows.

Specific new social media technologies carry their own strengths and protocols. The White House has attempted to adapt them to its own benefit.

The White House on the Web

The White House website serves as one potential place where a president and his staff could communicate with the public directly without having to worry about the selectivity of the media. They also do not have to worry about representation in short, edited news bites. Different presidents used the website in different ways, especially when it came to interactivity. Presidential websites have largely been used as broadcast media in which the president and his staff can control the content. Whitehouse.gov has adapted to new technological capabilities by allowing faster downloads and adding audio, pictures, and video. No matter the format, the White House website is more a series of press releases than a decision-enhancing tool. Over time, the White House website has focused more on the incumbent president and his accomplishments, as opposed to a general guide to the White House and its operations.[93]

President Clinton's website provided a large amount of information but lacked interactive capabilities. President George W. Bush's site included no vehicle for expressing policy interests but did have a section where members of the public could ask questions and have the answers distributed publicly.[94] The administration officials did:

> appear on the Web site from time to time to participate in "conversations" with the viewers, the questions are all deliberately selected to maximize the administration's ability to promote his policies. Old strategies of White House media management, in other words, [were] applied to new technologies.[95]

President Obama created a "We the People" petition section, where individuals could create or respond to petitions on public policy alternatives. Hundreds of thousands of people often responded to such petitions.[96] President Trump continued the "We the People" petition initiative.[97] In the detailed description of the issue involved in the petition, the administration has the ability to insert its own arguments. While the petition vehicle exists, there is no guarantee that it will affect a president's policy. Interactivity may well be a mixed blessing. Inviting input from the public "may generate unrealistic or unattainable expectations."[98] A president would be wise not to ask for advice from the public unless he is willing to listen to it.

The Web also became important to President Obama in his attempt to target messages to particular online audiences. When he wanted to talk about housing, he granted interviews to Zillow, or he chose WebMD for health care news.[99]

The official whitehouse.gov website designation belongs to the current occupant of 1600 Pennsylvania Avenue. Archived versions of previous presidents' websites are available[100] (see Box 7.5).

The President in 280 Characters

The arrival of Twitter during President Obama's administration offered presidents a new tool for using its 280 characters to present succinct and relatively simplistic messages. As the first president to use Twitter (then limited to 140 characters), President Obama's tweets were rare and carefully crafted, obviously having gone through a serious vetting process by his staff for format and content. President Trump's tweets, on the other hand, have an "off the top of the head" character.

The Tweeter in Chief

Donald Trump's affection for Twitter usage as president stems from his effective usage during the 2016 campaign to bypass the legacy media. Active tweeting has been likened to having "a president with his own printing press."[101] His unbridled tweets showed him to be a man of firm commitments willing to make strong assertions. Trump concluded "maybe I wouldn't be here if it was not for Twitter . . . I have my own form of media."[102] Trump was not the first president to see a new technology and use its advantages. John Kennedy turned to television. Both "mastered the megaphones of their eras, allowing them often to bypass the traditional media and speak directly to the electorate."[103] Few expected that Twitter would become the mainstay of Donald Trump's media strategy once in office. During the campaign he even asserted, "Don't worry. I'll give it up after I'm president. We won't tweet anymore. . . . Not presidential."[104] He obviously changed his mind, with his constant barrage of tweets on a wide variety of subjects.

Trump as a Tweeter

President Trump operates with two Twitter accounts. The @POTUS45 came with the office and is used primarily with official pronouncements and retweets from @realDonaldTrump. The latter account best represents the president's thinking.

President Trump has not been parsimonious with his tweets, sending out messages an average of eleven times a day during his first six months in office.[105] With over 45 million direct followers at the six-month point, he ranked twenty-first in the world in popularity.[106] While the presidency is a 24/7 job, we expect most of the work to be done during working hours. With the time stamp on tweets, we can now monitor what the president is thinking and when he is thinking it. More than half of President Trump's tweets originate outside of normal business hours.[107] President Trump is apparently an early riser, sending out tweets before most Americans are awake. Many of his tweets react to stories on the morning news programs. When it comes to tweets, Trump micromanages, writing most of them himself and badgering his staff, wanting to know "Did you get that stuff out?"[108]

It is not only the volume of Presidents Trump's tweets that bear attention. The content of his tweets "represent Trump at his most authentic and defiant, lashing out when he feels he is under attack, and [appear] to reflect a belief that only he, and not his staff, is qualified to speak in his own defense."[109] Unlike other politicians, his messages have not been tried out on focus groups and reviewed by many levels of the communications staff. The fact that President Trump has had to delete a number of his tweets because of spelling or grammatical errors seems to prove that the "Twitter feed really is a raw insight into his thought process without much input from aides."[110] Even supporters like former House Speaker Newt Gingrich bemoan the fact that "The president of the United States can't randomly tweet without having somebody check it out."[111] The media and other political observers hang on every word of a president, expecting careful parsing to reveal true goals and strategies. When those words are emotionally charged, conflicting, or confusing, they begin a firestorm of interpretation.

Punctuation marks mean something and President Trump is especially fond of emphasizing his tweets with exclamation points. Whereas only 22% of President Obama's tweets contained an exclamation point, 59% of President Trump's tweets used them for emphasis. Trump went a step further, using multiple exclamation points in about 10% of his tweets.[112] Among the characteristics of President Trump's tweets is the use of all capital letters to emphasize certain words in the text. Far removed from FDR's conversational "fireside chats," Trump's tweets tend to be "flamethrower bursts,"[113] capable of causing the media and the public to stand up and listen. To his supporters, he "tells is like it is," while his opponents view them as irresponsible.

In Defense of Presidential Tweeting

Both President Trump and his staff staunchly defend his activity on Twitter. As a benefit to the political process, White House counselor Kellyanne Conway sees his tweets as a "democratization of information" in which "everybody sees it at the same time."[114] From a more strategic perspective, former White House strategist Steve Bannon argues, "I think what [President Trump] does on Twitter is extraordinary. He disintermediates the media. He goes above their head and talks directly to the American people."[115] Former press secretary Sean Spicer sees Twitter as a way President Trump has "this direct line to the American people where he can communicate accomplishments, thoughts, and push back false narratives and false stories that frustrate people who want to control that narrative."[116] The bottom line from the White House is that President Trump sees social media tools such as Twitter useful for his purposes. To those critics of his Twitter use, President Trump flatly asserts, "it's my voice. They want to take away my voice. They're not going to take away my social media."[117]

The Dangers of Tweeting

As a communications platform, Twitter has a number of downsides. First of all, the 280-character limit makes presenting a cogent case for anything very difficult. It is best a blasting out assertions and catch-words, with little rational or justification.

Second, unless tweets are carefully vetted, spelling errors, gibberish, and unintended policy positions may be broadcast. President Trump controls his own tweeting activity, much to the consternation of some of his supporters. A partial early-morning tweet from President Trump stated "Despite the constant negative press confefe." While the president might have started typing "coverage," the made-up word led to concern about how seriously his tweets should be taken. Since Trump's tweets often include misstatements and grammatical and spelling errors, they have the potential for giving his opposition (and the media) fodder for negative reaction and may well undermine his veracity.[118] When one of his tweets misspelled "counsel" as "councel," it became the focus of many media stories, overshadowing the intended content of the tweet.[119]

Third, tweeting could have another downside; individuals targeted in a president's tweets can react using the same platform, giving them a vehicle for their protest. President Trump's Twitter battle with Senator Bob Corker (R-TN) dominated the media for weeks, with increasingly bitter and personal charges and countercharges.[120]

Fourth, presidents are the primary spokespersons for U.S. foreign policy. Diplomacy involves carefully constructed positions designed to protect American interests and keep bargaining options open. As one former CIA analyst argued, President Trump's tweets "are a gold mine for foreign spies."[121] The president's "unfiltered thoughts are available night and day . . . without much obvious mediation by diplomats, strategists or handlers."[122] At times, his tweets have been at odds with policy statements by other members of his administration in the State or Defense Departments. To add confusion, the White House has declared President Trump's tweets as "official statements."[123]

Finally, while brash tweets are titillating to the media and draw their attention, they add some confusion as to where even the president stands on issues. Unlike press conferences, the media cannot get clarification of the president's thinking through a tweet.[124] Also, reporters could once count on the printed and electronic *Daily Compilation of Presidential Documents* for all official White House statements. It includes press releases, speeches, toasts to foreign leaders, informal remarks to reporters, and much more.[125] With the arrival of Donald Trump as tweeter in chief, it is now necessary to explore a parallel universe of presidential communications.[126]

The Impact of Tweets

While the direct impact of tweets is hard to measure, the indirect impact on the mainstream media may well be more important. As former White House press secretary Sean Spicer sees it,

> When he tweets . . . it gets picked up by everybody, it gets read live on the news, you guys will cover it in the paper. . . . We put out a press release and it gets covered much less than when he send out a single tweet.[127]

Presidential tweets are like rocks thrown in a pool, with the reaction culminating in ripples of media attention. "Once the president tweets it, it's undeniably news, picked up everywhere and re-amplified—especially by right wing sites."[128] As one journalist put it, President Trump has the "ability to act as America's national news assignment editor from his bathrobe."[129] "Starting each morning with a tweetstorm [President Trump] often upends the news cycle."[130] Research has shown the effectiveness of tweets in generating news stories in the legacy media. When traditional coverage is low, presidents may well be encouraged to unleash at a series of tweets designed to recover the initiative.[131]

Most of President Trump's tweets are immediate reactions to recent events in which he challenges others or attempts to counter the conventional story line of the media. When stories appeared that Trump failed to receive the popularity honeymoon of his predecessors, Trump simply tweeted that the figures were fake.[132] Television news gravitated particularly to questionable tweets, quoting them more than twice as often as other tweets.[133]

President Trump's constant tweeting is almost too good to be true for journalists faced with finding and disseminating stories on a 24/7 basis. Increasingly White House correspondents face deadlines from their editors to file timely online stories. The tone and content of President Trump's tweets make good fodder for breaking news.[134]

How Others See Tweets

Despite his commitment to Twitter, the public reaction to President Trump's tweeting tends to be negative, with a significant partisan bias. Whereas only about one-quarter of voters evaluate his tweets as "effective and informative," that evaluation is voiced by 54% of Republicans but only 6% of Democrats.[135] The majority of voters feel that President Trump should stop tweeting.[136] Concern with presidential tweeting focuses on national security. Half of the American public feels that President Trump's tweets hurt national security, while only 13% feel it helps. An even greater percentage (57%) believes it hurts the presidency rather than helping it (20%).[137]

President Trump's tweets often catch even his supporters off guard while giving ammunition to those who oppose him. The tweets lead to a classic "flee or glee"[138] response, with Republicans demurring from answering reporters' questions about specific tweets and Democrats seeking members of the press to make damaging comments. After a set of tweet blasts about Donald Trump Jr.'s contacts with Russia, "Republican senators race-walked with haunted eyes while Democrats struggled to keep the pie-eating grins off their faces."[139] Numerous members of Congress, especially among the Republicans, have expressed consternation with President Trump's tweeting, pointing out how it makes their jobs more difficult.[140]

Conclusion

The White House uses the traditional public relations strategies of mandate-claiming, spinning, and framing in an attempt to control the message transmitted by the media to the public. The media counter with their own attempts at framing. Concern has arisen over the purported rise of "fake news" and the lack of veracity of political leaders. New technologies such as websites and Twitter accounts provide presidents with new ways to reach the public more directly. Each technology carries with it both advantages and disadvantages. While the very use of a technology identifies a president as "with it," effective utilization is more difficult.

Notes

1. Julia R. Azari, *Delivering the People's Message: The Changing Politics of the Presidential Mandate*, Ithaca, NY: Cornell University Press, 2014, pp. 35, 166.

2. Ibid., pp. 166, 177.

3. Ibid., p. 33.

4. Quoted in Ibid., p. 129.

5. Ibid., pp. 143–144.

6. Ibid., p. 150.

7. Ibid., p. 174.

8. www.whitehouse.gov/the-press-office/2017/02/28/remarks-president-trump-joint-address-congress.

9. Ibid., pp. 141, 149, 155.

10. www.cnn.com/2017/04/11/politics/sean-spicer-hitler-assad-gas-chemical-weapons/index.html.

11. George C. Edwards, III, *Governing By Campaigning: The Politics of the Bush Presidency*, New York, NY: Pearson/Longman, 2007, p. 39.

12. Quoted in Paul Farhi, "A Deputy Press Secretary's Baptism by Firing," *Washington Post*, May 12, 2017, p. C1.

13. Matthew A. Baum and Samuel Kernell, "Has Cable Ended the Golden Age of Presidential Television?" *American Political Science Review*, 93, 1999 (March), p. 99.

14. Ibid.

15. Ari Fleischer, *Taking Heat: The President, The Press, and My Years in the White House*, New York, NY: HarperCollins, 2005, pp. 45–46.

16. Martha Joynt Kumar, *Managing the President's Message: The White House Communication Operation*, Baltimore, MD: Johns Hopkins University Press, 2007, p. 285.

17. Marlin Fitzwater, *Call the Briefing*, New York, NY: Times Books, 1995, p. 216.

18. Stephen Farnsworth, *Spinner in Chief: How Presidents Sell Their Policies and Themselves*, Boulder, CO: Paradigm, 2009, p. 44.

19. www.bbc.com/news/world-us-canada-40010706.

20. http://thehill.com/policy/national-security/346613-trumps-charlottesville-response-stirs-debate-on-domestic-terrorism.

21. Philip Rucker, Ashley Parker, and Devlin Barrett, "Trump Lawyers Finding He Prefers His Own Advice," *Washington Post*, July 14, 2017, p. A1

22. Kumar, p. 58.

23. Lawrence R. Jacobs, "The Presidency and the Press: The Paradox of the White House Communications War," in Michael Nelson (ed.), *The Presidency and the Political System*, Washington, DC: Congressional Quarterly Press, 2010, p. 253.

24. George Edwards III, *On Deaf Ears: The Limits of the Bully Pulpit*, New Haven, CT: Yale University Press, 2003, p. 173.

25. Howard Kurtz, *Spin Cycle: Inside the Clinton Propaganda Machine*, New York, NY: The Free Press, 1998, p. 187.

26. Iyengar, Shanto, *Is Anyone Responsible? How Television Frames Political Issues*, Chicago, IL: University of Chicago Press, 1991; Rosenstiel, p. 26.

27. Joseph R. Hayden, *A Dubya in the Headlights*, Lanham, MD: Lexington Books, 2009, p. 225.

28. Ibid.

29. Margaret Sullivan, "Spicer's Exit Was Long Overdue," *Washington Post*, July 22, 2017, p. C2.

30. Stephanie Mansfield, "Ron Ziegler: The Loyalists and the Lobbyist," *Washington Post*, February 17, 1981. Available online at www.washingtonpost.com/archive/lifestyle/1981/02/17/ron-ziegler-the-loyalists-and-the-lobbyist/a326891d-5672–4d3f-8215–8939e6bf8b67/?utm_term=.807e6a11a898.

31. http://time.com/magazine/us/4710599/april-3rd-2017-vol-189-no-12-u-s.

32. www.nytimes.com/interactive/2017/06/23/opinion/trumps-lies.html.

33. https://shorensteincenter.org/news-coverage-donald-trumps-first-100-days.

34. http://time.com/4710614/donald-trump-fbi-surveillance-house-intelligence-committee.

35. Quoted in Margaret Sullivan, "Scott Pelly Is Showing His Bias for the Truth," *Washington Post*, March 26, 2017, p. C1.

36. David Nakamura, "Bush Denounces 'Bigotry', 'Fabrication,'" *Washington Post*, October 20, 2017, p. A1.

37. http://time.com/magazine/us/4710599/april-3rd-2017-vol-189-no-12-u-s.

38. http://time.com/4710614/donald-trump-fbi-surveillance-house-intelligence-committee.

39. https://shorensteincenter.org/wp-content/uploads/2017/05/Combating-Fake-News-Agenda-for-Research-1.pdf; www.merriam-webster.com/words-at-play/the-real-story-of-fake-news.

40. www.slate.com/articles/news_and_politics/press_box/2010/08/who_said_it_first.html.

41. Gregory S. Schneider, "Fake News Is Nothing New: Just Ask George Washington," *Washington Post*, April 16, 2017, p. C5.

42. Ellen Hunt, "What Is Fake News? How to Spot It and What You Can Do to Stop It," *The Guardian*, December 17, 2016.

43. Negative Polls Are 'Fake News,' Trump Tweets," *Vancouver Province*, February 7, 2017, p. A15.

44. Ibid.

45. Margaret Sullivan, "Even When the Facts Are Clear, Defense Is Still 'Fake News,'" *Washington Post*, July 17, 2017, p. C1.

46. Paul Farhi, "The Story behind the Story that Vexed CNN," *Washington Post*, August 18, 2017, p. C1; www.washingtontimes.com/news/2017/jun/26/three-journalists-resign-cnn-after-retracted-trump/#.

47. Ibid.

48. Addy Hatch, "What's Behind the Rise of 'Fake News'?" *Spokesman-Review*, February 8, 2017, p. A10.

49. shorensteincenter.org.

50. www.monmouth.edu/polling-institute/reports/MonmouthPoll_US_032917.

51. www.journalism.org/2016/12/15/many-americans-believe-fake-news-is-sowing-confusion.

52. Ibid.

53. Bret Stephens, "Don't Dismiss President Trump's Attacks on the Media as Mere Stupidity," *Time Magazine*, February 18, 201.

54. *New York Times*, September 4, 1927, p. 11.

55. Lawrence R. Jacobs, "The Presidency and the Press: The Paradox of the White House Communications War," in Michael Nelson (ed.), *The Presidency and the Political System*, Washington, DC: Congressional Quarterly Press, 2010, p. 239.

56. Quoted in Tom Rosenstiel, *The Beat Goes On: President Clinton's First Year with the Media*, New York, NY: The Twentieth Century Fund, 1994, p. 44.

57. Samuel Kernell, *Going Public: New Strategies of Presidential Leadership*, Washington, DC: Congressional Quarterly Press, 1997, p. 127.

58. www.reuters.com/article/us-usa-trump-mcconnell-exclusive-idUSKBN18K2MM.

59. www.politico.com/story/2016/12/trumps-tweet-shaming-corporate-america-232274.

60. Much of the information comes from Phil Patton, "Disk-Drive Democrats," *New York Times*, 28 November 1993, p. 7. Specific radio and television innovations are described in John Tebbel and Sarah Miles Watts, *The Press and the Presidency*, New York: Oxford University Press, 1985. See also: www.huffingtonpost.com/2010/10/11/obama-to-take-first-ever-_n_758571.html; www.theguardian.com/world/2008/nov/17/barack-obama-white-house-blackberry; www.voanews.com/a/white-house-presidential-facebook-page/3050421.html.

61. John Wagner, "Trump Quiet on Revamp of ACA," *Washington Post*, July 3, 2017, p. 1.

62. Alan Paller, "Deleting Those Embarrassing Files...Completely," *Government Executive*, February 1991, 50.

63. "Memories," *Government Computer News*, 16 (April 24, 1987), p. 30.

64. Charles Press and Kenneth Verberg, *American Politicians and Journalists*, Glenview, IL: Scott, Foresman/Little, Brown, 1988, p. 128.

65. John E. Yang, "Bush's Unintended Postscript: Open Mike Reveals Group Q & A Sessions Are Far from Spontaneous," *Washington Post*, 27 November 1991, A4.

66. www.washingtontimes.com/news/2000/sep/7/20000907–012025–9707r/.

67. Richard Adams, "This is a Big Fucking Deal," *Guardian Unlimited*, March 23, 2010.

68. Joshua Berlinger, CNN, May 31, 2017. Available online at www.cnn.com/2017/05/31/politics/donald-trump-covfefe/index.html.

69. White House staff member, quoted in Kumar, p. 138.

70. Kumar, p. 140.

71. James E. Katz, Michael Barris, and Anshul Jain, *The Social Media President: Barack Obama and the Politics of Digital Engagement*, New York, NY: Palgrave Macmillan, 2013, pp. 160–163.

72. http://opensiuc.lib.siu.edu/cgi/viewcontent.cgi?article=1042&context=pn_wp, p. 11.

73. Jeffrey E. Cohen, *The Presidency in the Era of 24-Hour News,*" Princeton, NJ: Princeton University Press, 2008, p. 137.

74. Katz, et al., p. 157.

75. https://shorensteincenter.org/wp-content/uploads/2017/05/Combating-Fake-News-Agenda-for-Research-1.pdf.

76. Dan Balz, "Scholar Asks," Can Democracy Survive the Internet?'" *Washington Post,* April 23, 2017, p. A2.

77. C.R. Sunstein et al., *How People Update Beliefs about Climate Change; Good News and Bad News,* SSRN Scholarly Paper No. 2821919, NY: Social Science Research Network, 2016.

78. Katz, et al., p. 50.

79. Ibid., p. 51.

80. Ibid., p. 50.

81. Jacobs, p. 240.

82. Ibid.

83. Ibid.

84. Ibid., p. 243.

85. Ibid., pp. 243–244.

86. Ibid., p. 244.

87. Newseum, "President and the Press" conference, Session 6, p. 9. Available online at www.newseum.org/2017/04/12/diverse-opinions-spark-conversation-at-the-president-and-the-press.

88. https://shorensteincenter.org/wp-content/uploads/2017/05/Combating-Fake-News-Agenda-for-Research-1.pdf.

89. ww--w.washingtontimes.com/news/2017/jun/27/voter-fraud-and-suppression-commission-to-meet-in-.

90. Farnsworth, p. 124; Julia R. Azari, *Delivering the People's Message: The Changing Politics of the Presidential Mandate*, Ithaca, NY: Cornell University Press, 2014, p. 156.

91. Katz et al., p. 24.

92. Ibid.

93. Farnsworth, p. 106.

94. https://georgewbush-whitehouse.archives.gov/interactive.

95. Farnsworth, p. 124.

96. See https://petitions.obamawhitehouse.archives.gov.

97. See https://petitions.whitehouse.gov.

98. Jacobs, p. 257.

99. Zachary A. Goldfarb and Juliet Eilperin, "Obama Tries to Tap Polarized News Media," *Washington Post*, May 6, 2014. Available online at www.washingtonpost.com/politics/white-house-looking-for-new-ways-to-penetrate-polarized-media/2014/05/06/ebd39b6c-d532–11e3-aae8-c2d44bd79778_story.html?utm_term=.ee8936205181.

100. See https://clinton5.nara.gov/; https://georgewbush-whitehouse.archives.gov/; https://obamawhitehouse.archives.gov.

101. Newseum, Session 4, p. 10.

102. Quoted in Steven Levingston, "The Communicators," *Washington Post Magazine.* May 21, 2017, p. 30.

103. Ibid.

104. Christopher Ingraham, "Trump Is Still Tweeting, but He's Toned Down the

Exclamation Marks, Sad!," *Washington Post*, April 4, 2017, p. B2.

105. www.cnn.com/2017/07/19/politics/donald-trump-six-months/index.html.

106. https://twittercounter.com/realDonaldTrump.

107. George Bennett, "Breaking down Trump's first 100 tweets as president," *Palm Beach Post*, February 7, 2017; http://twitaholic.com/realDonaldTrump.

108. Michael Sherer and Zeke J. Miller, "Trump After Hours," *Time Magazine*, May 22, 2017, p. 34.

109. Joshua Berlinger, CNN, May 31, 2017. Available online at www.cnn.com/2017/05/31/politics/donald-trump-covfefe/index.html.

110. Nada Bakos, "Raw Intelligence, 140 Characters at a Time," *Washington Post*, June 25, 2017, p. B5.

111. Bennett.

112. Ingraham, p. B2.

113. Ibid.

114. Newseum, Session 5, p. 2.

115. www.cnn.com/2017/09/11/politics/bannon-60-minutes/index.html.

116. Newseum, Session 3, p. 6.

117. Philip Rucker, Ashley Parker, and Devlin Barrett, "Trump Lawyers Finding He prefers His Own Advice," *Washington Post*, July 14, 2017, p. A2.

118. See Levingston, p. 32.

119. Noah Bierman and Brian Bennet, "Trump Turns Out to Be His Own Worst Enemy," *Capital Gazette*, May 19, 2017, p. A2.

120. www.nbcnews.com/politics/politics-news/trump-sen-corker-couldn-t-get-elected-dog-catcher-n813621.

121. Bakos, p. B1.

122. Ibid.

123. *Washington Post* editorial, "We've Got Some Questions for Mr. Trump," June 19, 2017, p. A20.

124. Newseum, Session 6, p. 4.

125. www.archives.gov/federal-register/publications/presidential-compilation.html.

126. https://twitter.com/realDonaldTrump.

127. Quoted in Marc Fisher, "Trump Has Long History of Secretly Recording Calls, Ex-associates Say," *Washington Post*, May 13, 2017, p. A1.

128. Margaret Sullivan, "The Lies Have It, But the Press Can Take Back," *Washington Post*, March 13, 2017, p. C1.

129. Newseum, Session 1, p. 1.

130. Philip Elliot, "White House: Chaos Theory," *Time Magazine*, February 27, 2017, p. 34.

131. Dan Balz, p. A2.

132. Ibid.

133. Sherer, p. 37; Frizell, et. al, p. 37.

134. www.nytimes.com/2017/02/04/opinion/sunday/why-nobody-cares-the-president-is-lying.html.

135. www.pollingreport.com/trump_ad.htm.

136. https://poll.qu.edu/national/release-detail?ReleaseID=2471.

137. www.aol.com/article/news/2017/06/07/poll-president-trumps-tweets-hurt-presidency-country/22130849.

138. Monica Hesse and Ben Terris, "No Comments from One Side, but Lots for the Other, about Donald Jr.'s Emails," *Washington Post*, July 12, 2017, p. C1.

139. Ibid.

140. www.reuters.com/article/us-usa-trump-mcconnell-exclusive-idUSKBN18K2MM.

CHAPTER 8

THE PRESIDENT AND POPULAR MEDIA

M uch analysis of the media limits its attention to traditional and emerging news platforms. Such an approach may well miss other ways in which the public is informed. For information "snobs," gaining valuable information through popular culture is an anathema. They prefer—both for themselves and others—reliance on traditional sources such as serious books and prestige newspapers. Such critics miss the point that movies, television, and other entertainment venues may well introduce people "to ideas and concepts they never thought about before . . . Popular culture offers a way of connecting the apathetically disinterested to a political system that very much needs them."[1] Representative government needs small "r" republicans who study the issues and express their preferences. Popular culture is the only way to reach some of these people. Evidence shows that entertainment media are able to inform usually disinterested people.[2] Writing off "infotainment" and soft news about the president may well miss an important point. Some people may garner important news as a by-product of their consumption of entertainment programming and soft news.[3]

To a large degree, "a nation *is* its stories,"[4] and the entertainment media are the key story tellers. Presidents play the lead character in many of these stories. Principles such as honesty (George Washington and the cherry tree), opportunity (Abraham Lincoln's "log cabin to White House" ascent), or overcoming disability (Franklin Roosevelt's polio) establish our ideals and set stands for presidents' successors. "The stories that Americans tell and have told about presidents are part of what makes America the nation that it is."[5] Movies and television are two of the key vehicles for telling stories. We expect that movies and television entertainment programs will explore the nature of the players, face them with challenges, and assess their ability to solve the problems. It is expected that the audience will walk away from the experience with a clear idea of who is the "good guy" and who is the villain. Subtlety seldom sells.

The President Goes to the Movies

"Hollywood, more than any other force in society, has determined how people think a president should act and look . . . [it] has given us a standard by which to measure the actual people holding the office."[6] Movies "reflect cultural norms and can play a role in shaping public attitudes. . . . [T]he same audiences that [go] to the movie theater also assesses a president's actions, motives, policies and choices."[7] With major exceptions, Hollywood and Broadway have traditionally treated presidents reverentially. They were portrayed as "[f]orceful, wise and selfless."[8] The 1933 box office hit *Gabriel Over the White House* focused on a president who had a life-changing experience after a confrontation with the angel Gabriel, leading him to heroically face the key issues of unemployment and homelessness.[9] In *Fail Safe* (1964), (President) Henry Fonda orders a nuclear strike on New York to stop Soviet retaliation, even though his wife is in the city. In the Broadway show (1977), and later the movie, *Annie*, President Franklin Roosevelt is portrayed as rising above partisanship to help Daddy Warbucks save Annie. At times the president comes across as an action-figure hero. In *Independence Day* (1996), (President) Bill Pullman uses his combat ace experiences to block an alien invasion.[10] A similar heroic tale emerges in *Air Force One* (1997), when (President) Harrison Ford, the ultimate hero, manages to fly a crippled aircraft and protect his wife and daughter, all while running the country.[11] The heroic president story line in movies has the potential for raising expectations too high for any president to accomplish. To the degree that the public buys into the image of a good president doing the right things for the right and moral reasons, they will be dissatisfied with the messy real world of politics.[12] Many of the movies focus on the fictional president's character and his ability to make principled decisions. Scholars point out that even the term "president" comes from the idea of "presiding," which means to "guard over" principles of behavior.[13]

Other movies, take the position that all it takes is well-meaning goodwill to perform well as president. In *Dave* (1993), a look-alike ordinary citizen secretly takes over for an ailing president. He runs the country well with a little humility, common sense, and plain speaking.[14]

At times positive movies emerge from unexpected quarters. During the 2000 campaign Alexandra Pelosi created the documentary *Travels with George*. Since her mother was a Democratic leader in the House, one might expect a hatchet job attempting to uncover George W. Bush's shortcomings. Instead it shows the human side of a campaign featuring the candidate's interaction with the media. After an inside look at the "bubble" of day-to-day campaigning the viewer is left with the impression that many of the members of the media, Pelosi included, may not have voted for Bush, but they liked him as a person.

Increasingly presidential movies leave the audience with a negative feeling about the president. Fanciful movies such as *Dr. Strangelove or: How I Learned to Stop Worrying and Love the Bomb* (1964) told the story of an incompetent president unable to control his staff while facing a nuclear attack.[15]

Movies laced with a tinge of truth about real presidents surrounded Richard Nixon and Bill Clinton. Nixon's weaknesses were graphically pointed out in movies such as *Milhouse* (1971), a scathing documentary.[16] In 1976, *All the President's Men* followed the investigation of corruption in the Nixon White House, reminding the public of why the president was forced to resign. The movie *Primary Colors* (1998) followed a slightly camouflaged Clinton-like campaign involving chicanery and sexual impropriety. For Clinton supporters, it asked the crucial moral question "should we forgive his personal shortcomings because we support his ideals, or are those ideals corrupted by his shortcomings?"[17] One of the most transparent presidential films was *Wag the Dog* (1998). In it, a president much like Bill Clinton is faced with declining popularity. His advisors come up with the idea of distracting the public through military activity diversion. With a small war going on, the media would take its attention off the president's other problems. The term "wag the dog" became part of the lexicon describing strategic chicanery in the White House and was applied to subsequent presidencies (see Chapter 5).

During the 2004 campaign, director Michael Moore released *Fahrenheit 9/11*. Presented as a documentary, it was more of a movie with little attempt at balance, targeting George W. Bush and his administration as the clear villains. Moore himself "was clear and plainspoken about his and the movie's motives—to help drive Bush out of office."[18] With its focus on Bush's ties with the Saudi royal family, it implied that Bush's pro-oil motives led to the 9/11 attack, and that his administration used fear of a future attack to pass right-wing legislation.[19] Questioning a president's motives helps knock him from his pedestal and is quite different from disagreement over the means of reaching widely held goals.

In a retrospective on the presidency, the 2012 movie *Lincoln* went beyond the usual "log cabin to White House" story line to portray a real-life pragmatist not above buying votes to reach his policy goals.[20]

Movies "operate in the realm of cliché and simplification. Their stock in trade is white hats and black hats and the good triumphing over evil by remaining true to itself."[21] Such distinctions seldom face politicians in the real world. There is no assurance that movie goers will be able to distinguish fact from fiction. For many viewers fiction may well preclude reality.[22] If the public buys into the more negative images of the presidency portrayed in contemporary movies, there is the potential for greater public cynicism and its negative impact of citizen interest and participations in politics.

The most important thing about presidential movies is not the impact of any one movie on public evaluation of a particular president. In reality, only a small segment of the population sees any specific movie. Films either directly or indirectly about the presidency do relatively poorly at the box office.[23] More importantly, the pattern of growing negativity toward presidents as represented in movie plots tells us a great deal about what movie producers feel they can portray without public backlash.

Presidents on Entertainment Television

Television serves as a primary source of both news and entertainment for most Americans. Presidents serve as interesting subjects for entertainment programs, and they attempt to use entertainment television to espouse their own message.

The President as the Story Focus

One recent example of popular culture focusing on the White House was *The West Wing* (1999–2006). It presented an image of what could be the best in presidential behavior. The fictionalized President Bartlet is portrayed as a wise and caring individual with the ability to rise above the worse aspects of politics. Bartlet seems "serenely above the moral compromises that are an inescapable part of real-life politics . . . the idea that in politics one must be satisfied to choose the lesser of two evils is anathema."[24] President Bartlet is a hero who does his job efficiently while at the same time maintaining human relationships with his family and staff.[25] The program even included a story about a film crew following the press secretary around for a day, explaining his function in relatively glowing terms.[26] The portrayal of such a perfect president on *The West Wing* begs comparison with previous and subsequent occupants of the office. The president-as-hero creates a "superman" image that no real-world president can live up to. A program like *The West Wing* fosters "an image that is unattainable by any public servant, making it seem like failure when the president does not live up to these standards."[27]

The President Uses Entertainment Venues

Increasingly presidents have found it useful to follow the audience. It does little good to have a positive message and no way to effectively spread it. With the decline of traditional news program ratings, the reduced number of newspaper readers and a fragmentation of the media landscape, presidents have to "scramble to chase viewers and voters."[28] While once seen as "unpresidential" for an incumbent president to utilize entertainment venues, necessity has required crossing that barrier. Visits to the late-night comedy or interview shows are no longer out of the question. Venturing into the entertainment venues also seems to have opened the door to allowing the treatment of the president in humorous ways.

Appearance by the president on entertainment programs not only allows him to communicate directly with the viewing audiences but also becomes news in and of itself. Other legacy media outlets create stories about the president's performance on air and promote the image of a leader accessible to the public and interested in communicating with them. The effectiveness of such events, of course depends on the president's performance. An on-air gaffe may well damage a president's image.

In the early years of late-night television, some candidates for the presidency saw television appearances on this emerging venue as useful. Senator John Kennedy appeared on the *Tonight Show Starring Jack Paar*, but the questions and answers were entirely serious.[29] In 1976, Ronald Reagan appeared on the Johnny Carson show in a light-hearted banter that focused on political strategy.[30] In a memorable moment from the 1992 presidential campaign, Bill Clinton, then governor of Arkansas and Democratic candidate, played "Heartbreak Hotel" on his saxophone during *The Arsenio Hall Show* on cable television.[31] While already seen as the mostly likely Democratic nominee, the performance helped him reach a different audience and to portray him as a unique and forward-looking candidate. As one of Clinton's political consultants, Mandy Grunwald, put it, "It was the end of one way of communicating with voters and the beginning of another."[32]

Former president Jimmy Carter eschewed late-night television as a candidate or president, but turned to *The Late Show With David Letterman* in 2014 to promote a new book.[33]

George W. Bush read his own "top ten list" (a staple of the program) on the *David Letterman Show* in October of 2000, allowing the topics to waver from purely serious to the funny.[34] Until late in President Obama's term, candidates conspicuously sought exposure on late-night television, but stopped the practice once in office.

Barack Obama appeared in cameos on *Saturday Night Live* prior to the 2008 election (2007) in an attempt to blunt the large number of impersonations of him done on the air.[35] Candidate Donald Trump hosted *Saturday Night Live* in November 2015, facing a number of his impersonators.[36]

The use of late-night television by candidates makes sense:

> Candidates regularly appear on late night comedy shows to display their "human" sides and to appeal to younger voters. It's often a smart political decision, since many independent voters base their decisions primarily on personal factors, not policy or ideological ones.[37]

The appearance of sitting presidents on entertainment television is a relatively new phenomenon. President Clinton sat for an hour-long interview with Larry King, billed as a news interview rather than entertainment even though King was known for his softball questioning of entertainers.[38] George W. Bush ventured into the popular culture venue at a time when his popularity was declining.

When the purple-heart winning Army Captain Joseph Kobes appeared as a contestant on the April 21, 2008, episode of *Deal or No Deal*, host Howie Mandel told the Iraq war veteran that someone wanted to come on the program to acknowledge his service. Appearing via satellite, Bush thanked Kobes, and then went on to offer up a joke or two at his own expense. "I am thrilled to be anywhere with high ratings," he said.[39]

After much discussion, President Obama went on *Between Two Ferns* with Zach Galifianakis for an irreverent discussion which Obama attempted to valiantly steer toward a discussion of Obamacare.[40] Obama sought to reach the younger demographics of the show and introduce them to the new health care options. When criticized for choosing such an unpresidential free-for-all comedy program, Obama responded that he was seeking out younger citizens "That's what young people like to watch."[41]

The pomp and circumstance surrounding the president tend to isolate him from intimate public ties. As society has become more informal, the presidency has been slow to adapt. The playing of "ruffles and flourishes" when the president enters a room and the personal space given by his entourage of aides tend to mark him as other than human. In recent years there

seems to be a relaxing of social norms around the presidency. In what was self-consciously styled as something of a farewell interview on Jimmy Fallon's *onight Show*, Obama exhibited all of the traits that defined him in the public eye—including a sort of TV-ready accessibility.[42]

Watching a president trade good-natured barbs with a talk show host makes him seem less other-worldly.

President Obama holds the record for late-night television appearances, visiting all of the major venues such as the *Tonight Show* and *David Letterman*. He did not limit himself to late-night television interviews. He took the risk of appearing on satirical programs such as *The Colbert Report*.[43] He also appeared on daytime television's *The View*, aimed at a more female audience. "No president has ever been quite so omnipresent—or, perhaps, so present both to older *Ellen* viewers and to younger *Between Two Ferns* viewers—in order to convey his message."[44] President Trump has not shown the desire to use entertainment venues as president.

Satirical and Humorous Representation of the President

Making fun of the president in the entertainment media was relatively rare until recently. Prior to the arrival of *Saturday Night Live* (*SNL*) in 1975, political "satire, let alone presidential satire, was hard to find on prime time television."[45] President Reagan, known as the "Teflon president," was not a good target for humorists, who found that their jokes would not stick any better than negative news stories. A few of the variety shows did venture into political criticism associated with Vietnam. Throughout the Clinton years, *SNL*'s "satire moved from satire about events and decisions to focus on the presidential scandals."[46]

Later faux news programs such as *The Daily Show* (1996) and *The Colbert Report* (2005), presented satirical stories designed to look like actual news. For many younger viewers they took the place of actual news. At the same time, late-night comedians such as David Letterman and Jay Leno placed the president in their sights with a panoply of jokes at the presidents' expense.

The longest-running sitcom on American television, the animated *The Simpsons*, indirectly took on President George W. Bush with an ironic skit in 2008 using a flashback to the 1990s, with Homer assuring Marge saying, "At least we know there'll never be a president worse than Bill Clinton. Imagine lying in a deposition in a civil lawsuit. That's the worst sin a president could commit," with Marge responding, "There'll never be a worse president. Never."[47] The implication was that Bush's actions surpassed that infraction.

Lest one think that political humor reaches relatively few individuals, it must be pointed out that ratings for programs such as *Saturday Night Live* sometimes exceed that of the evening news programs. *SNL* has boasted audiences of over 10 million viewers, while each of the network news programs reaches 6–8 million.[48] While the formats might vary, presidents are no longer immune from humorous attacks.

The President as the Target of Jokes on Late-Night Television

Presidents serve as the most popular political foil for late-night comedians. An analysis of Jay Leno's targets found that in eight years Bill Clinton was the subject of 4,607 jokes, while George W. Bush came in second with 3,239 during his term. No one else came even close to those totals. In his first six years, Barack Obama was not on track to supersede the two leaders, with his 1,011 jokes on the same programs.[49]

There are two basic approaches to political humor on television, that of Johnny Carson (1960s–1980s) and that of Jon Stewart (1999–2005):

> Carson stayed away from partisanship, leaving viewers guessing as to what side of the aisle he was on and making jabs that mirrored public opinion. "Once Carson started joking about Watergate, Nixon was completely doomed because that deathblow came from the public, not from being partisan."[50]

Jon Stewart on *The Daily Show* took on the president more directly, paying little attention to the status of the office. In today's offerings, Jimmy Fallon and Jimmy Kimmel take more of the Carson approach, while Stephen Colbert and Seth

Meyers take the more strident Jon Stewart path. There is some evidence that the more critical approach is winning out during the Trump era, with the edgier programs moving up in the ratings game.[51]

Parodying the President

It is one thing to humorously report stories or tell jokes about the president, and another to present a caricature of the president in intentionally funny sketches. The president as the target of satire on pop culture reached its first peak in the 1970s. Gerald Ford's tumble while walking down an airplane ramp in Austria in 1975 became grist for Chevy Chase, who depicted the former college football player turned president as a klutz on *Saturday Night Live*. Ford and other presidents even took to looking at *SNL* portrayals to identify weaknesses in how they presented themselves.[52] Every president since Ford has had to suffer the indignities of *SNL*'s parodies. Its caricatures of presidents and those around them have permeated the general culture, often making it difficult to separate fact from satire. *SNL* tends not to play political favorites proving to be "an equal opportunity offender"[53] skewering any president who happens to be in power.

President Trump and his staff quickly became targets for parody with imitators showing up on *Saturday Night Live* (Alec Baldwin), Comedy Central's *The President Show* (Anthony Atamanuik) and *America's Got Talent*. The signature hairdo and pursed lips made the characters readily recognizable. In Comedy Central's opening routine, the fake president proclaimed:

> A me-first country gets a me-first president. . .me. I've ruined everything I've ever touched—companies, citizens, marriages, toilets. I will use this office to enrich myself and my weirdo family, then tweet us into a war with Hawaii, I have the power to destroy any country on Earth, but I promise you it'll be America first.[54]

Early on, some of the most powerful *SNL* sketches portrayed the relationship between President Trump and his then press secretary Sean Spicer, played by Melissa McCarthy. Few people could be more heartbroken about Sean Spicer's departure as press secretary than Melissa McCarthy since her portrayal of the beleaguered Spicer earned her an Emmy award and great notoriety.

Reacting to Humor

Most modern presidents have graciously accepted political humor at their expense as part of the job. After his numerous unflattering portrayals of the president, Chevy Chase and Gerald Ford even became friends. Ford played the good sport while appearing on both *Saturday Night Live* and at the White House Correspondent's Dinner with Chase.[55] President Ford laughed along with the crowd at public events, even inviting the comedian to the White House to perform. Having a president able to laugh at himself was such a breath of fresh air after the agony of President Nixon's tenure that the Ford White House attempted to capitalize on it. Ford's press secretary, Ron Nessen, even took his turn at hosting *Saturday Night Live.*

George H.W. Bush invited his doppelganger—Dana Carvey—to the White House. Playing Bush on *SNL*, Carvey helped create the image of Bush as the type of man who said things like, "It wouldn't be prudent at this juncture."[56]

President George W. Bush appeared at the White House Correspondents' Dinner with Steve Bridges, his uncanny look-alike.[57] In the process, Bush showed "that he is after all a regular guy with a sense of humor."[58] Bill Clinton largely ignored the *SNL* sketches about his jogging to McDonalds and his relationship with Monica Lewinsky. As president, Obama made regular appearances on Jon Stewart's show and even invited the comedian to the White House.[59]

While other presidents have appeared to be good sports in public, *SNL* does seem to be getting under Trump's skin with its caricature and irreverence. In Washington, where one stands often depends on where one sits, his view might be understandable. Ironically, even though Trump hosted the program a number of times before the 2016 election,[60] his post-election encounters triggered tweets calling *Saturday Night Live* "biased," "unwatchable," and "always a complete hit job."[61] In a broader condemnation, President Trump tweeted, "NBC News is bad but *Saturday Night Live* is the worst of NBC. Not funny, cast is terrible, always a complete hit job. Really bad television!"[62] While that all may be true, *SNL* receives some of its highest ratings when Trump's foibles are presented. President Trump's seeming thin skin about criticism spawned additional unflattering media coverage.[63]

Emerging Venues

While our discussion has focused on television, the line between television per se as a distribution mechanism and the role of the Internet increasingly diminishes. Material initially created for television is now searchable and retrievable in the Web through services such as YouTube. Television shows create their own websites to distribute their programs. Video segments go viral, increasing their impact. Through video archives, the shelf life of television programs has been extended, while on demand services allow viewers to pick the time they want to watch.

The Impact of Presidential Humor on Television

While some may dismiss late-night television comedians and parodies of presidents as harmless distractions, the evidence is clear that such entertainment-based political information stimulates political education and forges perceptions of political leaders.[64] Individuals do gather important political information from the "soft news" presented through late-night comedy routines and pseudo-news programs.[65] The overall tone and impact of political humor is negative. Making fun of political leaders "lowers evaluations of, or attitudes toward its target(s)."[66] On the more positive side, movies and television programs that allow viewers to look behind the scenes in the White House could potentially have a positive educational impact. Understanding the important role played by spin doctors, political strategists, and pollsters in the modern White House could make those that see them more discriminatory consumers of White House news.[67]

While individuals may learn a great deal from political comedy, the end result may be more attitude stability. Research has shown that, "[i]f anything, comedic news encouraged less exposure to counter-attitudinal political viewpoints in comparison to hard news."[68] Thus opponents of presidents are more likely to find negative portrayals of him legitimate, bolstering their already negative views.

Editorial Cartoons

A long-standing staple of political humor has been editorial cartoons. While the number of cartoonists employed by individual papers has declined as the result of financial constraints, syndicated cartooning assures that most readers have access to a humorous take on the day's political events by turning to their paper's editorial page. Presidents serve as prominent subjects for editorial cartoonists, especially in this day and age when they hope to sell their cartoons to a national audience. As a national figure, the president is more saleable than the local political figures cartoonists once focused on.

Editorial cartoonists seldom break a news story but rather amplify story lines already in the news. They help build generalizations about a president and his behavior. Although both liberal and conservative cartoonists pen their ideas, most editorial cartoons are negative, pointing out the shortcomings and foibles of the president and his staff. Recognizing the importance of editorial cartoons in encapsulating political issues and influencing public opinion, George H.W. Bush tasked his staff with creating a weekly compilation (*The Friday Follies*) of cartoons focusing on him and his administration. Undoubtedly echoing the private thoughts of many presidents, "Boss" Tweed of Tammany Hall commented, "I don't care a straw for your newspaper articles; my constituents don't know how to read, but they can't help seeing them damned pictures!"[69]

The cartoonist's task is difficult in their attempt to take a complex issue and simplify it using a simple drawing and perhaps some text. They use a variety of tried and true techniques in their assault on the president. Some of the most clever cartons combine a variety of approaches to increase the chances that one of them will hit home.

Caricature

Most presidential cartoons involve *caricature*. In this mode, actual physical characteristics of the president are defined and exaggerated. Presidents Bush and Obama were drawn with big ears, growing bigger over their term in office. President Trump's unique hairstyle became his defining characteristic, with his overly long tie and pursed lips rounding out many representations.

The caricature is both funny in and of itself, and defines who the cartoon is talking about. Certainly within a president's few weeks in office most cartoonists have developed a clearly identifiable caricature (see Photo 8.1).

Metaphor

A metaphor implies that the president and his behavior are like something from history or popular culture. Presidents have been associated with a number of common metaphors from the animal world (a sneaky snake, sly fox, or clumsy

Photo 8.1 Caricatures Exaggerate Physical Characteristics of Their Subjects
Source: Cagle Cartoons/Adam Zyglis, *The Buffalo News*, NY

Photo 8.2 Metaphors Compare Presidential Actions to Well-Known Symbols
Source: Cagle Cartoons/Bill Day, Tallahassee, FL

bull in a china shop), participants in activities (a knocked out fighter, kids fighting
in a sandbox), job holders (a clown, an executioner), and literary or historical
figures (Pinocchio lying, Washington telling the truth), etc. Most often these
metaphors are negative(see Photo 8.2).

While metaphors are seldom perfect, they do impart a feeling about the president as the cartoonist evaluates him.

Sarcasm and Irony

Sarcasm portrays the worst possible interpretations of the president as if they were
the norm. The focus falls on questionable motives and inconsistency. Presidential
actions are ironic when observers point out how their actions or policy positions if
followed to their logical conclusion would lead to embarrassment (see Photo 8.3).

Word Play

Word play involves using the meaning (or double meaning) of a word to encourage
readers to see the president and/or his actions in a new or different way. In these

Photo 8.3 Full Commitment to Some Principles Lead to Ironical Outcomes
Source: Creator's Syndicate/ M. Lukovich

cases the visuals of the cartoon are less important than the words. President Trump's name lends itself to humorous usage, with observers of failures quick to point out how he was "trumped" in his efforts (see Photo 8.4).

Sight Gag

Sight gags put the emphasis on the visual aspect of the cartoon, portraying the president in a clever and new way (see Photo 8.5).

Whatever the particular tool, editorial cartoonists have the potential for sending a simplified yet powerfully negative messages about the president. In the media-rich environment of presidential news coverage, it is impossible to isolate the impact of a particular cartoon or set of cartoons. Few cartoons create a political mindset, but rather build on and reinforce other stories in the news. They tend to drive home assumptions about the president in a dramatic matter. Over the long haul, consistent themes captured in editorial cartoons reinforce opinions developed from other forms of media.

Photo 8.4 Clever Use of Words Creates Humor

Source: Cagle Cartoons/Steve Sack, *The Minneapolis Star-Tribune*, MN

Photo 8.5 Clever Visuals Make a Point without Words

Source: A.F. Branco

Conclusion

Individuals develop opinions about the president from a variety of sources. Popular media such as movies, television, and editorial cartoons often focus on the president. Humor serves as a mainstay of the entertainment media, with the president the frequent butt of jokes. Presidents themselves have attempted to capitalize on popular media with mixed success. Over time treatment of the president in the popular media has tended to be more negative. There is little hard evidence that the negativity of the popular media *causes* diminished respect for the president. A more reasonable conclusion is that the negative tone *reflects* and perhaps *reinforces* existing negative public evaluations. The amalgam of news stories and popular media helps create conventional wisdom that eventually emerges as undeniable truth.

Notes

1. Joseph Foy (ed.), *Homer Simpson Goes To Washington*, Lexington, KY: University of Kentucky Press, 2008, p. 3.

2. Christopher Cooper and Mandi Bates Bailey, "Entertainment Media and Political Knowledge," in Joseph Foy (ed.), *Homer Simpson Goes To Washington*, Lexington, KY: University of Kentucky Press, 2008, p. 146.

3. Matthew A. Baum, "Soft News and Political Knowledge: Evidence or Absence of Evidence," *Political Communications*, Vol. 20 (April/June), 2003.

4. Jeff Smith, *The Presidents We Imagine*, Madison, WI: University of Wisconsin Press, 2009, p. 4.

5. Ibid., p. 9.

6. Richard Shenkman," Forward" in Peter C. Rollins and John E. O'Connor (eds.), *Hollywood's White House*, Lexington, KY: University of Kentucky Press, 2003, p. xiv.

7. Lane Crothers, "Get Off My Plane: Presidents and the Movies," *White House Studies*, Vol. 10, no. 3, p. 1.

8. "Nuke the Wife," *The Economist*, Aug. 16, 1997, p. 66.

9. Peter C. Rollins and John E. O'Connor, *Hollywood's White House*, Lexington, KY: University of Kentucky Press, 2003, p. 9; www.tcm.com/this-month/article/64130%7C0/Gabriel-Over-the-White-House.html.

10. "Nuke the wife," p. 66.

11. www.rogerebert.com/reviews/air-force-one-1997; Smith, p. 217.

12. Crothers, p. 11.

13. Peter C. Rollins, "Hollywood's Presidents: 1944–1996," in Peter C. Rollins and John E. O'Connor (eds.), *Hollywood's White House*, Lexington, KY: University of Kentucky Press, 2003, pp. 252–253.

14. Smith, p. 224.

15. www.rogerebert.com/reviews/great-movie-dr-strangelove-1964.

16. www.rogerebert.com/reviews/millhouse-1971.

17. Sam Roggeveen, "Hollywood and the President," *Quadrant*, Vol. 46, No. 4, 2002, p. 64; www.rogerebert.com/reviews/primary-colors-1998.

18. Joseph R. Hayden, *A Dubya in the Headlights*, Lanham, MD: Lexington Books, 2009, p. 244.

19. Ibid.

20. www.rogerebert.com/reviews/lincoln-2012.

21. Crothers, p. 11.

22. See Smith.

23. Hayden, p. 251.

24. Roggeveen, p. 64.

25. Jennifer Hora, "The President as Hero," in Joseph Foy (ed.), *Homer Simpson Goes To Washington*, Lexington, KY: University of Kentucky Press, 2008, p. 89.

26. Smith, p. 285.

27. Hora, p. 94.

28. Caitlin Gibson, "When Trump Tweets, a Chorus of Squawks" *Washington Post*, May 9, 2017.

29. www.newsweek.com/late-night-politicians-presidential-candidates-371394.

30. www.mrmediatraining.com/2012/04/26/did-barack-obama-demean-his-office-on-jimmy-fallons-show.

31. www.latimes.com/entertainment/tv/showtracker/la-et-0619-arsenio-hall-010-photo.html.

32. www.tvinsider.com/2979/rerun-bill-clinton-on-arsenio-hall.

33. http://tvbythenumbers.zap2it.com/late-night/president-jimmy-carter-to-visit-cbs-late-show-with-david-letterman-on-monday-march-24.

34. time.com/3892131/david-letterman-late-show-finale-obama-presidents.

35. http://snl.wikia.com/wiki/Barack_Obama?file=SNL_Jay_Pharoah_-_Barack_Obama.jpg.

36. www.nbcnews.com/politics/2016-election/donald-trump-hosts-saturday-night-live-amid-protests-n459341.

37. www.mrmediatraining.com/2012/04/26/did-barack-obama-demean-his-office-on-jimmy-fallons-show.

38. www.presidency.ucsb.edu/ws/?pid=57113.

39. http://content.time.com/time/specials/packages/article/0,28804,2007228_2007230_2007254,00.html.

40. www.funnyordie.com/videos/18e820ec3f/between-two-ferns-with-zach-galifianakis-president-barack-obama.

41. www.newsweek.com/late-night-politicians-presidential-candidates-371394.

42. http://time.com/4363973/barack-obama-tonight-show-jimmy-fallon.

43. www.newsweek.com/late-night-politicians-presidential-candidates-371394.

44. http://time.com/4363973/barack-obama-tonight-show-jimmy-fallon.

45. John Matviko, "Television Satire and the Presidency," in Peter C. Rollins and John E. O'Connor (eds.), *Hollywood's White House*, Lexington, KY: University of Kentucky Press, 2003, p, 334.

46. Ibid., p. 343.

47. Hayden, p. 254.

48. www.washingtontimes.com/news/2017/feb/9/saturday-night-live-boasts-best-season-22-years-de; www.adweek.com/tvnewser/evening-news-ratings-week-of-oct-16-2/346113.

49. http://cmpa.gmu.edu/study-lenos-top-joke-target-was-bill-clinton.

50. www.forbes.com/sites/maddieberg/2017/02/03/john-oliver-stephen-colbert-jimmy-fallon-daily-show-in-late-night-tv-it-pays-off-to-dump-on-trump/#781bcd5135d7.

51. Ibid.

52. David Haven Blake, "Hollywood, Impersonation and Presidential Celebrity in the 1990s," in Peter C. Rollins and John E. O'Connor (eds.), *Hollywood's White House*, Lexington, KY: University of Kentucky Press, 2003, p. 323.

53. Jody C. Baumgartner and Jonathan S. Morris, "'It's Just a Joke!'. . .Or is it?" *Extensions*, Winter, 2014, p. 18.

54. Hank Stuever, "The Trump-Inspired Comedy Bubble Might Be about to Burst," Washington Post, May 2, 2017, p. C1.

55. http://content.time.com/time/specials/packages/article/0,28804,2007228_2007230_2007261,00.html.

56. http://abcnews.go.com/Politics/video/dana-carvey-performs-president-bush-impression-white-house-29003450; http://content.time.com/time/specials/packages/article/0,28804,2007228_2007230_2007252,00.html.

57. www.nytimes.com/2012/03/06/arts/steve-bridges-impersonator-of-presidents-dies-at-48.html.

58. Lisa Coletta, "Political Satire and Postmodern Irony in the Age of Stephen Colbert and John Stewart," *Journal of Popular Culture*, Vol. 42, No. 5, 2009, p. 856.

59. www.newsweek.com/late-night-politicians-presidential-candidates-371394.

60. www.nbcnews.com/politics/2016-election/donald-trump-host-snl-november-7-n443726.

61. Daniel D'Addario, The Uncanny Catharsis of *Saturday Night Live*," *Time* February 27, 2017, p. 24.

62. http://thehill.com/homenews/administration/314430-trump-tweets-snl-is-worst-of-nbc.

63. Elahe Izadi, "Trump Bits Helped Make SNL Ratings Great Again," *Washington Post*, May 24, 2017, p. C1.

64. See Jody C. Baumgartner and Jonathan S. Morris, Jody C. Baumgartner, and Jonathan S. Morris "The Daily Show Effect," *American Politics Research*, Vol. 34, No. 3, 2006, p. 341 and *Laughing Matters: Humor and American Politics in the Media Age*, New York: Routledge, 2008.

65. Danagal Young, "Laughing, Learning or Enlightenment?: Viewing and Avoidance Motivations Behind the Daily Show and Colbert Report," *Journal of Broadcasting and Electronic Media*, Vol. 57, No. 2, 2013, p. 153.

66. Baumgartner and Morris, p. 19.

67. Blake, p. 329.

68. Natalie Stroud, "Niche News, Selective Exposure, and Political Partisanship," *Extensions*, Winter, 2014, p. 9.

69. www.nytimes.com/learning/general/onthisday/harp/0819.html.

CHAPTER 9

ONGOING MEDIA RELATIONSHIPS AND HOW TO DEAL WITH THEM

It is natural and important to seek understanding of which political participants hold the upper hand and which outcomes are subservient to their initiatives. Sorting out the cause and effect when dealing with the president, the public, and the media is difficult. The typical model of the president "proclaiming," the media "transmitting," and the public "receiving" underestimates the complexity of the relationship.

At times presidents clearly lead, but the evidence is relatively weak that the president can unilaterally affect public opinion. On the other hand, working through the news media the president has significant power to influence the public.[1]

At other times, the media act as the agenda setter, bringing issues to the forefront and affecting both the president and the public. Alternatively, the public, largely through organized interests and polls, may take the lead. "When public opinion moves, elected officials [and the media] are never far behind."[2] It is reminiscent of the classic cartoon of a politician running down the street alongside a moving crowd saying, "Those are my people, I have to get ahead of them to lead."

Policy Leadership

Public policy is the ultimate outcome of the political process. Presidents, the media, and the public all have stakes in how policy is made, its content, and its application.

The President as a Policy Leader

In his classic work on public opinion, journalist Walter Lippman pointed out that the media may not be able to tell us what to think but they have an advantage in telling us what to think about.[3] His assertion spawned generations of research on agenda setting, with the president allegedly playing a key role. The media became seen as a key instrument for enhancing the president's impact. Research has shown that the "presidents' efforts at public leadership are not geared so much at changing public preferences, that is *moving* public opinion, but rather at influencing issues that the public considers important."[4] By analyzing presidential speeches and public opinion polls on issues of most importance to the public, Eshbaugh-Soha and Peake conclude that the "news media offer opportunities for presidential leadership of the public's agenda. By influencing what the media cover, presidents can affect the importance the public attributes to issues. [Furthermore] presidents respond to shifts in the public's agenda."[5] If presidents cannot directly lead public opinion, they can have indirect potential for using the media to set the public's agenda.

While presidents have an advantage as news makers, their control of the political agenda is limited. Approximately 90% of presidential appeals for legislative action fail to make it into the news.[6] The president is more likely to affect the agenda when faced with a relatively blank slate. Presidents are more effective in setting the public agenda on issues which the media have ignored and are low on the public's concern. On issues of higher salience to either the media or the public, the president is more likely to respond than lead.[7]

Contemporary presidents are hampered in their ability to change public opinion by four key factors. First, the audience for political news has diminished. Second, trust in the media is so low that it may well taint any message they try to communicate. Third, more of the coverage the president receives is negative, making it unlikely that the president will receive the volume and kind of coverage he desires.[8] Finally, presidents are not the only key players on the public stage. "Events have a way of drawing attention away from what presidents want to emphasize."[9] Presidents and their staff are forced to react to real-world events such as mass shooters, economic reports, and initiatives by foreign leaders.

Presidential ability to lead public opinion tends to vary depending on the subject matter and the venue. "Agenda-building by a president is an important but limited activity . . . presidents are most effective at 'agenda surfing,' simultaneously riding the waves of a story within the original news cycle."[10]

Presidents tend to have greater success in dominating foreign policy crisis news than domestic news.[11] Within the domestic realm, presidents tend to lead media attention to issues such as health care and education, while responding to media attention to crime and unemployment.[12] Despite the limitations, "[i]f presidents devote enough attention to a policy priority, offering an innovative and newsworthy policy agenda, then they will have a good chance to lead the media."[13]

The Media as Policy Leaders

The media play two important roles in the political process. By highlighting problems in need of solution they are critical in determining which issues public officials will confront. In this *agenda-setting* role they scan society for potential problems and assess which are solvable. Two kinds of problems emerge. *Relative problems* begin with a comparison to another time period ("things are worse than they were in the past") or to some other political entity ("the U.S. has more gun deaths than other developed countries"). On the other hand, *absolute* problems compare the current situation with a desired standard ("no child should be left behind" or "What don't you understand about 'illegal'?"). It is easier for the media to set the agenda on issues defined as absolute problems.

Agenda setting is a two-way street. At times the media forces items on the president's agenda by their reporting (see Box 9.1). Media questions can force a president and his staff to ask "What are we doing about this?" Real-world events such as natural disasters or international challenges impinge on the national agenda in ways outside the control of either the media or the president. At other times, the president seeks to use the media to move his items to the forefront of the American people and other policy-makers.

A second role of the media can be seen as "priming." There is too much information floating around for individuals to absorb it all, so the public depends on the media to send signals as to what is important and what can be ignored. Headlines, the placement of stories on the front page of a newspaper or web site or early in a news broadcast, and the amount of coverage provided alert the reader or viewer as to what is critical. News alerts on smartphones capture the attention of users, telling them what news is trending. Most people follow a "satisficing" strategy, gathering just enough information to perform necessary tasks and/or not look foolish to others around them.[14] Although the quote might sound strange coming from a representative of the Russian official news agency, Tass, it is important for all political participants to understand that when it comes to defining news "reporters always get the last word because they write it."[15]

While this analysis has focused on the president's relationship with the American press and the U.S. public, it is important to point out that interest in the U.S. president by foreign press and the world population has increased in recent years. While the number of U.S. reporters covering the White House has declined, the number of foreign correspondents has increased. Foreign reporters participate in White House briefings and presidential press conferences. They raise questions about their region of the world and alert the president and other journalists of impending policy problems.

What the president does and how he is portrayed affect his ability to serve as an international leader. Much of the world looks to the president for guidance. Presidents attempting to create international coalitions need to be seen as honest brokers good to their word. A key element of foreign policy has been the use of

---

Box 9.1
CNN Effect, Goading the President into Action

CNN has become the most comprehensive information-gathering news network, especially for the provision of foreign news. In many cases, CNN has a greater facility to cover international and breaking events than does the government itself. Former Secretary of State Colin Powell commented that "You would be lost in the West Wing of the White House . . . if you did not have C-SPAN and CNN to tell you what is happening around the country and around the world in real time."[16]

By covering atrocities, CNN stories are asserted to help set the agenda for U.S. action. When events are out of sight they are out of mind, especially when they occur thousands of miles away. Coverage can remind the public of the U.S. role in ameliorating hardship. For example, the U.S. did little to intervene in the ethnic cleansing taking place in Rwanda and Sudan until pictures of atrocities appeared on CNN.

Former Secretary of State James Baker explained that "the one thing it [CNN] does, is to drive policymakers to have a policy position. I would have to articulate it very quickly. You are in real-time mode. You don't have time to reflect." His former press secretary, Margaret Tutwiler, mirrors his sentiment: "Time for reaction is compressed. Analysis and intelligence gathering is out."[17]

Not all observers recognize the power of the CNN effect and assert the other factors that go into foreign policy–making.[18] Even if CNN coverage, and that of other news networks, are only one factor in setting the national agenda, they are worthy of consideration.

In the fast-moving era of real-time news there is the danger of not knowing the veracity of various statements. Policy-makers who are also watching CNN or other networks may be getting their information there, and then passing it on as their own take on the developing event. This gives the original information (or misinformation) more credibility.[19]

"soft power," a significant portion of which revolves around good presidential public relations transmitted by the media.

Competing Policy Influences

Presidents are not the only ones able to use the media to their advantage, nor can the media completely ignore issues brought forward by other political players. A dramatic story or unique presentation can challenge the president's story line and lure media attention. The sources of competing national stories may emerge from Congress, the courts, the bureaucracy, interest groups, political parties, or even individual citizens.

During the second Iraq war, the White House was quick to acknowledge parents who had lost a child in the conflict who still backed the administration's policy. Interviews expressed how their son or daughter "died while doing what they loved" or "contributed to a worthwhile cause." Then along came Cindy Sheehan, whose son died in Iraq. She felt the sacrifice was unnecessary and that her son had "died for [the Bush administrations'] lies."[20] Sheehan give a human face to the abstract idea of patriotic sacrifice and questioned its worth in Iraq. The image of a mother camped out in front of George W. Bush's ranch in Crawford, Texas, made for a good news story, especially for news crews hanging out without a lot to cover. In January, 2006, Sheehan was invited to the State of the Union message by a Democratic opponent of the war. She arrived in a T-shirt emblazoned with the phrase "2245 Dead. How many more?" The Capitol police quickly arrested her and roughly ushered her out of the chamber citing rules against protesting in the Capitol. The story became even more tantalizing when a Republican congressman's wife, wearing a "Support the troops defending our freedom," was handled much more gently. The media were quick to point out the double standard.[21]

For the president, media attention is a double-edged sword, at least partially out of his control. In many cases, presidents are almost forced to react, entering the dangerous zone of allowing one's opponents to choose the terrain of battle.

The Impact of the Media on the President

While we normally think of the president as the subject of media coverage, using the media to seek control over the policy process, the nature of presidential coverage also affects the nature of presidential support and the presidents' own agendas.

Presidential Popularity

Presidents popular with the general public are generally better able to have their policies passed by Congress. Members of Congress use a president's national popularity figures as surrogate measures of support within their own districts. A series of bad stories about the president are assumed to have a negative impact on the president's popularity.[22] Answering the crucial question as to whether bad news coverage causes diminished public support is clouded by the fact that as a president's popularity begins to wane, he and his staff begin to ramp up their public relations activities.[23] Low public support may well be correlated with extensive media coverage of this expanded activity and coverage. Much of this coverage is likely to be negative given the investigative penchant of the contemporary media. Thus low public support could be at least a partial cause of media coverage rather than the other way around.

Affecting the President's Agenda

We focus on news media coverage *of* the president rather than *for* the president. Part of the media's potential power lies in its impact on an elite audience of one, the president. Presidents serve as the responder in chief, reacting to stories brought to the surface by the media. Presidents who disregard news stories focusing on social problems put themselves in line for media criticism of unrresponsiveness.[24] Floods, tornadoes, and other natural disasters serve as stimulants for a presidential reaction both verbally and through the approval of federal grants. Presidents failing to recognize publicly emerging social problems such as drug use or school violence are painted as out of touch. Presidents also "often perceive public opinion changes through the news media."[25]

During the 2016 campaign, candidate Trump explained that he received his military advice from "the shows," referring to cable news, especially Fox News. Numerous examples exist of Trump reacting via Twitter almost immediately to stories presented on Fox. Long before receiving his official briefings, the early-rising president watches his favorite shows and reacts with what becomes interpreted as official policy.[26]

Part of President Trump's morning briefing includes a summary of news coverage, as was the case for previous presidents. The perceived importance of local news is reinforced by the fact that the Trump White House communications staff began "including local news clips in his daily news roundup partly to demonstrate how his message is playing outside the nation's capital and partly to help buoy his mood."[27]

But President Trump does not wait for his staff's summary of the news. He is arguably our first "real-time president." While previous presidents have been interested in the polls and news coverage of their actions, "Trump wants to know minute to minute how a decision is being received. He watches it on television. He reads it in the papers."[28] President Trump depends on the media for immediate information:

> [M]ost of his controversial utterances, are usually prompted by something he has seen on television just moments before . . . [he] also uses details gleaned from cable news as a starting point for policy discussion or a request for more information.[29]

Trump is especially fond of One America News and Fox News, conservative networks.[30]

By garnering a president's attention, the news media encourage him to act on the problem in question. Media stories thus can affect both the president and the public simultaneously.

Dealing with the Current Media Shortcomings

Few would argue that these are the best of times when it comes to the relationship between the president, the media and the public. To the degree that the current media environment fails to adequately serve the president, enhance the proper role of the media, and provide the public with the necessary information they need, there is plenty of blame to go around.

Presidential Responsibility

Presidents have the right and duty to present themselves and their policies in a positive light, but shortchange the political process when all of their energies focus on securing positive coverage. The president's inordinate focus on good news, either manufactured or real, cheats the American public out of true understanding of successes and failures. If everything is seen as spin, public trust in any story emanating from the White House becomes suspect. Presidents who emphasize public relations and rhetoric over accomplishments and failures may begin to trust their own press releases and misperceive the public and its problems.[31]

Evaluating recent presidencies, Stephen Farnsworth concludes that:

> [m]odern presidential communication . . . is both deceitful and counter-productive . . . [f]or the White House. There is a great temptation to manipulate appearances and tell only the most favorable part of the story. Presidents can and do appear before invitation-only crowds asking preselected questions that praise the chief executive's wisdom and foresight.[32]

The ultimate danger of presidential trickery is more than the bolstering of an unworthy and self-serving occupant of the White House. "The link between the public and the president is a tentative one and can be broken by betrayal. Once severed, the links cannot quickly be restored."[33]

The media and citizens have a right to honesty regarding continuing social problems and to learn both from the president's successes and mistakes. Short-term misrepresentation undermines the office of the presidency in the minds of citizens. Presidents have the duty to pass on to successive presidents an office unsullied by scandal.

To some degree presidents are captives of the media environment in which they are expected to operate. The speeding up of news production and the 24/7 news cycle almost forces presidents and their staffs to focus on short-term reactions rather than long-term planning.[34] Short-term goals often fail to match long-term objectives. Expending effort on short-term initiatives takes time and effort away from longer and more comprehensive enterprises. The attempt to look good in the short run by winning minor skirmishes tends to portray the White House as secretive and manipulative.[35] The media's focus on who "wins" and who "loses" in policy or public relations battles exacerbates the problem. Presidents and their surrogates seldom admit failures. The loss of a policy battle with Congress is explained as a "moral victory" or with an attempted redirection toward those portions of the decision that were successes for the White House. Weak polls measuring public support are either ignored or met by striking out at the messenger (the media) or demeaning the polls themselves. While the subjects of negative news coverage might find some solace in the condemning the messenger, simple condemnation does little to rectify the situation. "Everyone loses if political leaders must communicate with citizens via information media that much of the public doesn't trust."[36]

It is possible for presidents to try too hard to get their message out. One of the paradoxes "is that the more the president publicly promotes controversial policies to create favorable news, the more likely is an increase in the volume of damaging press coverage and web chatter."[37] Like in physics, for every action there is an equal and opposite reaction—although, unlike the physical world, the reactions often are not equal. Opponents tend to counterorganize, reacting to presidential initiatives. The media adds to the potential danger of presidential public relations initiatives by redoubling their efforts to tell both sides of the story, and framing the president's actions in terms of political strategies rather than policy perspectives.[38]

Some structural changes could improve the stories coming from the White House. More regular presidential press conferences with follow-up questions would provide the acquisition of more nuanced information. Expanding the number and variety of participants in daily briefings would allow more voices to be heard. There is a practical problem with broadening the nature of reporters having access to the White House through press briefings. With approximately 750 reporters credentialed to cover the White House and only forty-nine seats in the briefing room, some tough choices need to be made. So far, the vast majority of seats go to the mainstream legacy media. One solution might be to use revolving groups of reporters from wider groups of ideological and dissemination venues.[39] As media audiences become more fragmented, this will become more and more important.

While structural changes could help improve the information flow, most of the problems stem from attitudinal factors and perceptions of the other players. Presidents and their staffs need to recognize the legitimate role of the media in honestly and objectively questioning White House assertions. The current communications warfare tends to generate more heat rather than casting light on important problems and their possible solutions. Treating the public as uninformed and easily persuadable children does little to enhance either the presidency or the public debate. A useful exercise for the White House communications staff would be to ask "What kind of information would you want to make an intelligent decision on this issue?" Providing that information would go a long way to better informing the media and the public.

Media Responsibility

Looking at the media reveals several shortcomings. The profit-oriented bottom line of most news sources leads to pandering to the audience by only reporting what "sells." When ratings are king, public problems and policy solutions are shortchanged. There is little or no chance that this characteristic of American media will change. The best hope comes from harnessing the profit motive by educating the public as to the information they need, and reeducating the media about the potential real desires of the public. It is possible that the media has misread the public's interest.

Seeing everything from the horserace perspective and emphasizing conflict and bad presidential behavior is not a benign influence on American politics. As the late *Washington Post* senior reporter David Broder put it,

[c]ynicism is epidemic right now. It saps people's confidence in politics and public officials. . . . If the assumption is that nothing is on the level, nothing is what it seems, then citizenship becomes a game for fools and there is no point in staying informed.[40]

As one former press secretary put it,

[t]he press have a mission to find the bad [news], and in the process, they help us correct it. They're right to expose wrongdoing so it to can be seen and fixed. In doing so, they protect the Republic itself. But that shouldn't be their only mission.[41]

The presidency offers a large number of possible story lines. With the panoply of subjects that might be considered news, the media is drawn to stories which often should deem little attention. "[R]eporters are better at aggressive real-time coverage of less significant matters, such as personal scandals, than they are at challenging a commander in chief in time to affect the debate over whether the nation should go to war,"[42] or some other national policy issue. The media tends to frame everything in political terms, ignoring other aspects of the president's goals and behavior.[43] A challenge for the media lies in providing context for ongoing news stories. "Too often events are presented as isolated news bites, unconnected to the larger narrative of the long-term story."[44]

The 24/7 news cycle impacts on the emphasis on scandals and conflict. White House reporters for cable news asked to report from the White House lawn perhaps a dozen times a day must dredge up new stories continuously. "For news organization thirsty for fresh material, conflict is often the fire that gets stoked. Many people in politics are happy to provide it and cable TV reporters know a juicy piece of criticism will get them on the air."[45] The news media also tend to momentarily focus on an issue and then to move onto the next piece of alleged "breaking news." The job of the journalist is not just to break the story but to also "create and sustain the public conversations democracy demands."[46] When everything is breaking news, nothing is breaking news.

The media can be an easy target for presidents and their staffs to play the "blame game." It is important to remember the childhood admonition that when you point your finger at someone else, there are three fingers pointing back to you. Bad press may be well deserved by a White House doing the wrong things or presenting them in the wrong way.

Some journalists remind their colleagues in the media that they:

> need to take some time for introspection and realize that we, too, are part of the problem. . . . The stories we choose to cover, how we cover issues, the headlines we write, the op-eds we publish, the balance in perspective offered and the word choices we use are all part of this discussion.[47]

Just as the general population and political leaders have shown a deepened ideological and partisan divide, a similar split has occurred in the media. While bemoaning these divisions, the media may well be part of the cause as they reinforce the cleavages.[48] With the rise of more clearly conservative and liberal media, journalists with those bents gravitated to those outlets. News gathering, dissemination and reception increasingly resemble "echo chambers" of reinforcing bias more than open exchanges of neutral information.

One positive step for improving media coverage lies in re-raising the flag of objectivity that seems so tattered in this age of increased partisanship in society, the media and public office. On the one hand, the role of journalists does not lie in dishing out adulation to those with whom their organization agrees. As one conservative journalist explained about his organization's coverage of President Trump, "[W]e have a bigger responsibility to tackle his work here and hold him accountable to the promises he made to our readers."[49] On the other hand, an unyielding criticism of particular political leaders without recognizing their positive characteristics does little to inform. As one liberal columnist puts it, "If journalism is to do its job fully, as the founders intended, it can't speak primarily to one side of the political aisle."[50] It is dangerous for the media to act or be perceived as the opposition to the government, a political party, or a political leader. It is the competition between the party or politicians in power and the party or politicians who hope to replace them that deserves adequate and even-handed coverage. The reemergence of opinionated journalism carries with it significant danger. Although complete objectivity is impossible, "[s]ycophantically cheerleading every governmental action is no better than cynically criticizing every action of government. Both paint a false picture of government and help instill either a naive trust or cynical disdain for government and its leaders."[51] The media should stand on the sidelines like good referees, pointing out errors and successful plays to the gathered audience.

Being objective does not mean presenting toothless stories accommodating the preferred story lines from the White House. Steve Scully of C-SPAN clearly outlines how journalists see their role by saying:

> [t]he press has a simple job: to ask questions, search for the facts and hold public officials accountable to their promises. An adversarial relationship between the press and the presidency is healthy for democracy. . . . No president, no public official should ever restrict what our Founding Fathers wanted to guarantee; a free press that offers our system of government checks and balances.[52]

The importance of objective coverage of the president is as high as its challenge:

> Although neither journalists nor citizens can compel presidents to govern responsibly, journalists can raise the costs of bad behavior. Presidents can and often do surround themselves with sheep bleating in unison about the wondrous nature and sage judgment of the national shepherd.[53]

Cutting through the White House public relations machine takes skill and perseverance.

There are a number of steps journalists could take to allow recipients to more effectively determine the validity of the information they disseminate:

- Increasing transparency by describing the newsgathering process would give recipients a better idea of potential strengths and weakness of the news product. A clarion call to the contemporary media has been described as to "Give people an accurate picture of government actions, show your work and make it transparent about how you verified your facts, and be willing to risk ridicule and censure and surveillance and arrest by public officials who prefer supremacy to scrutiny."[54]
- Reassessing of what is legitimate news would send a more valid signal to the public of what they should pay attention to. By "not barking at every car," the importance of the stories that are covered increases.[55]

- Giving the president a chance to speak in something other than sound bites would help put issues into context. Presidential frustration with media "talking heads," and bloggers anticipating their message and criticizing it before it permeates the public is not lost on some journalists. As *Washington Post* correspondent Ann Devroy put it, "The president ought to be allowed to say what he wants to say to the American people before it is dissected and taken apart."[56]
- Having the media more clearly distinguish objective news from opinion would increase the public's trust in the news.[57]

Public Responsibility

Supreme Court Justice Louis Brandeis once argued that "the only title in our democracy superior to that of president is the title of citizen."[58] He was obviously thinking of well-informed individuals assessing politicians and their policies with the intention of taking action on those of importance to them. To be well-informed means knowing the multiple sides of issues and running them through the forge of critical analysis.

In the broad sweep of things, American society and the media within have become victims of acceleration in the sharing of information and the demand to reach conclusions. For those so inclined, virtual real-time news alerts on computers and cell phones inundate us. Many political events can be viewed in real time on outlets such as C-SPAN. If problems and alternative solutions hit us with such immediacy, it is natural to desire eventual solutions to emerge with similar speed. "It is far easier to spin forward with speculation than to wait patiently"[59] for the political process to create a reasonable response.

News consumers can be faulted both for failing to gather the necessary volume of information to make rational judgments and for only gathering information supporting sparsely defined goals. Opinions without factual underpinnings contribute little to the citizen's ability to participate in the political dialogue.

Countering the lack of adequate information or misinformation is not for the fainthearted. While we can encourage presidents to be more forthcoming and journalists to be more responsible in providing more useful and correct information, news consumers have their own challenging responsibilities. We all need to become smarter consumers. Without becoming so cynical that we leave the playing field in disgust, we need to delve into the adequacy of our sources and hone our skills for discovering bias and other misrepresentation. Although it is easy to blame the media for misguiding us, some responsibility falls on our shoulders. Arthur Hays Sulzberger, former publisher of the *New York Times*, reminds us that "Along with responsible newspapers we must have responsible readers . . . the fountain serves no useful purpose if the horse refuses to drink."[60] It is important to remember that the "We" in our vaunted goal of "We the people" is us.

While it is true that "presidents will try to manipulate the political conversation, as they are convinced that it is in their advantage,"[61] consumers are not powerless. Consuming news from multiple sources, learning to recognize spin and other techniques of persuasion, and voicing our own opinions all will help to bolster our representative democracy. Media bias and spin will never disappear, but an informed and active citizenry can still prevent the worst excesses of PR-driven deception from corrupting our democracy.[62]

Much of the problem with becoming an open-minded and informed news consumer stems from our unwillingness to admit our own shortcomings. Many members of the public are often thwarted by the "third-person effect." Individuals tend to believe that the biased media finds easy targets among the general population but has little or no effect on them. They see the media as brainwashing the masses but that they are able to navigate toward the truth.[63]

The challenge of becoming legitimately informed has increased with the explosion of news venues. The very volume of media sources may keep the timid from even trying to make sense out of the political world. Emerging from the "data smog"[64] requires effort.

Established media have a track record of veracity and/or bias that serve as a benchmark for evaluation. Where one gets presidential news today is affected by where one goes for the news. Fox News has consistently been more positive toward Republican presidents, while MSNBC favors Democrats[65] (see Box 9.2). Critics of these more opinionated sources point out that in justifying their favored president conservative sources have tended to overlook profoundly unconservative policies, while liberal outlets fail to blow the whistle on illiberal initiatives.[66] Audiences tend to gravitate toward media sources that reaffirm their political biases.

The media are not the only framers. We as consumers take the raw material from the media and frame our own images of desirable presidential action and how the incumbent lives up to it. Once we have a particular frame, we selectively collect, perceive, and retain information that backs up our predisposition.[67] When the public simply gravitates toward media sources that bolster their existing biases, they approach politics with a false sense of assurance that only their view is correct, and contribute to the partisan and ideological gridlock that has gripped the nation. Actively seeking out countervailing information takes effort, but may well be enlightening. There is little question that to the degree citizens can urge policy-makers to tone down their partisan rhetoric by limiting their own name calling and argumentativeness the political dialogue will improve.

The arrival of new networks, websites, blogs, and news alerts lacking a widely understood track record allows consumers to be misled and to mislead others. The most basic step lies in giving priority to sites and sources known to be legitimate. Looking for stories which provide direct quotes, figures, and citations of sources provides good clues for avoiding fake news. On the Web, watch out for "clickbait," outrageous headlines designed to lure in the uninformed. Checking

BOX 9.2
Watching the Media Watchers

Photo 9.1 FAIR Logo

Source: FAIR

Photo 9.2 Accuracy in Media Logo

Source: Accuracy in Media

Photo 9.4 Media Matters Logo

Source: Media Matters for America

**Photo 9.3 Media Research Center
Logo**

Source: Media Research Center

Just as it is important to watch the media, it is important to watch the watchers. A number of media watchdog groups have developed. Each sees the media through its own ideological lens. In making subjective judgments about the media through selection of stories and content analysis methodology, they often come out with different conclusions.

On the liberal side one finds Fairness and Accuracy in Reporting (fair.org) and Media Matters for America (mediamatters.org).

Viewing the media world from a more conservative position are the Media Research Center (mrc.org) and Accuracy in Media (aim.org).

the "about us" sections of a website often gives clues as to its veracity. The impact of misinformation depends on the degree to which it is spread. Responsible consumers "only post or share stories [they] know to be true, from sources [they] know to be responsible."[68]

The Critical Connection

We live in a representative democracy. Most decisions are not made directly by the public but rather delegated to the legislative and executive branches of government. In order to live up to the "representative" label, public officials need to have some way to assess and influence the public's policy preferences. Both the president and the media can lay claim to representing the public, albeit in different ways. The president can assert a mandate from the election, arguing that his policy positions were the ones favored by the majority and deserve passage. As new problems emerge, the president can go to the public to affirm the existence of a problem and support his tendered solution. An informed public has the potential to choose preferred leaders and help direct those in power. Through polls and other less empirical observations, the media seek to chime in and express what the public really thinks about public policy. Competing politicians and interest groups use the media to influence the public and generate support for their policy preferences. The media's ability to serve as honest brokers providing both the public and political activists with the information they need plays a big role in determining the effectiveness of representation.

Conclusion

Both the president and the media play important roles in establishing the American policy agenda, with the media playing a special role in alerting the public as to what is important. The president serves as both the source of media stories and a consumer of their coverage.

The current media relationship between the president, media, and the public is far from ideal—and never has been. "Fixing" the situation is not the responsibility of only one of the components. Presidents, the media, and the public all have a stake in improving media coverage and increasing the reservoir of media support that is necessary in a democratic society.[69] There are surely enough tasks to make improvements to go around. Not everything is grim. America is blessed with a largely free press and with an increasing multitude of competing venues. Our separation of powers and two-party system increase the chances that presidential and media misconduct will be discovered. While some structural changes might make a difference, what needs to be increased is the will to change the negative aspects while enhancing the positive characteristics.

Notes

1. Han Soo Lee, "Analyzing the Multidirectional Relationships between the President, News Media, and the Public: Who Affects Whom?" *Political Communication*, Vol. 31, No. 2, 2014, p. 275.

2. Samuel Kernell, *Going Public*, Washington, DC: CQ Press, 2007, p. 220.

3. Walter Lippmann, *Public Opinion*, New York: Macmillan, 1922. See also Maxwell E. McCombs and Donald L. Shaw, "The Evolution of Agenda-setting Research," *Journal of Communications*, Vol. 43, No. 2.

4. Matthew Eshbaugh-Soha and Jeffrey S. Peake, *Breaking Through the Noise: Presidential Leadership. Public Opinion and the News Media*, Stanford, CA: Stanford University Press, 2011, p. 5.

5. Eshbaugh-Soha and Peake, p. 181.

6. Andrew Barrett, "Press Coverage of Legislative Appeals by the President," *Political Research Quarterly*, Vol. 60, No. 4, p. 655.

7. Eshbaugh-Soha and Peake, p. 185.

8. Jeffrey E. Cohen, *The Presidency in the Era of 24-Hour News*," Princeton, NJ: Princeton University Press, 2008, pp. 89, 175 and 176.

9. Stephen Farnsworth, *Spinner in Chief: How Presidents Sell Their Policies and Themselves*, Boulder, CO: Paradigm, 2009, p. 4.

10. Wayne Wanta and Joe Foote, "The Presidential-News Media Relationship: A Time-Series Analysis of Agenda-Setting," *Journal of Broadcasting and Electronic Media*, Vol. 38, No. 4, 1994, p. 437.

11. Eshbaugh-Soha and Peake, pp. 17, 75. See also George Edwards and B.D. Wood, "Who Influences Whom? The President, Congress and the Media," *American Political Science Review*, Vol. 93, 1999, pp. 108–134.

12. Eschbaugh-Soha and Peake, pp. 19, 151.

13. Ibid., p. 185.

14. Christopher Cooper and Mandi Bates Bailey, "Entertainment Media and Political Knowledge," in Joseph Foy (ed.), *Homer Simpson Goes To Washington*, Lexington, KY: University of Kentucky Press, 2008, p. 134.

15. www.politico.com/magazine/story/2016/04/2016-white-house-press-corps-reporters-media-survey-poll-politics-213849.

16. Author's interview with a Powell aide. See also Colin Powell, *My American Journey*, New York: NY, Random House, 1995, pp. 505–506.

17. Quoted in Steven Livingston. *Clarifying the CNN Effect: An Examination of Media Effects According to Type of Military Intervention*, John F. Kennedy School of Government's Joan Shorenstein Center on the Press, Politics and Public Policy at Harvard University. 1997. For online, see http://genocidewatch.info/images/1997ClarifyingtheCNNEffect-Livingston.pdf.

18. www.globalpolicy.org/component/content/article/176/31233.html.

19. Jeff Smith, *The Presidents We Imagine: Two Centuries of White House Fictions on the Page, the Stage, Onscreen and Online*, Madison, WI: University of Wisconsin Press, 2009, p. 251.

20. Ray Quintanilla, "Cindy Sheehan: In Losing a Son, She Inspired a Movement," *Chicago Tribune*, August 6, 2006.

21. www.wsws.org/en/articles/2006/02/shee-f02.html.

22. Michael Baruch Grossman and Martha Joynt Kumar, *Portraying the President: The White House and the News Media*, Baltimore, MD: Johns Hopkins University Press, 1981, p. 317.

23. Samual Kernell, *Going Public: New Strategies of Presidential Leadership*, Washington, DC: Congressional Quarterly Press, 1997, p. 104.

24. Lee, p. 262.

25. Ibid.

26. Dana Milbank, "TV shows Trump Should Watch Instead of Fox News," *Washington Post*, March 12, 2017, p. A21.

27. John Wagner, Robert Cost, and Ashley Parker, "Trump May Retool His Staff," *Washington Post*, May 28, 2017, p. A2.

28. Newseum, "President and the Press" conference, Session 4, p. 9, available at www.newseum.org/2017/04/12/diverse-opinions-spark-conversation-at-the-president-and-the-press.

29. Ashley Parker and Robert Costa, "In a Reality Star's Presidency, Cable TV Is the Guiding Light," *Washington Post*, April 24, 2017, P. A1.

30. Ibid.

31. Kernell, 2007, p. 228.

32. Farnsworth, p. 144.

33. Ibid., p. 146.

34. Ibid., p. 128.

35. Ibid.

36. S. Robert Lichter and Richard Noyes, *Good Intentions Make Bad News*, Lanham, MD: Rowman and Littlefield, 1996, p. 271.

37. Lawrence R. Jacobs, "The Presidency and the Press: The Paradox of the White House Communications War," in Michael Nelson (ed.), *The Presidency and the Political System*, Washington, DC: Congressional Quarterly Press, 2010 p. 246.

38. Ibid.

39. Mike McCurry [Bill Clinton's press secretary] and Ari Fleischer [G.W. Bush's press secretary], "Advice for Media and Trump from Two Former Presidential Press Secretaries," *Columbia Journalism* Review. Available online at www.cjr.org/covering_trump/white_house_press_corps_trump.php.

40. David Broder, "War on Cynicism," *Washington Post*, July 6, 1994, p. A19.

41. Ari Fleischer, *Taking Heat: The President, The Press, and My Years in the White House*, New York, NY: HarperCollins, 2005, p. 361.

42. Farnsworth, p. 149.

43. Howard Kurtz, *Spin Cycle: Inside the Clinton Propaganda Machine*, New York, NY: The Free Press, 1998, p. 184.

44. Farnsworth, p. 150.

45. Fleischer, p. 77.

46. http://news.stanford.edu/2017/01/30/stanford-experts-president-trump-media.

47. *San Bernardino Sun* editorial, "Trump's War with the Media Divides Nation," March 5, 2017, p. A21.

48. Richard Rubin, *Press, Party and Presidency*, New York, NY: Norton, 1981, p. 10.

49. Newseum, Session 4, p. 4.

50. Margaret Sullivan, "The Media Has High Negatives, but Positives Are on the Rise," *Washington Post*, July 11, 2017, p. C3.

51. Cohen, pp. 204–205.

52. www.politico.com/magazine/story/2016/04/2016-white-house-press-corps-reporters-media-survey-poll-politics-213849.

53. Farnsworth, p. 148.

54. http://news.stanford.edu/2017/01/30/stanford-experts-president-trump-media.

55. Margaret Sullivan, "The Lies Have It, but the Press Can Take Back," *Washington Post*, March 13, 2017, p. C1.

56. Quoted in Matthew Kerbel, Dom Bonafede, Martha Joynt Kumar, and John L. Moore, "The President and the News Media," in Michael Nelson (ed.), *Guide to the Presidency*, Washington, DC: CQ Press, 2008, p. 985.

57. Sullivan, "The Lies. . .," p. C1.

58. www.azquotes.com/author/1818-Louis_D_Brandeis.

59. Dan Balz, "Accelerating investigations are a test of Democrat's restraint," *Washington Post*, May 18, 2017, p. A16.

60. Quoted in Max Frankel, "Beyond the Shroud," *New York Times Magazine*, March 19, 1995, p. 30.

61. Farnsworth, p. 151.

62. Ben Fritz, Bryan Keefer, and Brendan Nyhan, *All the President's Spin: George W. Bush, the Media and the Truth*, New York, NY: Touchstone, p. 255.

63. David Niven, "Bias in the News," *Press/Politics*, Vol. 6, No. 3, 2001, p. 31.

64. A term coined by David Shenk, *Data Smog: Surviving the Data Glut*, San Francisco, CA: Harper Edge, 1997.

65. Stephen J. Farnsworth and S Robert Lichter, *The Mediated Presidency: Television News and Presidential Governance*, Lanham, MD: Rowman and Littlefield, 2006, p. 97.

66. www.theatlantic.com/politics/archive/2013/02/why-does-the-media-go-easy-on-barack-obama/272807.

67. David Paletz, *The Media in American Politics: Contents and Consequences*, New York, NY: Longman, 1998, pp. 105–106.

68. Ellen Hunt, "What Is Fake News? How to Spot It and What You Can Do to Stop It," *The Guardian*, December 17, 2016.

69. Andrew Kohut and Robert Toth, "The Central Conundrum: How Can People Like What They Distrust?" *Harvard International Journal of Press/Politics*, Vol. 3, Winter 1998, p. 112.

INDEX

Speakes, Larry 97
special interest groups 8
Spicer, Sean: departure of as press
secretary 80; as director of
communications 69; on horserace-type
coverage 38; as press secretary 75, 78,
82–84; on press secretary role 154;
Saturday Night Live parody of 187;
Trump administration approach to
press briefings and 67; on Trump's
Twitter use 174; White House leaks
and 97
State of the Union Address 122–124, *123*
Stephanopoulos, George 68
Sununu, John 79
Supreme Court 27, 123
surrogates 103–107
symbolic leadership, role of 8–10
symbolism 97–101, 125

tapes 164
Tapper, Jake 59
technology: advances in White House
162–163; dangers of 161; electronic
archiving of presidential statements
164; fact checking and 163; going
public strategy and 7; loss of
information control and 164–165;
presidential adoption of 161–166;
twenty-four hour news cycle and
166; *see also* Internet; social media;
Twitter
television *see* broadcast television; cable
television; entertainment television
terHorst, J.F. 80
Time Magazine 157
timing of communications 91–92
town hall meetings 133–134
Trump, Donald: advertising while in
office and 136; amount of media
coverage of 28, 31; ceremonial events
and 107; Charlottesville
demonstrations and 132; Comey
firing communications and 77–78, 81,
92; communications operations of 68,
81; conflict frame of coverage and 37;
coverage of first 100 days *33*, 35;
entertainment television and 184;
falsehoods and 157–158; gaffes of 42;
gaggle briefings and 82; going public
strategy and 8; horserace-type coverage
and 39; hurricane response and 10;

impromptu shouted questions and 121;
leaked information and 96–97;
mandate rhetoric and 152; media effect
on policy of 202–203; negative
coverage and 31, 32–33, *33*; North
Korea statements and 132; parodies of
187; personal interviews and 133;
photo ops and 136; presidential press
conferences of 117, 118, 119; press
briefings under 82–86, *84*; press pool
norms and 59; public trust in 47–48;
public view of coverage of 47–48;
reaction of to humor at his expense
188; reaction of to media coverage
137, 138; redirection and 93;
relationship with media and 16, 67,
142–144, 160; relationships with
reporters 61; themed news stories and
16–17; timing of communications and
92; Twitter use and 14, 161, 163,
165–166, *168*, 171–175; use of media
to communicate with 6; use of
repetition and 93; use of sound bites
and 93; use of speeches and 126; use
of Twitter and 161; use of visual images
and 101–103, *101*; White House
Correspondents' Association dinner
and 135–136
Twitter: archives of presidential tweets
164; Obama and 14, 161; presidential
usage of 14, 161, 171–175; Trump and
14, 161, 163, 165–166, *168*, 169,
171–175

USS *Abraham Lincoln* event (George W.
Bush) 108–109

VCR 12
video clips, from White House 106
Vietnam Conflict 20
visual images, as PR strategy 97–103, *98*,
99, *100*, *102*

Wall Street Journal 33, 144
Washington, George 3, 30
Washington Post 31, 33, 37, 144
Watergate: effect on objective journalism
and 20; leaking and 94–96; rise in
investigative journalism and 31; taped
records and 164
weapons of mass destruction 31, 36, 44
welfare state 7

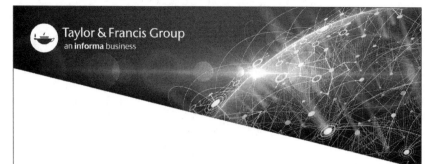